A Politics of the Ordinary

D1189558

A Politics of the Ordinary

Thomas L. Dumm

NEW YORK UNIVERSITY PRESS

New York and London

NEW YORK UNIVERSITY PRESS
New York and London

Library of Congress Cataloging-in-Publication Data
Dumm, Thomas L.
A politics of the ordinary / by Thomas L. Dumm
p.   cm.
Includes bibliographical references and index.
ISBN 0-8147-1896-5 (alk. paper)
ISBN 0-8147-1897-3 (pbk. : alk. paper)
1. Civil society. 2. Common sense—Political aspects.
3. Consumption (Economics)—Political aspects.
4. Ordinary-language philosophy.   I. Title.
JC336 .D86 1999
320—dc21   98-40234
                 CIP

New York University Press books are printed on acid-free paper,
and their binding materials are chosen for strength and durability.

Manufactured in the United States of America

10 9 8 7 6 5 4 3 2 1

To
James Eugene Dumm
and
Eileen Jane O'Leary Dumm,
with love

Contents

Acknowledgments

In this book I try to present evidence or proofs of a way of thinking about certain kinds of experience. The way of thinking is suggested by the book's title, *A Politics of the Ordinary*. Such a title has some obvious resonances, most directly with the project of ordinary language philosophy. And it is true, though probably not of much use to note, that some of what is attempted here has to do with my thinking about affinities between certain poststructuralist writers, such as Michel Foucault and Jacques Derrida; other writers identified with a philosophy of the ordinary, such as Stanley Cavell; and some writers who might be said to underwrite such a philosophy, especially Ralph Waldo Emerson and Henry David Thoreau.

But I hope that the readers of this book will attend as closely to the first part of the title, especially the indefinite article that modifies my use of the term *politics*. I use the indefinite article as a gesture to a democratic ethos, to projects of participation and active interest that do not stake claims to strong grounds of certainty. Instead, while trying to proceed with my feet on the ground, I want to make no claims that the ground will never shift beneath my feet. When thought about in reference to the ordinary, the question of the grounding of politics might open up to an indefinite series of questions concerning the comings and goings of political action, the traversals of public and private, the limits of language, the varying roles of mood and desire, and the embodiment of self. These issues are at stake in a politics of the ordinary and consistently open us to a discussion that is too often arrested before it is begun. Out on parole, maybe we can begin again.

The concerns I have about the ordinary have been in place for a very long time, in one way or another. As some may already know from some of my earlier work, one way has been through elements of French poststructuralism, a mode of analysis that I have found of crucial importance for coming to understand the condition of our lives together and alone. Another way has been through a kind of liberalism; but not the liberalism championed by mechanics of procedure who calculate the common as transparent communication, nor the liberalism of those who retreat behind barricades of legal rights into zones of private privilege. Instead, I am interested in those who tend a spirit of liberalism, who recognize, for example, that when Emerson writes of our rejected thoughts coming back to us with a certain alienated majesty, he is writing not with regret but with an ecstasy born of the realization of common greatness, acknowledging the extraordinary ordinary that may always be only partially realized but that, in being acknowledged, helps us go on with our lives.

Coming to a way of thinking and writing about the ordinary that is anywhere close to adequate to the task—and that remains to be seen, for that is the wager of this book—has been the result of my good fortune to be writing in reference to and with the help and advice of a group of thinkers and writers who sometimes go so far as to put the words in my mouth. To whom do I owe thanks this time?

Institutionally, the trustees of Amherst College allowed me to take a semester sabbatical out of turn so I could join my family in California in the spring of 1997, while my wife was a postdoctoral fellow at the Getty Center for the Study of Arts and the Humanities. It was during that period I first thought that I really ought to try to write this book. While in California, the denizens of the Getty Center provided me with a desk in the scholars' offices in Santa Monica, though I ended up spending more time in our apartment kitchen learning how to bake bread while writing.

Even before knowing I would try to write this book, in the summer of 1996, Norton Batkin invited me to participate in a conference on "Transcendentalism and American Culture" at Bard College in Annandale-on-Hudson, New York, during their summer music festival, which was focused that year on the world of Charles Ives. Norton was especially generous as a host, keeping the invitation open even when he learned I would not be driving over from Amherst but flying in from coastal Texas. At Bard, I presented the material that appears here in chapter 5, "Toy Stories." In April 1997, I was invited by the Honor's Program at Portland State University to give a lecture as a University Scholar and to attend an honor's seminar that was reading some of my work on Michel Foucault. Michael Flowers, who was most responsible for the invitation, proved a generous and gregarious host. My first attempt to discuss the relationship between Heaven's Gate and *Moby-Dick*, which appears as part of chapter 1, "A Politics of the Ordinary," was undertaken in my lecture at Portland State. In the autumn of 1996, I was invited by Mark Reinhardt to speak at Williams College on presidential sovereignty, where I was able to explore the nuances of the film

Independence Day in front of a lively audience. In March 1997, I accepted the invitation of Tiffany Lopez to present a slightly more developed version of the same material at the University of California, Riverside. This material appears here in chapter 6, "Aliens." All these speaking opportunities were great listening opportunities as well, and I thank the members of audiences at all these events who made them memorable occasions.

At Amherst College my intellectual life is enriched by having an office in Clark House, the home of my colleague Austin Sarat, who shares with me an awful lot of ordinary life, which includes his passionate concern for the conditions of ordinary injustice. Other companions through the long march at Amherst College and Amherst town who have helped my thinking on this book include Bob Gooding-Williams, Janet Gyatso, Nat Herold, Adriene Hill, Stephanie Sandler, and Kim Townsend.

Outside in the big world (made smaller by E-mail and telephone), the correspondents and friends who have helped me think about the status of the ordinary include Lauren Berlant, Wendy Brown, Simon Critchley, Bill Chaloupka, Jodi Dean, Fred Dolan, Kathy Ferguson, Kennan Ferguson, Dick Flathman, Larry George, Paul Gilroy, Bonnie Honig, George Kateb, David Lenson, Bill Mohr, Mort Schoolman, Mark Reinhardt, Michael Rogin, and Michael Shapiro. Jane Bennett has been a careful reader of much of this manuscript and has provided as well the example of her inspired reading of Thoreau, *Thoreau's Nature: Ethics, Politics, and the Wild.* Anne Norton has provided regular encouragement, especially by insisting that this book has a life at times when I really needed to hear that it did. At New York University Press, Eric Zinner has been a patient and calm voice, a fine editor who insists that I try to be more reader friendly than I sometimes can muster. Try again, fail again.

When Norton Batkin invited me to Bard's music festival, I was delighted especially because Stanley Cavell was to be there. Until that conference I had met Cavell on only one occasion, at an American Political Science Association panel devoted to discussing George Kateb's important work on Emerson, since published as *Emerson and Self-Reliance.* So I looked forward to learning more about Cavell's understanding of the (repressed) role of Emerson's thought in the development of American thinking. Since the occasion of that lucky invitation, Stanley has been especially generous with his time and advice. I would be in debt to him had I never had occasion ever to meet him, simply for his powerfully effective efforts to make philosophy speak across the ocean. That he has been so encouraging to this project has been of great help to me, and I am grateful to him.

Ann Lauterbauch was also a participant at the Bard conference, and shortly after that meeting she and I began a correspondence on questions of integrity, care, doubt, and what Ann refers to as "the it of it" that has provided me great solace, especially, and inevitably, at moments of greatest uncertainty. Some small bit of what I have learned from reading her poetry and prose also might be found in these pages.

Bill Connolly has read bits and pieces of this manuscript, listened to lines of it over the telephone, pointed me toward new and old sources, shared his work with me unstintingly and patiently, warned me of pitfalls, guided me to kindred spirits, been a kindred spirit, and I am running out of ways to thank him. But I'll keep trying.

I have been following Brenda Bright around the United States for some fourteen years now. This is a price I pay for having convinced her to come to live with me in Amherst in the first place. I have spent considerable chunks of time with her (and our children Irene and Jimmy now) in Chimayo, New Mexico; East Los Angeles, California; Port O'Connor, Texas; and the Brentwood section of Los Angeles, California, when what I most wanted was to be chained to my desk in Amherst. This book is a wan reflection of some of the experiences that she has opened to me. I acknowledge these travels as a gift of love.

Acknowledgment can be an embarrassingly overfull exercise, because it is a gesture that lies between the deadly certainty of one kind of truth and the solipsistic abyss that is the end of another. We can't know for certain, and we can't live without one another. It is a wonder, isn't it, how we get along at all.

Earlier or alternative versions of parts of the following chapters appeared in the publications that I acknowledge here: chapter 2, "Resignation," appears in *Critical Inquiry* 25, 1 (fall 1998); parts of chapter 3, "Compensation," appear in Austin Sarat and Dana Villa, eds., *Liberal Modernism and Democratic Individuality* (Princeton: Princeton University Press, 1996); parts of chapter 5, "Toy Stories," appear in *Cultural Values* 1, 1 (fall 1996).

Introduction

Ordinary life, the life-world, the everyday, the quotidian, the low, the common, the private, the personal—everybody knows what the ordinary is. The ordinary is what everybody knows. The ordinary gives us a sense of comfort; it allows us to make certain predictions about what will happen; it provides the context for the text we provide. The ordinary allows us to assume a certain constancy of life. It is reliable. We can count on it. The sun sets, the sun rises, another day of life begins. No matter what else happens, we live our lives in the manner of ordinary people. And so we celebrate the ordinary as the practical form that peaceable living takes when life is good, and we cling to any vestiges of the ordinary that survive when catastrophe takes hold of us or when our circumstances are diminished, when life is bad.

The modern celebration of the ordinary is especially intense in the United States, a polity where it has achieved almost fetishistic significance. And that makes sense. In the United States the pursuit of happiness is famously inscribed as a fundamental right in the founding document of the polity, the Declaration of Independence.[1] And because the pursuit of happiness carries its practitioners away from lives devoted to dramas of conquest and war or selfless devotion to others and instead toward the private gratification of desire, where conquest and service become means of achieving the end of happiness, the ordinary seems to express commonwealth as merely the common denominator of wealth. If we want to be happy, we win the lottery; we invest in Microsoft early; we live in a big house, with a big car, with a beautiful family. This hedonism is channeled and controlled by our recourse to an image of the ordinary as the limit of allowable pleasures and the form that pleasures might take. In this sense, the ordinary emerges in the United States as both the benchmark of the morality of convention and the end of material wealth. The ordinary becomes the bland and stultifying ground of American values.

At least by this common measure of its own founding benchmark of happiness—material wealth—the United States can be said to have succeeded in its most basic aspiration, becoming a veritable heaven on earth. Here it is more possible than anywhere else in the world for anyone to live an ordinary life saturated with goods. Here quotidian pleasures spill from the cornucopia of consumer society and become touchstones of commonality. In millions of kitchens, living rooms, and baths, little pieces of plastic bear their objecthood as the signs of the good life. The formal emergence in the second half of the twentieth century of "consumer society" might be said to have marked the penultimate shift away from the Protestant ethic of production to a post-Protestant ethic of consumption. This great transformation has occurred even as virtue itself has become a more problematic category of moral discernment. In the self-reinforcing representations of television and film; in the uninterrupted flow of advertising that informs the structures of private choice and the articulations of public good; in the contemporary senses of self that are shaped by consumption and its shadow, indebtedness; in the press of debt that in turn reshapes desires and aversions; in the styles of existence represented through all sorts of media as the contested terrains of truth; in the whispered needs Americans have constructed out of the information that passes, seemingly unhampered, through the ears and eyes of multitudes; in the cacophony that shapes our dreams of good lives in these United States, the common sense of ordinary life as the pursuit of material good might be read.

But this aspect of the ordinary, not quite fully captured by the equation of happiness with the acquisition of material goods, threatens to obscure another sense of the ordinary that is thoroughly entangled in the pursuit of happiness through consumption. This other aspect of the ordinary, what could be called its "mysterious indeterminacy," disappears under a crush of goods and their pursuit. As many of us would tacitly acknowledge—though this acknowledgment fails to influence most of our practical reasoning—the crush of goods is never so good as to save any of us from the need to pursue more of them. In fact, perhaps the most commonly recurring theme in the pursuit of happiness in the United States is the general failure by Americans to achieve the happiness we pursue. Entire genres of literature and film present us instead with the serendipitous discovery of happiness where it has been overlooked, staring us right in the face, enjoying a fugitive existence that somehow escapes or disdains achievement through its pursuit.[2] To the extent that we imagine our goods actually determine who we are, to the extent that the constitution of necessity itself is calculated in terms of political economy, another sense of the ordinary—as the serendipitous repository of happiness, as that which lies between us in our commonality, and as an alternative common sense existing behind and beyond our acquisitiveness—becomes a sentimental alternative to the acquisitive character of modern life, the X factor that melts the heart of Scrooge on Christmas Day.

Thus the ordinary is sentimentalized by those who would make it a synonym for common sense.[3] When it is celebrated as the commonsensical substance of modern liberal democracy, the ordinary is comprehended as a primary repository of meaning, a dimension of life from which the raw material of happiness might be drawn. The ordinary so construed is thus praised as the essence of democratic good. A picture of ordinary people pursuing ordinary goods and leading ordinary lives constitutes an ideal vision of liberal-democratic society.

When we think of the ordinary as being a force that would help us resist a false sense of good by posing itself as the alternative, authentic good, we may become aware of the most prominent ways in which it is under attack by other forces, some of which—for instance, consumer capitalism—will claim the status of a false idol of ordinariness, others of which—for instance, entertainment spectacles or spectacle wars (like the Persian Gulf War)—will tempt us to become contemptuous of the ordinary as not worthy of consideration. We could say that the ordinary exists in an uneasy relationship to the forces of events and the deadening practices of consumer capitalism. But even more than this, if we pose the ordinary as an alternative to these forces, we sooner or later must begin to explore how the ordinary comes into being, and hence how it might be diminished and displaced. On such occasions we would be forced to think through our sentimental understanding and reach toward a better sense of a politics of the ordinary.

Constantly threatened by the habits it sustains, the ordinary might be said to (con)front the forces of its diminishment, a metaphysical resource analogically akin to the great rain forests, which produce the oxygen that supports their destroyers. (Tropologically, it dangerously achieves a similar illusion, attaining a magical persistence in the face of effacement.)[4] When we open the question of a politics of the ordinary, we might then think back to those who have touched on it as a theme. The ordinary has been approached in relationship to a transcendentalist vision of nature, discussed as a front of the wild we mortals supposedly revere. It has cautiously been apprehended as a font of common meaning, an immeasurable measure of common sense, unerring because it has no fixed point that might subject it to refutation, frustrating to think about for the same reason; confused with the sites that surround and yet never contain it; an aspect of language, yes, but not yet or ever synonymous with language; infinite in aspect, resistant to totality.[5] One feature can be noted in the writing of most of those who have contemplated the ordinary—inflections of tentativeness and caution carry great weight in thinking about the ordinary. Surprisingly, this is so not only because of its delicacy but because of its dangerousness. The ordinary is to be reckoned, and to be reckoned with.

Many students of the ordinary within the academies are quick to note that something like the ordinary—common sense, basic decency, human nature, or even moral truth—underwrites what they would call civil society. Yet some of these students are frustrated by the ordinary's elusive character. One such group—let us call them disciplinarians—tries to comprehend the paradoxical character of the ordinary as the underwriting instrument of civil society. But precisely because of their commitment to clarity and un-ambiguous ends, they cannot unravel the paradox they want to know. The act of knowing itself becomes a barrier for them. So while the quality of re-lationships pursued under the auspices of the ordinary inflects the shape and tonalities of common lingo and publicly held values, the ordinary re-mains a repository of the unknown. This fact frustrates disciplinarians and often renders them dangerous to democracy, as they try to whip us into their truth.

The mysterious indeterminacy of the ordinary is not simply a feature that frustrates the rigid and fearful. It troubles the imaginative designs of some of the least disciplined of academics, political theorists, who struggle mightily against the ordinary even as they valorize and romanticize its pow-ers. For some reason political theorists (especially those who have followed Jean-Jacques Rousseau's path) seem to seek as much to overcome the ordi-nary as to celebrate it. (Celebration generally appears as a suspicious sign of attempted burial.) More recently, thinkers such as Hannah Arendt have seen in the ordinary a danger to the autonomy of political action, which ex-ists for them as a force that has its own hazard openness, its own majestic unpredictability. Arendt most clearly expresses a respectful hostility to the ordinary in *The Human Condition* by way of her hierarchizing of labor, work and action, where she explicitly expresses her concern about the dis-persal of "the political" throughout the social body.[6] This concern is re-peated and elaborated on by others, some of whom summarize this worry by repeating the now oft-used syllogism "For where everything is political, nothing is."[7] This quip, as intended, kills the possibility of a politics of the ordinary, because the ordinary insinuates itself into every where and touches every thing.

But, as other political theorists have pointed out, reliance on such a dualism to characterize that which is political misconstrues the protean character of political action by overlooking how power operates as a force in a field of intensities and spaces. One might take a page from some of the most imaginative and funny of such thinkers, Gilles Deleuze and Félix Guattari.[8] Borrowing vocabulary from their thinking regarding the distinctions between arboreal and rhizomatic linkages, we may respond to formulations that absolutize the boundaries between something called the political and the rest of life by shifting terms from a concern for *the political* to a concern for *politics* and by suggesting an alternative, though less succinct, aphorism to the one so favored by serious thinkers. To the claim "Where everything is political, nothing is" we could respond: Where politics is arboreal, institutions hierarchize and colonize meaning, establishing zones of legitimacy for privileged kinds of politics. Where politics is rhizomatic, institutions disperse meaning and pluralize the dangers and powers of politics. In all cases, politics exists as a capacity and as a yearning.

A Politics of the Ordinary is devoted to exploring this other sense of the ordinary as it expresses and mediates politics, understood as a capacity and a yearning. In the chapters that follow I explore the idea that a politics of the ordinary is to be located in processes through which a kind of constitution and amendation of human existence unfolds. I wish to provide some evidence for the claim that struggles most directly identifiable as political in character deeply intertwine the ordinary with two other important dimensions of life, what I call *the eventful* and *the normalized*; that ordinary aspects of life are never purely one thing or another but are shaped through the struggles and pleasures that constitute human existence at its most persistent and common levels; and that the ordinary in turn reshapes the terms through which struggles (and pleasures) unfold. Because I understand the constitution and amendation of existence to be a political matter, my interest in the ordinary is broadly political, rooted in a sense that a better understanding of the ordinary may lead to a better apprehension of some the most important political struggles of this era. These struggles concern the fate of the ordinary as an aspect of existence.

One concern is that it may be possible the ordinary is becoming lost to us before a discussion of its value can even begin, through what might be called the "logical hegemony of the discourse of disenchantment."[9] For instance, if the commodification of existence is reducing the range of what can be thought of as ordinary by drastically simplifying the realm of necessity, eliminating what may be called ordinary things by substituting for them the products of mass consumption, then the range of common practices of life is diminished. Or, for instance, if the codification of existence through the digitalization of information is reducing the complexity of ordinary things by creating a normal language of numbers that reduces the relationship of things to a common denominator, then we may well be losing the ambiguities of ordinary language. Both of these instances are consequences of the emergence of sophisticated practices of normalization. By reducing and threatening to eliminate the seedbed of the ordinary, by repressing and demonizing things that processes of normalization do not constrain or capture, forces of normalization, sometimes obviously but more often through subtle insinuations, operate politically. They are articulations of power as control. That the ordering of the ordinary is attempted in the name of something other than politics does not matter. To the extent that normalization reduces the unpredictability and unknowability of the ordinary, it operates as a form of politics.

But if it is the case that the ordinary has been overlooked as a subject of politics, this may be because politics is being conceptually confined these days by thinkers who identify themselves most firmly with the idea that "the political" is an autonomous form of and forum for human action. Beyond issues concerning the capaciousness of a theoretical analysis that limits political meaning to a rarified sphere of existential possibilities, I believe there is an elitism in the concern for "the political" that, in the end, shows itself most directly by ruling *ex cathedra* on what counts and what doesn't as politics. This elitism expresses itself more indirectly as a narrow academic concern for the canon.[10] But its effects are felt all along the convoluted paths by which the various cultures of nationhood find expression. Indeed, this claim for the importance of such academic concern may have been the most significant point Allan Bloom had to make in his 1987 condemnation of American toleration and pluralism.[11] And it may well be that the most important successors to Bloom are not the obvious propagandists against higher education, whose hostility to the academy is palpable, but rather those disciplinarians who in their practical activities would foreclose discussion and silently limit the terms of discourse by dismissing not only the ordinary but also those who would take it seriously.

Constituting Proof, Recovering Surprise

Aside from the conscious efforts of academicians to repress what they more or less accurately estimate as the force of the ordinary, the ordinary can be obscured, reduced, or eliminated by the underestimation of its importance in light of the more obvious import of events, or by its subordination to the demands of normalizing principles, or by a lack of appreciation of the richness of its connections to the larger world it composes. One difficulty in reckoning the ordinary concerns establishing its sense in contrast to the power of these other forces, which would emphasize the triviality of the quotidian. But proof of the obscure power of the ordinary cannot be found through the results of surveys or polls, which in this context only participate in the process of normalizing the ordinary, shaping its constitutive elements into pieces of norms, aiding in the destruction of life through its observation.

There is, however, another way of thinking about the process of proofing, what might be called proof through exemplification. This notion of proof is inspired by the original idea of a proof being an "illustration of forms," rather than the later "showing to be true."[12] The former idea concerns itself with the quality of illustration, while the latter is implicated in an attempt to fix a truth, in the sense of pinning down a definite meaning by way of placing. In the field of the ordinary, such a fixing destroys the object being analyzed in order to save its meaning. In this sense exemplification may be understood as the detailed description of an incident or phenomenon that shows the thing's characteristic status as common or low while respecting its integrity. The idea that there may be exemplary instances of the ordinary—common (enough), recurring instances of ordinary actions that are examples of a wildly contextualized exercise in freedom—may be illustrated through a method of proof that disdains the tracing of regularities for another kind of generalization. Proof through exemplification could thus be an alternative to the idea of the "ideal type" that Max Weber famously advanced,[13] in that in proofing no attempt is made to elevate a useful generalization to a rule of action. Instead, in making proofs we might focus on the particularity of an example derived from a sometimes more and sometimes less generalizable context.

This method, to the extent that it even ought to be called one, tries to allow for the recovery of surprise. That is, the technique of proofing fits well with the idea that the ordinary might be a repository not so much of essentially contested concepts but of indefinitely variable experiences, so that what is often understood as mundanely definite, settled, and routinized on further reflection can be appreciated for the contingent depth and multiplicity of connections to each life it is a part of.[14] And there is another way to understand "proof," one I have learned from baking bread. Many recipes call on the baker to "proof the yeast" while gathering together the other ingredients for making the dough. In this sense, one may also understand proof to be a process of testing the potency and life of something. Of the proofing by example that I undertake in this book, it might be said that I am trying to test the metaphors of the ordinary to see if they are alive and to enliven what may have seemed dead.[15]

So my proofs are examples. The examples I offer are incidental, contingent on observation and intuition, occurring at the conjunction of events, inciding into the course of things. It cannot be otherwise given the object of this study and my desire to protect its strange integrity, an integrity that depends on a kind of impurity. So whether the discussion concerns the appearance of a new child's story at a moment of corporate downsizing, of an audience breaking into one song instead of another, of an electrician in New Mexico and a cult leader in southern California expressing the same sense of boredom, of a professor and president both writing letters of resignation, or even of a fictional president's interaction with a hostile alien, the proofs of *A Politics of the Ordinary* do not lend themselves to definitive statements of political endings. Instead, I am guided throughout this book by the concern to see how glimpses of the ordinary, not in a pre-given form compatible or congruent with an upright moment of truth but as elusive bits of becoming and seemliness, might encourage new ways to reflect on how we begin politics. The ordinary does seem not to permit itself to be ordered without disappearing from view. But my hope is that the ordinary may be exemplified through a particular method of proofing. Plainly put, this is a book of proofs, selectively culled from observation and interpretation of common circumstance.

Why I'm Not a Patriot

As with earlier explorations I have attempted into themes that blur or erase distinctions between public and private matters, I have found the locale from which I work to be inseparable from the substance of my concerns.[16] My local knowledge is American, which means that the low I love is predominantly American in its inflections. Given recent remonstrances by at least one prominent American philosopher toward the unpatriotic academy—when Richard Rorty fulminates against the unpatriotic Left,[17] I want to ask, not unlike Travis Bickle in Martin Scorsese's *Taxi-Driver*, "Are *you* talking to *me*?"—it seems important to clarify some of the presumptions I bring with me when I think about the politics of the ordinary in the United States. I do not think I am a patriot of the political entity of which I am a citizen, the United States of America, at least as I understand an important meaning of that strange term *patriot:* someone whose ruling passion is love of country. I do not think it wise to be so governed. The unreflective embrace of a patriarchal ordering, which is implicitly conveyed in the word by its etymological associations (from the Greek for "of one's fathers" or "one's fatherland"),[18] still carries with it meanings that are all too clear to me regarding *how* one is to love what one loves. I do, however, recognize that I am best able to take seriously (if not too seriously) artifacts and works that have their origin and trajectory in the loosely configured cultures of the United States. Maybe this is a different kind of love that dares not speak its name, out of a sense not of shame but of wonder. Or perhaps the answer is even simpler: that I am condemned to think about this country as some are said to be condemned to think philosophically.

I hope that the awkwardness of this confession will not distract readers from the seriousness of the charge it attempts to answer. Like all times, the years closing the twentieth century are tough times as well as opportune times for those of us who want to learn to be self-reliant thinkers. Our pleas for understanding are too often used against us to interrogate our best intentions. Yet we benefit from misunderstanding as well, to the extent that we are left to our own devices and may not be taken too seriously. So I try to strike a balance in writing about the politics of the ordinary, using the United States as the place I write about and the place I write toward: I do not suggest that the explicit recognition of the parochial character of the source of my thinking about the ordinary operates as a limit on its value, any more than I imply that the supposedly more worldly character of the thinking of those who stake a claim to the universality of the thoughts they pursue prevents them from seeing the particulars of the world beneath them. The claims that any of us might make are to be assessed by others who more or less share the perspectives of one side or another in this ancient debate. But I plan to remain on guard, for I am not the first person to have observed that universal thinkers usually descend to a more familiar partiality when the universalisms they espouse are challenged in practical ways.

1

A Politics of the Ordinary

And it does look, after the death of kings and out of the ironies of revolutions and in the putrefactions of God, as if our trouble is that there used to be answers and now there are not. The case is rather that there used not to be an unlimited question and now there is.

—Stanley Cavell, *Must We Mean What We Say?*

Being Bored, Living Here

The television set is on in the middle of the day in western Massachusetts; it is deep in the winter of 1991. *CNN Headline News* tells its viewers about a multiple murder that has occurred somewhere in northern New Mexico. The outline of a mesa serves as a backdrop for a reporter on the scene set along an arroyo in Chimayo, a village in the heart of the Sangre de Christo Mountains. The reporter tells of a man who has just slain his estranged common-law wife, her sister, her mother, his daughter, and a sheriff and deputy who had come to the house to arrest him for violating a restraining order. This is an ordinary mass murder: the man is distraught and crazed in the way that men dispossessed of their (minimal and compensatory) privilege can become; his heartbreak is as violent as it can be; no court order is able to keep him away, and technologies of death are ready at hand. Murder is in his heart and murder is on his mind when he drives out that dirt road. Even as the reporter speaks, this man, now a fugitive, has so far eluded state law enforcement officials. He is arrested a couple days later, about one hundred miles west in Albuquerque, where he turns himself in. He had run to a safer place, having feared death at the hands of local policemen in the nearby town of Española. These comrades of the fallen policemen might have expressed *their* loss, their rage and heartbreak, and demonstrated the strength of the still unbroken, subterranean, and ancient chain of blood justice.

Chimayo is located on the "high road" to Taos, which wends its way through tiny villages, mountain meadows, and canyons to end near an ancient pueblo/modern resort. In Chimayo one can find "lowriders"—Chicano car customizers, young men and some women, families even sometimes, who cruise the main drag in Española on Route 68, the "low road" to Taos.[1] The lowriders are a reminder of urban space in a rural locale. (Española is called Little L.A. by locals.) Up the road from this larger town, Chimayo's small fame rests on three tourist attractions associated not with lowriders but with peasant life: a shop that sells high-quality blankets woven at the same site by eleven successive generations of a single family, a well-regarded restaurant specializing in New Mexican cuisine, and a chapel of miracles. The last of these, the Sanctuario de Chimayo, is the destination of pilgrims who come thousands of miles to eat the sacred dirt and who leave behind crutches, white canes, messages of praise and thanks, and small gifts for the Holy Virgin. A secret society of *penitentes,* mystics who engage in rituals of self-flagellation, organizes an annual procession commemorating the Passion of the Cross, in which a young man carries a crucifix some twenty miles from Sante Fe to the Sanctuario on Good Friday in memory of the horrible suffering endured by Jesus Christ. (The *penitentes* have been known in the past to have crucified one another in secret ceremonies, a sign of their ecstatically intense worship.)

Chimayo is also a place of desperate poverty and the kind of violence that accompanies such despair. In 1990, Chimayo's county of Rio Arriba was said to have the second highest rate of death from unnatural causes of all counties in the United States. Between drunken accidents on narrow highways, suicides, and murders, the area is known throughout New Mexico as a dangerous place. It is wise not to travel the road between Chimayo and Española after dark on Saturday nights; the drunken drivers make travel too hazardous.

In Chimayo the farmers' fields are irrigated by *acequias,* irrigation ditches. Many *acequias* date back to the sixteenth century, and some of them predate the Spanish Conquest and exploration. For as long as the *acequias* have existed, local people have chosen major domos to regulate their flow. Water from the *acequias* irrigates the chili fields and orchards of apricot trees. The man who killed his family first drove up the arroyo, which was called Daniel's after the name on the mobile home court that marked the turnoff from the blacktop road. The summer before his rampage, telephone company employees in cooperation with the county had numbered the arroyos and the homes along them, establishing addresses for everyone there. By establishing addresses, the telephone company would be able to find their customers more easily. Of course, it also made it easier for government authorities to track down people who previously had enjoyed a greater anonymity.

This neighborhood looks out onto Truchas Peak, about twenty miles in the distance. At thirteen thousand feet, the peak is visible from many windows and is the backdrop for the drama of every unfolding day, every evolving season. Summer in the high desert is the monsoon season. Each morning begins crisp, clear and chilly, and during the course of the day the temperature rises to the mid-nineties. Then a touch of humidity perfumes the air with the complex scent of desert, and thunderheads, visible for many miles, build up. By late afternoon, with astonishing regularity, there are thunderstorms. Afterward the air clears, and after sunset the sky is bright with the glow of stars, brilliant at eight thousand feet. It is a wonderful place. People fall in love with it.

Sam and Angie Martinez lived on the very arroyo where the slaying occurred, in an adobe house where they were raising their three children. An electrician by trade, Sam is a resourceful and skilled craftsman, in the fashion of someone raised on a farm, someone who has lived in a rural area and often has had to improvise solutions to problems. A local person—the lineage of his family can be traced back over three centuries—he once worked in nearby Los Alamos as a maintenance man at the government laboratories. By 1990 he had his own electrical business and was always doing many other small things to make life comfortable for his family. (He could gather a winter's worth of wood chopping trees by permit in Kit Carson National Forest; he was remodeling another adobe house on his property; and with his cousin he was raising chilis—Chimayo chilis have a great reputation in New Mexico, though Hatch chilis are more famous and abundant.) Angie mainly stayed home, raising the kids, though she also did some housecleaning in the area.

One evening in the summer of 1990, Sam was doing some work in the house he was remodeling. A visitor from New England who was in Chimayo for the summer (and who was renting a small cabin on their property) offered to help him with some of the simpler chores. As they went about moving some sheets of chipboard into an empty room, Sam asked this easterner how he liked Chimayo so far. The visitor started talking about the beauty of the mountains, the silence of night, the stars, the desert, the fragrance of the air before a thunderstorm. Sam allowed him to go on in this vein for a while, and when the visitor had run out of things to say he responded, "Oh. Well, I was asking because we find it really boring living here."

What does it mean for Sam to find it boring living in Chimayo? Most obviously, there is the dull quietness that one experiences in the countryside in contrast to urban life. Does his experience correspond with the problem of many who have thought of boredom as a distinctly modern experience? For many such thinkers, to be bored is to suffer from tedium or ennui. But even here, there is no clear sense of what it means to be bored. Some of this incoherence is echoed in etymology. The word *bored* has no indisputable etymology that might move one beyond imagining the labor of drilling to explain how the idea of drilling a hole—*to bore*—could also describe the process of being dull and stupefied; how a meaningful activity can gradually be transformed into a drudgery; and how a more distant perspective that overlooks the details of the everyday might become desensitized to the time-boundedness of a meaningful activity becoming meaningless. Here is where some turn to Hannah Arendt's deprecation of labor and work to seek sustenance for meaning in some higher activity.[2] Sam's experience as a laborer may be connected to this sense of boredom: the repetitions of work, the enslavement to routine, the troubles of scrambling to keep up—with bills, with family obligations, with chores.

But a boring moment may be filled with meaning. Gilles Deleuze has noted that Samuel Beckett "spoke of 'drilling holes' in language in order to see or hear 'what was lurking behind.'"[3] And Jean-Luc Nancy can even be interpreted as having defined truth as a bore:

> Truth punctuates, sense enchains. Punctuation is a presentation, full or empty, full of emptiness, a point or a hole, an awl, and perhaps always the hole that is pierced by the sharp point of an accomplished present. It is always without spatial or temporal dimensions.[4]

Perhaps the acute observatory powers that accompany being bored suggest that the claim of seeing something behind language depends on the language itself. In this sense, the labor of boredom prepares one for an insight into something even deeper and stranger than meaninglessness. Boredom may be understood as a preparation for telling oneself something. In boredom, something is wanting explanation, and someone is refusing to be distracted from the wanting.

Of course, Sam may not have been as bored as he claimed to be—his life seemed full, busy, rich in incident and concerns. He was, in the words of Primo Levi, "unhappy in the manner of free men."[5] And yet he knew that rural life in New Mexico wasn't as the visitor from the east seemed to want it to be. The visitor's description, a sentimental tourist's description, was devoid of people, for one thing; and the people who were struggling to get by in that small village weren't simply characters in a travel sketch. The visitor started to wonder if Sam might have thought life in New England, for instance, was somehow more meaningful than the life he had made here in the town of his ancestors. Perhaps Sam wondered at the visitor's interest in the New Mexican desert.

The experience of boredom may be connected to the feeling of being uninterested, and hence uninteresting even to oneself; feeling left out, existing on the margins of events that powerful people represent as central to what matters in the world. Perhaps the opposite is also true: boredom may be understood as a symptomatic response to an unsought inclusion, a reaction to the invitation to observe, an expression of discomfort at not wanting to be a part of a larger narrative while being acutely aware that one is. In such a situation boredom becomes a recognition of the terror that prefaces the moment one is forced to see what might lurk behind language; the deadening power of the force of events as they are about to thrust themselves on ordinary life; the punctuation of truth as it is bearing down but before it has broken through, harrowing, inscribing—enlightening us in an untimely fashion, like a prisoner in Kafka's penal colony.

It is the moment *before* something happens that marks the apex of boredom. This is one reason we may be so often tempted by the comfort of television. Television distracts us from the boredom of anticipation by substituting a spectacle, a synthetic resolution, serially, with the regularity of a schedule. I once was suspicious of wide-screen televisions in desert villages, the ubiquitous satellite dishes that pull in Chicago superstations, because they seemed to contribute to making local life in lands of enchantment appear dull and idiotic by comparison. But I have come to think that my suspicion is misplaced, that in some ways the comparison of city and country is itself vacuous. If one recognizes the ordinary as existing below the threshold of a certain register of representation, then it is not to be found by television, nor overcome by the spectacles that television miniaturizes. But matters are not that simple. The entanglements of the ordinary in spectacular events and in entertainments are complicated and partial, not simple and pure: its losses and gains seem to be the negative images of what may matter and what may not. In fact, the spectacular event may be composed of bits and pieces of the exemplary ordinary—distorted, perhaps; destroyed, in some ways; but returning to the scene of the everyday. So it may be that the ordinary is not overshadowed by Michael Jordan floating above a basketball rim on television. The ordinary may actually sometimes be enhanced. The network of communications that allows us to compare ourselves to others is not by itself a threat to the ordinary. The ordinary does not exist on a simple scale of desire but is itself a compositor of desires.

Sam Martinez found it boring living in Chimayo. Would he have found it less boring living in Los Angeles? How would he like being part of that (much larger) desert village, a member of what one denizen of the city has found to be a "gesellschaft community?"[6] Many villagers from Chimayo have made the trek to Los Angeles to find work. Many have returned as soon as they could. Sam himself has done this. There are times when boredom is an accomplishment, the triumph of local carefulness over the recklessness of distance. Boredom seems to be the loss of a sense of the familiar in the presence of all that is familiar. This defamiliarization, the accompaniment of the drilled hole that exposes the death behind language, goes some way toward explaining how the experience of being bored is akin to the experience of fear. Both reflect a sense of a loss of familiarity. With fear, the loss is pronounced. With boredom, it is compounded by the presence of what should be familiar and hence is not easily perceivable as having anything directly to do with a trauma.

The anxiety that boredom expresses may be appreciated as a loss of the familiar by its absorption into a larger context. Boredom may be a response to a strange liminal state—when people find experience infiltrated by processes of ordering that diminish the uniqueness of their lives, on the one hand, and by the representation of events as being of overwhelming import, on the other. This sense of loss becomes a common denominator of ordinary life as it is invaded by the eventful and strip-mined by normalizing strategies. In the face of this loss, boredom expresses an anxiety that is distinctively modern. William Connolly has put it this way:

> Underlying persistent boredom is anxiety, a mood we are not encouraged to articulate in the subject-centered world, but which, once articulated, discloses or expresses something that had been obscurely present in the initial feeling. Anxiety is a vague malaise about the human condition itself . . . which is hidden when subjects are active, interested, involved, in charge of things, but which disturbs us vaguely and darkly when we step outside the hustle and bustle of everyday life . . . when we are bored, for instance.[7]

Outside the hustle and bustle, not distracted, we have trouble avoiding our condition. And what is that condition?

Sam Martinez's boredom may be a warning, a sign of the gradual diminishment of the ordinary. The losses he experiences in the village of Chimayo are repeated every day in city and in suburb. It is not the idiocy of the countryside that afflicts him: Karl Marx's idiots were not bored.[8] Their relationship to language, their familiarity with death, bespoke other terrors, but not the terror of boredom. They placed their faith in God, to be sure, but also more or less knew the practical wisdom of Thoreau, who, on being asked when dying if he saw anything beyond this life, replied, "One world at a time."[9] A particular kind of patience is required to work through boredom, to face the unease of a possible meaninglessness. A different recovery of the world is required of us. Here and now, the diagnosis of the condition itself might influence the action that could be taken. How do the conditions of boredom inflect a willingness to be patient?

Being Free, Averting Boredom

The problem of boredom is intimately linked to the question of how to be free. To be bored is too often to be free in one way and not to know what to do as a consequence; to face a truth and to assume a posture of despair; to be fixed in a place, not knowing how to move beyond what one knows. There is a place of boredom, and it is a place we make in our attempts to think of how to be in the world. The thought of a place of boredom coincides with the way in which we think about the categories of ordinary freedom. In this way, formal freedom may be thought of as the emergence of a neutral space, or even spaces, in which action occurs afterward, and the actor is bereft for not knowing what to do in this empty, completed space. Alternatively, ethical freedom may be understood as a complicatedly related set of practices and relationships that entail the creation, negotiation, and traversing of multiple and overlapping spaces.[10] Under the rubric of ethical freedom, the work of constructing spaces enables people to avert boredom by re-cognizing the space of boredom as a space in need of reworking, where one has the opportunity to turn around and reattain an interest in others and hence in oneself. One will never totally avert boredom, but one may be able to dissipate its effects by easing the anxiety it expresses, converting the tension of boredom into the quiet of meditation so as to prepare oneself to begin again.

We might hope that the practices of averting boredom will help preserve what may be called the hazard openness of the ordinary. For while it is through the construction and reconstruction of spaces of freedom that the emergence of the ordinary into the field of events and its exposure to ordering comes about, it is also by way of these fleeting moments when freedom is practiced that a certain confidence emerges concerning the democratic persistence of politics in the late modern era. When freedom is understood as a set of practices that involves such a respect for the ordinary, it becomes oriented toward what Connolly has called the cultivation of an ethos of pluralization.[11] This ethos embraces a recognition that new things are becoming, that the ontological commitment to security is the most serious front of danger in the late modern world, and that an infrastructural violence of silencing is the most powerful force that those most anxious to secure freedom deploy.

This ethos also embraces an acknowledgment of a difficult paradox— that the moment we are best able to recognize the ordinary is as it transmutes into events. Practices of freedom that are oriented toward a cultivation of the ethos of pluralization more closely couple freedom with democratic expression. To put it another way, democracy fronts the politics of events through ordinary life. This is especially so once the term *democracy* is supplemented by the idea of *representation*. Representations are acts of communal transmutation that make available the possibility of troping, a constant turning of words and phrases that enables habitations of meaning to develop and unfold.[12]

Out of the fecundity of representations, the ordinary embodies and gives shape to possibilities of meaning, providing a measure of the contents of people's concerns, techniques for developing the temporalities that inflect political action at given moments, and strategies for constituting and amending the spaces within which events unfold. To think about the ordinary as a contested space in which practices of representation occur links it to the forces of normalization and events. Because both the normalization of life and the emergence of events entail the control and deployment of representations that originate in the space of the ordinary, we must learn to distinguish a politics of the ordinary from the politics that attends events and norms. This is a difficult problem. We live with a fearful suspicion and a philosophical worry: in tandem with the development of normalizing practices that exfoliate the ordinary by reducing its elements to fixable points on an arbitrary scale, modern events have unfolded in such a way as to undermine the possibility that ordinary life might continue to exist as a space where truthful things may happen. Agents of normalization attempt to dominate or monopolize the content of meaning in the name of morality, efficiency, and democracy, and sometimes of the normal itself. In doing so, they wreak havoc with our aspirations to truthfulness.

This struggle concerning meaning constitutes a profound political project, perhaps the most important project of the late modern era, when more overt struggles over material goods have extended explicitly to the domains of language and communication, when the spectacular casts a large shadow over small and quotidian matters. To borrow from Nancy's nomenclature, both events and normalization punctuate, and the ordinary enchains. Events fix time, and normalization builds neutral spaces. Against the static actions of events and the composed behaviors of the normalized, the ordinary offers a dynamic waiting. While much of what is recorded as political struggle in the late modern era is the conflict between the event and the normalized, this conflict does not determine final expressions of truth. Nonetheless, the conflict is of intense importance: it shapes strategies of governance and the forms of violence imposed on people in their exercise of ordinary freedom. But in turn, the ordinary constantly dis-settles these governing powers. From the perspective of the ordinary, a rude and democratic impulse is always formally possible and may often be substantively necessary as the inspiration for the creation of sites of resistance against the forces of normalization and event.[13]

To the extent that the ordinary sustains itself in the face of normalization and events, we denizens of late modernity are freer than we think we are, even though, or perhaps even because, we do not too often fully assess the style of freedom we enjoy.[14] In this sense political action may not be limited to what we typically think of as the eventful but instead may be re-figured as the human activity that energizes the ordinary from surprising places, providing a key connecting thread between persons and events. Against the notion that there is an aesthetic of human existence that can be salvaged in the wake of the rarification or establishment of an exclusive realm of the political, I want to think about how to recover a political ethos that inheres in quotidian acts and small gestures, in what might be called the gist of ordinary life.

To suggest that such a political ethos may be at work in a politics of the ordinary is to lay a groundwork for seeking evidence of practices of freedom that ordinary people engage in as we lead our lives. The degree to which these always elusive ordinary people may be considered free is a very complicated question when considered in this light, a matter never finally decided but to be considered as of substantive evaluation. But even if one supposes this idea of the practice of freedom as a common thing is mistaken, I still take as axiomatic James Madison's famous assertion that liberty is the air that allows the fire of faction of burn.[15] In recognizing the possibility of faction in the presence of freedom (and the almost practical inevitability of freedom), Madison condescendingly enables democracy to exist. We might then be encouraged to seek out freedom and recognize democracy when we see it, even or especially in its fragmentary and inchoate expressions in ordinary life, if only so that we may better diagnose the conditions of our times in terms of our departures from the promises of politics. This may be one way to assess our status as citizens. Such an endless task is sometimes boring, but from this perspective, the alternative to boredom is worse.

The Ordinary and the Eventful

When the ordinary is invoked in reference to the conflict between the eventful and the normalized, it is usually considered to be outside politics, not a contestant in a political struggle regarding meaning and power. But the ordinary might come to light in the conflict between forces of normalization and events as an element that infiltrates events and opposes the normal. In this sense, the notion that the ordinary retains a sympathetic relationship to the event is suggested not only by the representational connection of the two but by characteristics the ordinary shares with events.

Stanley Cavell's various attempts to think about the ordinary aid in illuminating these complicated relationships between the ordinary and events. Consider, for instance, one of his most explicit attempts to think about the relationship between the two. In 1980, Cavell was asked to respond to a critique of the *Annales* historians that had been developed by the philosopher of history Paul Ricoeur (who later re-presented, in expanded form, similar themes in his study *Time and Narrative*).[16] Ricoeur argued against what he thought was the *Annales* historians' peculiar understanding of their project: he believed that they thought they had developed a kind of history that could oppose itself to the history of events. In his response, Cavell characterizes Ricoeur as wanting to suggest "that the writing of history cannot fully escape narrative discourse, and that since this discourse requires the concept of an event, the writing of history—if even of long timespans—cannot escape the thought of the subjects of those time spans as events."[17]

Cavell questions the role of the ordinary in the alleged submergence of the eventful. He begins his response by suggesting that Ricoeur's argument may be importantly mistaken on one key point. For Cavell, the sense of the capture of history under the concept of the event, where what is narrated is necessarily eventful even when the frame of narration is extended in space and time, does not adequately address an understanding of the event in which a more or less agreed upon public attaches importance to something. He contrasts the attachment of importance to something by an interested public to the individual desire to "escape the dictation of what it is interesting or important to think about . . . a demand to let one's own discourse determine its interest for itself."[18] This interest—an important kind of self-interest—establishes the beginning of the path that leads Cavell back to a defense of ordinary life. He writes, "What the ordinary language philosopher is sensing—but I mean to speak just for myself in this—is that our natural relation to the world's existence is—as I sometimes wish to express it—closer, or more intimate, than the ideas of believing and knowing are made to convey."[19]

Cavell's statement gestures toward an ontological perspective we might adopt concerning the various relationships to the world available to human beings. This "natural relationship"—a more intimate relationship to the world's existence than the idea of believing expresses—confronts the theocratic conceit that we can achieve some sort of certainty through the evocation (or invocation) of faith. A more intimate relationship to the world's existence than the idea of knowing challenges the epistemological conceit that we can achieve some sort of certainty through reference to facticity. Faith and facticity appear on the same side of certainty, bound to be resisted for the damage they threaten to do to another, more philosophically nuanced relationship we may enjoy with truth. In a space allowed by skepticism, a place between faith and facticity created by the need to live through the experience of radical doubt rather than repress it or evade it, acknowledgment may begin to establish itself as another way of existing in relation to the world, alongside knowing the world.

This intimate relationship to truth is on the side of being free in what I have called the ethical sense. Cavell's intent is to show how we might be freer in our relationship to truth by reaching a better understanding of what we may appreciate as the indefinite character of the relationship of the ordinary to the uneventful. A truth that comes of grasping—as opposed to a truth that one receives while waiting undistracted, while bored, for instance—is a truth that reflects a violence of conceptualization, which in that violence overwhelms the truth that comes *to* those who wait and who, by waiting, actively seek a more intimate relationship to the world. The condition of grasping is an unhandsome one.[20] From the ordinary we resist the unhandsome condition of grasping, oppose (or avert) the violence of conceptualization that can stop thinking in the name of thought.[21]

Cavell argues that Thoreau and Emerson authorize this kind of interest in the ordinary as a repository of existence's relationship to truth. He cites a passage from Emerson in which the ordinary is invoked in this way:

> I ask not for the great, the remote, the romantic; what is doing in Italy or Arabia; what is Greek art, or Provençal minstrelsy; I embrace the common, I explore and sit at the feet of the familiar, the low. Give me insight into today, and you may have the antique and future worlds.[22]

Cavell's main point in this citation is to support the contention that the ordinary is misconstrued if it is understood simply as the small and unnoticed opposed to the event or that drags the event back to the great rhythms of the normal. Instead, we need to understand that the uneventfulness of the ordinary is the inevitable ground from which we may come to a better appreciation of events. The relentless *presence* of the ordinary, even in, or especially because of, its elusive character, becomes the source of its validity. This presence repudiates or chastises the arrogance of the idea of the autonomy of history, as conceived by both the *Annales* school of history and Ricoeur, because it suggests that neither the history of regularities nor the history of events can adequately account for the ordinary, for the presence of an insistence on the dynamic of thinking over the stasis of thought.

In theorizing the uneventful as the ordinary, and the ordinary as the ground for events, Cavell reaches an implicit, if surprising, agreement with Michel Foucault, who may be construed as suggesting that the conditions of possibility for the emergence of events are threatened not by anything we would identify as ordinary but by processes of normalization that we fail to understand as normalizing. Indeed, Foucault gives the name *normalization*—which I have appropriated here—to the processes that threaten the common, the familiar, the low, the sites from which we humans might reach a more intimate relationship with nature and our selves.[23] And while Cavell invokes the ordinary in part to protect things that are not eventful from being reduced into things that may be ordered, Foucault invokes the idea of the anonymous to accomplish a similar ethical end.[24] Resistance to normalization is akin to what Cavell, relying on Emerson, calls escaping dictation; only for Foucault it proceeds as a resistance to that which is dictated as norms. Foucault's desire to enunciate ways of caring for the self so as to learn how to become freer is a project that emerged from his concern with the normalized conditions under which freedom is lived. Like Cavell, Foucault does not apprehend ordinary life as a threat to the eventful but worries instead about the conditions that either support it or suppress it. For Foucault, in the modern age processes of normalization operate as a primary means of destruction of the grounds of ordinary life, not simply by the prohibition and repression of events but by the work of distributing singular occasions around indeterminate norms so as to reduce events to facts.[25] This relentless positivity is the nexus of power/knowledge that he struggled to find a way out of in his late work.

Cavell and Foucault comparably implicate the grounding of events in the ordinary even as they raise the frightening possibility of the disappearance of ordinary life. But neither Cavell nor Foucault sees the primary threat to the ordinary as being posed by events in and of themselves. Instead, they suggest that secondary interpretations of the meaning of events distract from the possibility of understanding them as anything other than the eclipse of the ordinary, and these secondary interpretations—whether they take the form of normalization or dictation—disguise the ordinary, not in some essentialist form as a hidden history or natural metaphor but in an always indefinite relationship to the event. This play of appearance and disappearance not only is a matter for philosophers of history to sort out in their determination to judge the importance of what has happened in the past but is a concern for anyone who is interested in turning a new leaf, in the nomenclature of the American transcendentalists. Though writing in different vocabularies, then, Cavell and Foucault enunciate a common and immediate concern to protect the ordinary from that which is ordered so as to enable plural possibilities of ways of being free in an increasingly administered world.

In short, they are democrats, in the sense that Connolly has recently, and with intensifying vehemence, identified and identified with.[26] They recognize that democracy involves a kind of self-reliance, or care of self, if contemporary subjects are to avoid the new enclosures that threaten to arrest new ways of being free. They recognize the contemporary self as being more troubled than ever by forces that threaten to undermine and repress its looser, more artful forms.[27] To the extent that we accept the idea that boredom can be a symptom of how this threat finds expression at the level of the ordinary, the larger claim that there is always a relationship of the constitution of self to the constitution of the polity is freed from its Neoplatonic moorings and finds fresh expression. This is the idea of constitutional amendation.

Amending Constitutions

The ordinary appears in connection to the eventful as a kind of ground from which the event springs. But who is doing the springing? Who is making the history of events? It is perhaps inevitable that the relationship of the self to the event be troubled.[28] Emerson has noted this dialectic between the event and the person: "Person makes event, and event person," he writes in his essay on "Fate."[29] Cavell explains the extraordinary difficulties Emerson confronts when he attempts to describe the extent to which freedom is contained in the event and the limitations placed on freedom in the process of event-making.[30] He notes that in "Fate"—which many consider Emerson's most important essay on freedom—Emerson attaches freedom to fate through a certain recoiling (or springing) of language:

> "Man also is a part of [Fate], and can confront fate with fate." That is, I will now say, Emerson's way of confronting fate, his recoil of fate, is his writing, in every word; for example in every word of "Fate," each of which is to be a pen stroke, a common stroke of genius, because a counter stroke of fate.[31]

While Emerson supplements the opposition of "Fate against Fate" to associate freedom with the "revelation of Thought," seeing freedom exercised in an affirmative acceptance of life's experiences, of "truth that comes to our minds,"[32] this movement is made in the wake of a hard appreciation of the arduous task involved when cultivating the attitude necessary for such a receptivity. This attitude is available to each person as a play on their constitution (or character).

In this sense, Emerson chides Americans for a failure to appreciate how difficult freedom *is*, not only to attain but to live. He writes, "Our America has a bad name for superficialness. Great men, great nations, have not been boasters and buffoons, but perceivers of the terror of life, and have manned themselves to face it."[33] But for Emerson the terrors of life are not limited to those contingencies that exist beyond the human. They also are composed of fateful acts that confine the person in a life of his or her own making. He writes, "Every spirit makes its house, but afterwards the house confines the spirit."[34] This is a modern formulation of the framework within which being free is possible, a formula that can be adapted to contemporary experience without serious revision. To suggest that one might be confined in the house of one's spirit anticipates and parallels Foucault's later assertion that "The soul is the prison of the body."[35] Emerson suggests that this form of confinement also points toward the kind of freedom we enjoy. Freedom is constituted through the acts by which we overcome our confinement from within by coming to know our individual roles as builders of our fate. Emerson insists that we come to respect the terrors of fate as intrinsic to the exercise of freedom.

Cavell raises a concern that grows out of this terror, about the silence that might be encouraged as a kind of resistance to the violent clarity of normalization and the use of that silence to ignore or suppress knowledge of injustice while preserving the presence of the ordinary. Silence appears in Emerson's "Fate" as a silence concerning slavery. Cavell asks: How is it possible to write of the powers of freedom as an affirmation of life's experience when one is in the state of slavery? He worries about Emerson's silence in the face of the abnegation of freedom—worries about it for its own sake but also because a similar silence is exemplified in Martin Heidegger's postwar posture regarding the politics of Nazism and Heidegger's controverted Nazism, a silence that has put extreme pressure on Heidegger's philosophical commitments. Cavell sees how Heidegger is an important inheritor of Emerson by way of Nietzsche; so important, in fact, that in working out the *how* of the inheritance, the fate of Emerson as a resource for democratic thinking might be determined. In this reading, Emerson's fate becomes so closely associated with the fate of democracy as to be coterminous with it. (And this goes some way toward explaining what for some is Cavell's obsession with Emerson, with the fate of democracy and philosophy together.)

In response to the question of *how*, Cavell poses another question—too often staged in bad faith in recent years, the bad faith consisting of asking from a position politically and ethically removed from the basic concerns raised by it—about the latent power of one thinker's work to inflect the meaning of the work of another. He asks, "Does Heidegger's politics—by association, to say the least—taint Emerson's points of contact with it?"[36] If this is the case, the question of inheritance and precedence is crucial for Emerson, Heidegger, and Cavell himself, whose embrace of Emerson is, among other things, a public attempt to implicate himself in what he has suggested is the Emersonian project of underwriting philosophy. To the extent that we allow Cavell to stand in for those of us who see the question of the possibility of philosophy to be a political one, crucially concerning the prospects of democracy, the question of contamination threatens to spread like a stain through all our thinking about the ordinary and what it allows.

It is a concern with art's relationship to philosophy that leads to this other set of issues. When Cavell questions the conjoining of the fate of philosophy with the fate of art, he is directly led to the related question of the conjoining of philosophy and politics:

> Isn't Heidegger careful to deny that poetry and philosophy are the same? (He is careful to deny that philosophy and religion are the same, presumably on the ground that philosophy cannot acknowledge religion as letting—the way religion works to let—truth happen, say by authority or revelation. Then can philosophy acknowledge the work of politics—to what extent does it define Heidegger's curse to say that he saw politics—as letting truth happen?)[37]

Another way to put this matter is to ask under what set of circumstances is it warranted for someone to go about repudiating the association of action with grasping, with the desire to hold truths, to affix them to certain places, to engage in the violence of ordering in the name of justice, or in the ironical phrase, to work to "preserve freedom," if the alternative to such a grasping is *merely* letting truth happen? How can one go about doing that when "letting truth happen" means both to repudiate the grasping for oneself and to accept the grasping of others? It is almost an understatement to say that the stakes for both philosophy and the ordinary are high when the issue of the politics of the ordinary is raised in this way.

What is the character of this receptivity that marks the attempt to enter a relationship with truth and yet to avoid grasping? Is it a *mere* passivity? Cavell's Emersonian turn to the diurnal, to the rhythms of the everyday, confronts this question. He suggests that receptivity is an active mode, the passivity of passion being able to turn into activity, and is characterized by the daily return to the state of our lives. Such a thinking requires a severe discipline, the walking of a tightrope strung between two mistakes: the pessimism of cultural decline and the optimism of positive fact. The conditioning of this exercise, the formal requisites of the openness thus enabled, should be attached to a political posture that enables one to realize himself or herself as a citizen of a larger public, engaging through consent and dissent in the work of meliorating injustice, acting as no *mere* subject might.

A test of this Emersonian thinking can be made by retracing Emerson's response to the racism that accompanied the institution of chattel slavery in the antebellum era. Cornel West suggests a very direct tainting of Emerson when he attaches "Fate" to the essay "Race," a chapter from Emerson's *English Traits*. West argues that a severe circumscribing of Emerson's thought is entailed in what he suggests is Emerson's debilitating racism. The fear Cavell expresses concerning inheritance may be thought to be most relevant here, where Emerson seems to legitimize the limitations allegedly imposed on personality by race.[38] But examination of the essay in question suggests something otherwise. The tension Emerson expresses in "Fate" between freedom and circumstance appears in "Race" as a tension between embodiment and imagination. Emerson suggests that to pull oneself out of the limits of circumstance and to rise above the parochialism of one's immediate surroundings requires a betrayal of who one has previously been. The recommendation of the English that Emerson advances in "Race" has to do with their cosmopolitan capacity to be a mongrel nationality, in the sense of resisting the impulse to be any one thing or quality. They thus carry with them the sort of circumstances that might encourage a greater exercise of freedom. He writes, "The English derive their pedigree from such a range of nationalities, that there needs sea-room and land-room to unfold the varieties of talent and character."[39] This expansive notion of race, associated with the (de)constitution of nationality by way of its imperial spread, renders biological racialism moot even as it implicitly endorses an expansive nationalism (though even here one might wonder what a nation that never realizes itself as such—namely, America—is *qua* nation).

In general the idea of race as physicality, even when present in Emerson, may be minimized because what is most important for him is the freedom of thought, expressed as the overcoming of the limits imposed by the fact of embodiment, not as the crude expression of physical constitution or trait. Despite such an excuse, there remains the other question of what Emerson *allows* in connecting fate to race. Is he passively permissive of racism? Is the idea of freedom as an overcoming of fate, and this overcoming as located in the ordinary, in the uneventful, tainted by ordinary racism?[40]

This question points to the internal limits of one of the most favored metaphors of liberalism, the idea of self-ownership as self-determination. One path of this idea of freedom as self-ownership is stoicism, the embrace of inner freedom and renunciation of the world by the minimally impeded individual, who, to preserve a sense of self, turns away from the struggles of those who are owned by others. Even if not explicitly stoical in character, self-ownership most often resolves itself as a set of practical ethical questions concerning the various burdens different people can be asked to bear in the struggle to resist fate. In that reckoning, those who embrace self-ownership are disabled in calculating the burden for those who lack self-ownership. This disability echoes clearly in contemporary evaluations of ways to confront the malignant power of discrimination as an unjust barrier to the quest for freedom, the harmful inequality imposed contingently on a caste of people. This damage is yet another unwanted inheritance of chattel slavery.[41] At another level, the question returns us to the concern about the tainting that the ordinary can do to philosophy, and what that tainting means for the political inheritance of philosophy.

The existence of slavery disrupts the quest for self-reliance to the extent that self-reliance becomes synonomous with self-ownership. Those who think that Emerson is passively permissive of racism also comprehend self-reliance as a doctrine of self-ownership. But self-reliance as an aversion to conformity also averts some of the central claims of property relationships, because those claims are conformist in character. We might ask of those who would be self-reliant, those who would endorse Cavell's thoughts as somehow their own: How might there be a tutelage in self-reliance for those who, ceasing to be owned by others, find themselves un-owned, even by themselves?

This second question may enable a deeper understanding of the democratic impulse underlying political theories of freedom. Emerson's politics are a politics of constitutional amendation, in which the relationship between person and constitutive event is made an explicit subject of the willing of free persons, much freer than Kant would have them be.[42] For while subjects are constrained by the force of what Emerson still acknowledges as a universal voice, what separates Emerson from Kant as a moralist is the former's poetic recognition that the universe is a much more complicated place than even a Kant will allow, not to be presumed upon as if it *might* be known, even if one acknowledges it *cannot* be known. Emerson is deeply aware of the forces and directions of the language that bears human beings. His attempt is to suggest not a conformity with the demands of a universal imperative but something more strange, rather than more familiar, to make use of Nietzsche's distinction.[43] Referring to one of the famous lines from "Self-Reliance," Cavell writes, "The great difference from aesthetic and moral judgment is that the constitutional judgment demanding the amending of our lives (together) is to be found by each of us as a rejected thought returning to us."[44] Here Cavell is referring to one of Emerson's famous insights, when in "Self-Reliance" he writes, "In every work of genius we recognize our own rejected thoughts: they come back to us with a certain alienated majesty."[45] This appeal to the thoughts we have rejected gives Emerson's philosophy its esoteric quality and permits it to address, non-polemically, political issues as important as slavery. In this way Emersonian alienation requires the dependence of self-reliant individuals on others who will enunciate the thoughts rejected. This reliance on others to enunciate one's thoughts may be said to constitute the sociality of the self-reliant individual. (Constitutional judgment moves us away from Kant and toward Deleuze.)

The alienated relationship of self to others is the subject of Emersonian amendation.[46] Through a philosophical stance that is able to recoil from absolutes (one that recognizes in each of us our own rejected thoughts)—a philosophical stance suggested by Emerson—the absolute character of slavery, an absolute that silences, may be uncovered and opposed. But the achievement of this philosophical stance is deeply ambiguous in its references to the connections between person to event. The linkage between the two seems to be accomplished or frustrated by the degree of artfulness with which one engages in addressing the ordinary without ordering it in such a way as to re-enforce normalization.

Amendation is thus the subversion of the obvious. Cavell points to a passage in Emerson's West Indies address in which he says that "language must be raked, the secrets of the slaughter-houses and infamous holes that cannot front the day, must be ransacked, to tell what negro-slavery has been."[47] Cavell comments: "To think of language as raking and recoiling, is to think of it, though it may look tranquil, as aimed and fired—at itself, at us—as if the human creature of conditions, fated to language, exists in the condition of threat, the prize of unmarked battles, where every horizon—where the air of words (of what might be said) gravitates to the earth of assertion (of what actually has been said)—signifies a struggle between possession and dispossession, between speech and silence, between the unspeakable and the unsilenceable."[48] To rake language is to use it to tell, to count, to reckon. This telling or counting function bears on how amendation might be applied to the defect of thought in our constitution. In reckoning Emerson as a philosopher of freedom, Cavell points to a place where Emerson would think about what it means to count persons: the clause of the American Constitution that assesses representation—a clause that contains the infamous phrase "and excluding Indians not taxed, three fifths of all other Persons." From Emerson's perspective, the problem of amendation is the problem of constitution up and down, from the Constitution of the polity to the constitution of the person. Taking the Constitution this seriously, as a shaper of those citizen-subjects who are to amend it, is the stunningly open-ended, contingent, and terrifying achievement of the American scholar, who is anyone who would engage in the project not necessarily of founding but of amending. As Cavell puts it:

In the large we do not see how many we are; in the small we do not know, as Emerson put it in "The American Scholar," whether we add up to what the "old fable" calls "one Man." As if we do not know whether any of us, all and each, count. We are living our skepticism.[49]

This lived skepticism can be corrosive of will, paralyzing of any new effort in the face of constant and terrible loss. The more effort, the less movement. But amendation is partial, open, and incomplete, an acknowledgment that even skepticism is imperfect.

In the face of our skepticism we have, at least (and at the worst moments), a right to remain silent.[50] This silence disturbs Cavell, for it is a profound philosophical act—perhaps the most profound philosophical act. Deeply familiar with Wittgenstein, he surely recalls at this moment the final proposition of the *Tractatus*, the book that Wittgenstein was later to amend into *Philosophical Investigations*: "What we cannot speak about we must pass over in silence."[51] Can this sentence be an instruction to a way for philosophy to preserve itself in the face of conditions that negate philosophy? Cavell thinks it is important to consider silence and knows how fraught with danger the consideration of silence is. To want someone to say something can be to deny that person his or her voice, a point he makes in regard to Wittgenstein but that also applies here: "To interpret silence as delay— that is, to refuse to see that sometimes there is nothing to say—may be tragic."[52] Yet silence can simultaneously be known as philosophy's excuse.[53] For Emerson, the condition of slavery calls for us to speak out against it, but philosophically, it calls as well for a silence that will preserve the philosophical enterprise in the face of the tragic recognition of every person's entanglement in this injustice. In the case of Emerson we can observe a silence that is supplemented by references in his philosophical essays to the experience of the ordinary which is to be realized outside of injustice. We may understand from Emerson's silence that the separation between politics and philosophy is never complete.[54]

It isn't easy to remain silent. One may note the classic scenario of detective shows, which illustrates the compulsion of the criminal in the final act to tell someone of his crime—usually the successful detective, who comes upon the criminal, is trapped, and urges, "So tell me, how did you do it?" Then the criminal tells all, instead of quickly dispatching the detective (the sensible course of action, were it not for the compulsion to tell). Here, while it seems that the philosophical imperative to tell the truth overcomes the political counsel to protect one's secret, at a more complicated level silence is overcome so that the criminal will tell not only how but why he has committed the crime. Silence is overcome so that the criminal may justify the act, not simply to the detective but to herself or himself, whether it be through braggadocio or plea.[55] One doesn't overcome silence in the face of the evil one is complicit with; one cannot resist speaking, against prudence and truthfulness, in order to justify to oneself and others one's motives and actions, however delusionary the justification might be, in order to test oneself to others. To speak may be to justify what is unjustifiable.

This complex connection of political and philosophical actions applies to all acts of confession.[56] We are confessing animals, we human beings: confession is a primary mode through which we acknowledge each other and so acknowledge ourselves. In this context, silence is a powerfully passive action, a shaping resistance in the face of the desire to confess. The assertion of the right to remain silent, to decline to speak of one's crime or sin, itself speaks to us of a turn in modern thinking, of the rise of a protestant sensibility that suggests that one justifies oneself finally to the God of one's own self.

This sort of exercise of silence suggests a reverence for a self that is self-owned. In contrast, the grounding of politics and philosophy in the ordinary suggests that both must ascend from another place, the place of the low, the common, or, even more radically, from what both Emerson and Thoreau have called Nature (though their understandings of the nature of Nature were not exactly the same). That philosophy and politics may be claimed to ascend from something common to both is a disparagement not of the ordinary but of the pretense of politicians and philosophers when they elevate the love of power and truth above the ground from which they have grown, when the play of confession and silence tends to dominate public discourse. Put less tendentiously, amendation might be best comprehended as an aspect of a more generalizable inflection, the political face of the human ability to notice those things that may be called nature through a practice of (re)iteration. In practices of confession and silence, in the discourses through which we publicize ourselves and acknowledge each other, we develop and make claims about who we are and how we should be together and apart. In this sense, the natural becomes us politically.

In her study of Thoreau's political theory, Jane Bennett argues that he understands nature as a "heteroverse . . . a work of art reducible neither to creation nor discovery . . . an ideal that articulates the experience of being 'part and parcel' of one's surroundings even as those surroundings exceed full comprehension."[57] For Bennett, this expansive and complex sense of nature encompasses a sense both of volition and of contingency. Nature as heteroverse enables Thoreau (and us) to "front" the wild, that which is contingent and unpredictable, and to draw on the experience of nature by confronting its least predictable appearances and actions. The wildness we might experience on the frontier between our internal subjectivities and the external heteroverse of nature enables us to break with some of the patterns of meaningless repetition that can dominate our lives. The availability of such experience, the not quite *a priori* character of nature, can thus be considered a resource of the ordinary against the powers of normalization and eventfulness.

But to claim that we might draw on the wild as a resource is not to say how we might learn to do so. What resourcefulness is needed to turn us to the wild, to the common, to the low?

We might first notice what we ought not be tempted to do. The politics of amendation is subverted and repressed by the quest to achieve certainty, a quest undertaken on the part of those who place security above all other values and who see in constitution not only initiation but the end of all action. The events of contemporary times sometimes seem inflected with too many overripe meanings, overdeterminations of the ordinary that threaten to overwhelm the possibilities of free experiences of all sorts. In response to the proliferation of meaning, the desire for a sense of cloture—expressed most vehemently by the resurgence of various social, political, and religious fundamentalisms—operates within the heart of modern institutions of power to generate a mistaken sense of self-preservation, laying the groundwork for a bulwark against amendation.[58] Whether the impulse is located in a jurisprudence of original intent or in more direct appeals to the heavens above, the attempt to freeze truth into place, to establish certainty as a buttress for action by authority, becomes a secret expression of one of the more corrosive forms of contemporary nihilism, one that begins from above and ends with the destruction of democracy.[59] This might be called the nihilism of the master of the house.

Rather than live in such a house (even when one calls it home), it may be possible to embrace a kind of homelessness, a condition that could make the idea of home more palpable by showing more clearly the character of what home lacks. The play of home and homelessness is a process of a politics of the ordinary, fronting the ordering principles that would undermine the possibilities of their common disappearance. Both are spaces of happenstance privacy, one exposed, the other concealed; one composed of the discarded and wasted, the other elevated by modern politics as the privileged space to which we all might repair at the end of struggle. But both home and homelessness depend on a continued and persistent confrontation with a realm of the ordinary that would not be exhausted by the ordering of events and the normalization of selves.

And when one wants to be at home? Here we may think of a home as an always incomplete project, a place within which we may nonetheless dwell. Thoreau suggests how the open site of the incomplete building is a space of created obscurity:

> My house never pleased my eye so much after it was plastered, though I was obliged to confess that it was more comfortable. Should not every apartment in which man dwells be lofty enough to create some obscurity overhead, where flickering shadows may play at evening about the rafters?[60]

Thoreau's house at Walden becomes a home at moments when this space is obscure, when there is a moment's rest within the shelter of the incomplete, unplastered roof; no pleasing smoothness but a roughness that is indefinitely amendable. Here is a paradox: a home is most completely livable at those moments when it is unfinished, not quite comfortable. So with ourselves, and with the polity we make together.

Being Bored, Leaving Here

But what if home were finished, a deadly and dull place? What if being homeless, which is always a departure from some home, was an experience no longer available to someone, precisely because all homes were finished, all spaces presumed to be mapped, all trajectories measured? What if there were nothing left to do here? One explanation for the resurgence of fundamentalisms in the late modern age lies in their power to allay the dread of deadness. This is yet another kind of experience we may associate with boredom. This boredom is close to the bone, harsh and pitiless, a deep challenge to human being.

We come to boredom in quiet moments, when we are able to experience something unknown—holes in the sky, uncertain futures, forgotten pasts. Boredom once more gives us access to an important and strange question: In the face of boredom—or in spite of it—is there an unknown that might remain unknown? Might there yet be some obscurity overhead that would help us think about how to acknowledge the unknown without surrendering to the temptation to know it? Because the more common approaches to the ordinary are from places we believe we know, we offer to each other postures of partial certitude when facing different elements of our common existence. It might be possible to say that from our senses of the ordinary we go forth to make new spaces, to build a world of spaces, turning toward that world, embracing it, loving it. In moments of boredom, however, we may see something else: the meanness of the quest, the terrific harm we do to each other and ourselves out of the desire for a convincing love. This desire is responsible for the spread of the sense of certitude from its partial and *ad hoc* locality into various domains of imperial existence. As it comes to represent itself as a naturalistic position of truth, that certitude obscures the question of the unknown. But boredom brings us back to the unknown. Out of boredom, when we are resting from our labors of making our world, we can see how the unknown is a repository of freedom, a place we must somehow make untouched to give us a way of being free, a deferred resting place we may never reach but may always be approaching.[61]

The unknown thus presents an important set of challenges to thinking about freedom in the modern era. But the predominant response to the thought of the unknown, even at this late moment in the modern era, relies on the cultivation of theistic religious sensibilities, and the most common forums for expressing a sense of the ineffable and enacting its logic remain institutions of organized religions. Politically, religious values in countries such as the United States seem to conjoin with a particular notion of freedom that identifies it more and more closely with a kind of security.[62] To think of freedom as security encourages one to work to overcome uncertainty, to find a resting place, a home. The price of that certainty is that we turn away from the fecund pluralizations arising from the regions of human conduct that remain unthematized. Many turn away from these regions with regret, but usually their regret is outweighed by a fear of a loss of control and a hope of entering a state of a sort of peace that will place them safely beyond regret. This is a desperate kind of faith.

Freedom as security presents an illusion of stillness. But underneath the surface of certitude and the representation of freedom as security, agents of the late modern security state must be continuously in motion, mapping out and stabilizing constantly upwelling uncertainties. The peace that has been sought at least since Thomas Hobbes dreamed of it requires a lot of boundary maintenance, but the maintenance pays off to the extent that it becomes increasingly difficult to imagine other ways of being in the world.

So while the institutionalization of freedom as security inspires dreams of freedom by other religious seekers, they find themselves entangled in the ends of freedom as security.

Cultists serve as exemplary case studies in this regard. Against the dead hand of what they see as an overrationalized world, modern cultists have sought the kind of answers that will allow them to gain entry into something they want to know as the unknown. Their narrative myths involve superterrestrial beings, the infusion of bodies with alien spirits, possibilities of strangeling births, alternative dimensions of reality, and resurrected beings. Their aspirations are close enough to traditional religious beliefs that a nervous question presents itself: What distinguishes cultists from more conventional religious seekers? This is no easy question, for the disturbing implications as much for religionists as for cultists. Nietzsche warns against all such seekers when he has Zarathustra say, "I entreat you my brothers, *remain true to the earth*, and do not believe those who speak to you of superterrestrial hopes! They are poisoners, whether they know it or not."[63]

One might not condemn the act of seeking and still recognize the limits of the search. Perhaps this problem can be phrased another way: it may be that the institutional legitimacy of traditional religion compensates for a lack of passion, or that the cultists' lack of institutional legitimacy is compensated for by their surplus of passion. Maybe the affective history of religious belief is composed of no more than a series of transitions from passion to institution. In this sense a deep protestant sensibility, a trust in intuition as a way of finding one's self through a process of discovery, effectively opposes the tuition of leaders who tell lost souls what they must do in order to be found. One might even claim that the controversy concerning tuition versus intuition is at the heart of struggles concerning the way in which Americans are to lead their spiritual lives at the end of the millennium.[64]

One may think about the fatal narrative of the Heaven's Gate cult as a disturbing example of this loss of faith in the ability to escape the dictation of another's intuition, to be self-reliant in one's religious convictions. The bare facts of the story of this cult were widely publicized at the moment of the group's demise. At the end of March 1997, the mass news media's attention in southern California turned away from a court-ordered seizure of the personal goods of O. J. Simpson to a strange finding in Rancho Santa Fe, a "gated community" some thirty miles north of San Diego. In a rented mansion the bodies of thirty-nine members of Heaven's Gate were discovered.[65] Led by a former opera singer and music teacher, Marshall Herff Applewhite—who had renamed himself Do after the first note on the standard music scale—the members of Heaven's Gate believed it was possible for them to attain a form of virtual immortality, if only they were to abandon their vehicles, as they called their bodies, and in doing so to escape the Earth itself by transporting themselves onto a space vehicle hidden by and accompanying the Hale-Bopp comet.

Perhaps more important than the content of the cult's beliefs, which were in many ways quite close to Christian mythology, were the motivations that informed the choice of Do's followers to leave Earth by abandoning their bodies. Their desire identified the goal of reaching a higher plane of existence with a sense that nothing was left to exist for on Earth. Hitching a ride to the stars on the Hale-Bopp comet, abandoning their vehicles, was not only a step forward but a chance to leave a place that was already dead to them. On one of the videotaped messages many members left behind to explain their reasons for departure, one member of the cult was recorded as saying, "Maybe they're crazy, for all I know. But I don't have any choice but to go for it, because I've been on this planet for 31 years and there's nothing here for me." She was not worried about the idea of dying or leaving her vehicle because "if that is what it takes, that's better than being around here and doing absolutely nothing."[66]

Being around here, doing nothing. . . . Here the expression of boredom connects to a deep alienation, in this case to what Hannah Arendt once termed "earth alienation," attributing it to the dominance of the *telos* of science in late modernity.[67] For the members of the Heaven's Gate cult, the abandonment of bodies was synonymous with the abandonment of Earth. They engaged in a rigorous asceticism; many submitted to castration, and all embraced a powerful discipline of self-denial. Everything they did, including their major pleasure—watching *Star Trek* reruns on television—was oriented toward the goal of leaving the Earth behind. When heaven is understood as both a departure from and an extension of Earth, a utopian site where what is denied during one's life (especially the pleasure) is granted in an afterlife, Earth is better understood as a place of confinement, a closed and limited place. The terror facing those who might actually reach Heaven's Gate is that there may still be nothing for them in the new world they have overtaken. They fail to recognize a logic of compensation that allows no escape through the line of flight they seek, that their fantasy of escape is but the mirror image of freedom as security.[68] Still they seek it, engaging in a search for certainty that is also an attempt to master the unknown, to tame it, to overcome it. What would the members of Heaven's Gate think if life on a higher plane was no more or less than the life they currently enjoyed or despised? And what if they couldn't leave, even by exiting their vehicles? Surely this question, a version of Nietzsche's question concerning the eternal recurrence of the same, is indebted to Emerson and his America. This may be the deepest that boredom goes, and it goes to the heart of a politics of the ordinary.

The Unreasoning Mask

If Emerson gives us permission to think about the ordinary as something we may descend or aspire to, it may be that neither descent nor ascent is adequate as a metaphor for coming to an acknowledgment of the ordinary. In this sense, perhaps we can call Herman Melville, figured here as a philosophical descendant of Emerson, the (first) prodigal son in the American quest for the ordinary. Melville is a writer who marks the worst of the American experience and, in so doing, enables us to carry on. His novels, poems, and stories re-create and allegorize events; he represents these events in the context of a much larger cultural project, as they work through his sense of the ordinary and its connection to the politics of an expansionist vision of the United States.

Charles Olson has compared Melville to Whitman, suggesting that he moved beyond the positive flow of the transcendentalists' vision of America, braving the horrors that, as Cavell worried, would tear down the possibility of democracy if left unfaced and unchallenged. One could suggest that Melville complements Emerson's overcoming of the limitations imposed on us by that which is unknown, showing the consequences of abandoning the quest of the ordinary in the name of—what? Melville knows that in America, the name itself is too terrible to speak, even though we blaspheme every day in our failed attempts to say it.

One of Melville's accomplishments consists of his ability to show the space of American freedom *as space*, in this sense giving greater appreciation to the spatial dimension of the Emersonian project than Emerson himself may have allowed. "Melville went to space to probe and find man," Olson writes.[69] He later continues:

> Whitman we have called our greatest voice because he gave us hope. Melville is the truer man. He lived intensely his people's wrong, their guilt. But he remembered the first dream. The *White Whale* is more accurate than *Leaves of Grass*. Because it is America, all of her space, the malice, the root.[70]

Melville gives us a model for excavating key moments of everyday life, making the novel into an attempt to reckon the ordinary by making its space explicit. The depth of the surfaces we live and the most terrible things we do to one another in grasping, in expressing the most unhandsome aspects of our condition, become in the hands of Melville the backdrop for distinctly new kinds of tragedy and comedy. That is, Melville takes full measure of the Emersonian opening to a new yet unapproachable America and writes out of a sense of the wreckage that piles up as we attempt to approach it.

If there is a novel that represents the deepest moment of this sense of reckoning or accounting for the losses entailed in these gains, it is *Moby-Dick*, what may be the largest and most intimidating novel ever written on the subject of American evil. "Ego non baptizo in nomine patris, sed in nomine diaboli" is the blessing Ahab bestows on the harpoon tempered in his blood and the blood of his secret team; "I do not baptize you in the name of the father, but in the name of the devil." Olson suggests that the very world of Ahab, "Ahab-world," is an evil one, akin to the world of Macbeth, excluding God—not only the Father but the Son and Holy Spirit. Ahab's world is a plunge to the watery depths. This evil heart of Ahab, his raging desire—oh, where does it come from? Or even better, where *doesn't* it come from? For Ahab's world is a world of slaughter, right there on a boat in the middle of deep blue sea. This evil is grand, familiar, recognizable, and grows out of the claims that goodness makes on us. Ahab is every man who wants to be good by overcoming himself and his limits.

Olson suggests that Ahab is modeled on Shakespeare's King Lear. But how are we to take this observation, and how far? Ahab's madness seems akin to that displayed by the leader of Heaven's Gate, Do. A charismatic leader challenges his crew to go with him to the ends of the world in a quest to make the unknown knowable. Lear, Ahab, and Do all seem ashamed of being loved. Yet there are continents of madness, and oceans of madness, too. Lear tries to reach the sea, having imagined himself cast out by his ungrateful daughters. The American Lear, Ahab, leaves his young wife and child ashore. Do, a cult leader weaned on science fiction posing as religious revelation, terrified of his own desires, leaves the world altogether. In this spinning of love and hate, pride and shame, whose shame follows whom?[71]

We may comprehend Melville's politics through yet another lens. Michael Rogin has claimed that Melville is the American Marx, a Marx whose politics were displaced through the genealogy of his aristocratic family, so that in *Moby-Dick* he was able to refract the deeply racialized American version of class conflict that enveloped the European revolutions of

1848.[72] Indeed, Rogin suggests that the whole corpus of Melville's work may be understood as a response to and re-figuring of the wars of race, colonial expansion, and class conflict afflicting American society in the middle of the nineteenth century. Through its characterization of the racial divisions of labor on the *Pequod*; the violence that attends the monomania of Ahab, himself the grand allegorizer of this book; and a staggering array of racial, gender, and class interactions, conflicts, and loves, played out in an astonishingly simple, black-and-white, exclusively male seascape of surfaces and horizons, *Moby-Dick* becomes a simulacrum of the American 1848. Rogin writes, "Ahab brought into view the political and social crisis opened up by Manifest Destiny and slavery, and grounded that crisis in capitalist expansion and possession."[73]

Whether it be through Marx or Shakespeare, Melville's work serves as a great countervoice to Emerson and Thoreau in thinking about ordinary freedom. Like them, he represents the problem of the unknown as being somehow beyond the capacity of representation to capture. But in ways that move the question of America past all prior limits, making the found West of Emerson into yet another lost site, Melville emphasizes the tragic dimensions of the ontological fact of space itself.[74] His Ahab anticipates our struggle concerning the fate of the ordinary as it refers to and operates against a desire for security through enclosure and the wretched boredom that might attend a finished world. Ishmael is warned of this boredom when he first tries to sign on board the crew of the *Pequod*. Captain Peleg, one of the owners, asks him if he is signing up to see the world. He asks Ishmael to look over the weather-bow of the ship toward the ocean horizon and to report what he sees.

> "Well. What's the report?" Said Peleg when I came back; "what did ye see?"
> "Not much," I replied—"nothing but water; considerable horizon though, and there's a squall coming up, I think."
> "Well, what dost thou think then of seeing the world? Do ye wish to go round Cape Horn to see any more of it, eh? Can't ye see the world where you stand?"[75]

Ishmael admits being a "little staggered" by this observation. Through this exchange, Melville imagines the world as a great open space of sameness, ready to be gridded, cast as a plane where every place is the same as another. So the focus will depend on who we are but not where we are: how we come to be but not where we are going, which is only where we are.

Against this relentlessly open and homogeneous space, Melville posits his great regard for the event, in what appears to be a reverence for the agent, for what Ahab calls some unknown but still reasoning thing. In a justly famous rhapsody, Ahab explains why he must seek the whale and what the desperate character of his freedom is to be:

> All visible objects man, are but as pasteboard masks. But in each event—in the living act, the undoubted deed—there, some unknown but still reasoning thing puts forth the mouldings of its features from behind the unreasoning mask. If man will strike, strike through the mask! How can the prisoner reach outside, except by thrusting through the wall?[76]

Ahab seeks to thrust to through the mask, the gray sameness of the mapped world, to reach to a place on the other side of that plane. That place is one of reason, and we can see the shape of reason even behind the mask. Yet that shape is not enough; for Ahab, this truth cannot be veiled. (There is an only slightly disguised critique of Kantian common sense here, with its notions of an upright truth, a following of that which we can never see as though we can see it. How is one to see beneath the object?) The white whale frustrates Ahab, denying him the truth of his profession, becoming a wall between him and his authentic self. Nevertheless, Ahab's regard for the event—the lowering, the chase, and the kill—is also the enunciation of a principle of hope, made from right *there* on the surface of things. Ahab seeks to demonstrate that surfaces conceal depths, that somehow in the separate world of men represented in the voyage of the *Pequod* there might be a way to break through the visible world into an ideal one. This ideal, what can best be called an ideal of authentic manliness, is dependent on the powers of caste, class, and gender oppression and enslavement. Melville's attacks against his great tragic character are attacks on this manliness, because it expresses this untoward hope that there may yet be a freedom to be realized in a place beyond this imperfect world. Such an idealism is deadly, informing the most foolhardy projects in American life, our attempts to do something akin to the ends of that philosophy we maybe ought to be repudiating instead.

Ahab's profession is that of a whaler, and in *Moby-Dick*, because the whale is the repository of the deepest truths, the whaler is a philosopher. Ahab searches for truth, using all means available to him; he must come to possess it in order to overcome the wounds he has suffered in pursuit of it. He is dismembered in his pursuit of truth and can hope to re-member only in the presence of the animal, the pagan of seas, that "dismasted" him.

What does Ahab hope to re-member? Only that which he cannot know.

It seems as though Melville fears and loathes Ahab and all that he represents—his monomania, his destructive power, his attraction to death, and his willingness to play a role in the master's game. But he must also be deeply attracted to him. It is a measure of the extraordinary imaginative power of Melville that he creates so strong an argument on behalf of what he must fear the most. Melville figures Ahab's principle of hope as vainglory, the hubris that leads to calamity, the solipsism that establishes a tragic distance between the quotidian humanity of Starbuck, on the one hand, and the equally quotidian and raucously joyous carnality of Ahab's Patagonian crew, on the other. And yet Ahab is never given less than his due, even by Starbuck, who eventually bonds with him in what might be considered an Emersonian hermaphroditic marriage of betters.[77] Melville's intense representation of a quest for perfection that ends with the death of all (save Ishmael) may be said to call into question the entire trajectory of the polity Melville is a part of, and apart from. And while rejection may be evaluated apart from the method of representation that conveys its force, it is not to be separated from it completely. Otherwise, Melville would become what he criticizes.

For Rogin, the key to reading Melville lies in this paradox, in how the play of fiction and realism approaches but never quite realizes a representative truth. Commenting on Melville's essay on bookbinding, he notes both the power of Melville's imagination and the seeming futility of his project to create a world in writing.

> Melville . . . defended the unadorned book . . . when he insisted that his early narratives were in fact not fiction. That claim collapses the distinction between a work of art and its social referents. It seems to promise that the book offers an escape from the world. Melville's pretense that he was simply reporting his own experience was itself fictional, however. He never intended that his tales should merely reproduce a reality existing outside of them. But the relationship of his fiction to the material from which it was constructed changed over time. Melville's withdrawal from social reality into the text and the state came in the later stages of his development. His imaginative origins took him, by way of his family, out into the central political and social issues of his time.[78]

This imaginative project resulted in Melville's increasingly intense isolation from social life. In this interpretation of the failed impact of *Moby-Dick* on cultural politics and the subsequent trajectory of Melville's work, Rogin argues that because Melville failed to influence the political reality he was most concerned about, he became increasingly self-referential, retreating from the political origins of his artistic inspiration, and even, at the end of his writing life, providing ironical acknowledgment of his final defeat by having Billy Budd bless Captain Vere. (But this fall into poetry, seen by Rogin as a defeat, may also hint of something else.)

The evil heart of Ahab, his terrible rage—where does it come from? Where Rogin sees Marx's 1848, Olson sees Shakespeare's Lear. But perhaps they are not so far apart. In Lear, Shakespeare represented a character whose extraordinary largeness, in Olson's rendering, inspired the creation not only of Ahab but of Moby-Dick, the unknowable writ large. The unknowable is what Ahab wants to strike through to reach some other side. The unknowable, in the form of what we call love, is what Lear wants to evade in his shame. But Ahab is shameless. So is Melville, who wrote to Hawthorne on finishing the writing of the book, "I have written a wicked book, and feel spotless as the lamb."[79]

This wickedness sinks into the details of the everyday. In *Moby-Dick*, Melville describes in loving detail the various membranes, the soft tissues, bones, and various bodily products of the largest animal in the world; he tells us how it is stripped and cooked in the floating charnel house of nineteenth-century American industry, melted into oil, stowed in barrels, ballasted in the hold of the ship circumnavigating the globe, a nineteenth-century ancestor of twentieth-century oil tankers. (And all this is prefaced by "Etymology and Extracts,"elevating the low subject of whaling to a place of immortal import.) Melville gives us a heavenly/hellish world of the ordinary (from beginning to end), of abstract planes occasionally confronted with mists of blood, the bodies of whales (and men) cast to the sharks when used up, as the great birds of the sea wheel above in azure skies, occasionally descending to feed.

In this book Melville may be said to have read and recoiled from the space of modern, abstract freedom in order to pursue a more substantively democratic course. This democratic aspiration is often noted but more rarely explored in its substance. In one attempt to find the place of contemporary poetry between the respective powers of sight and voice, Ann Lauterbach refers back to Olson's attempt to comprehend Melville in this way. She writes:

> Olson, I think, wanted to claim for poetry a terrain, a mental geography, which would collapse the separation between, and privileging of, sight over sound, giving each equal status on the linguistic field of the poem. . . . The

structures that would come from such a vocabulary would move laterally, metynomically, rather than vertically, suggesting American ideals of democratic mobility rather than European ideals of hierarchy.[80]

Such democratic movements of language are peppered throughout the narrative of *Moby-Dick*: in the most wholesome love of Ishmael and Queequeg, in the rude solidarity of the crew in search of the whale, in the common and low meals served at the Try Pots chowder shop, and in the watery death shared by the crew with Ahab. And opposed to democracy, it is easy enough to note the factory-like division of ship's labor and the rated division of profits (Ishmael was offered the seven hundred and seventy-seventh *lay*, as it was strangely termed), the command hierarchy of officers and crew, and the teleology of the quest, to kill the whale. *Moby-Dick* may be considered a poetical novel of democracy, at its best and worst. But *Moby-Dick* is also a tragedy, which suggests something tragic about the democratic project as a whole.

Unless one takes the side of the whale. Then some of this novel's most democratic aspirations may become more visible. To take the side of the whale is to try to comprehend the whale as a subject. And Melville does take the side of the whale in passages of extraordinary weirdness and brutal humor. In the midst of a series of chapters that provide details of the physiology and behavior of the whale, he imagines the subjectivity of the whale, assessing its intellect and character. These are the chapters titled "The Prairie," a seemingly whimsical parody of the "science" of physiognomy applied to the sperm whale, and "The Nut," in which the physiognomical interpretation of the whale is discarded as delusional and its substitute, the phrenological study of the skull, is rendered useless unless radically modified.[81]

In "The Prairie," the whale's head is represented as a "mystical brow." Comparing the whale to Shakespeare, Melville writes:

> But in the great Sperm Whale, this high and mighty god-like dignity inherent in the brow is so immensely amplified, that gazing upon it, in that full front view, you feel the Deity and the dread powers more forcibly than in beholding any other object in living nature. For you see no one point precisely; not one distinct feature is revealed; no nose, eyes, ears, or mouth; no face; he has none, proper; nothing but that one broad firmament of forehead, pleated with riddles; dumbly lowering with the doom of boats, and ships, and men. . . . Has the Sperm Whale ever written a book, spoken a speech? No, his great genius is declared in his doing nothing particular to prove it.[82]

This stillness of genius may be compared to Emerson's characterization of genius as believing that what is true for oneself is true for all, coupled with the admonishment "Speak your latent conviction and it will become the universal sense; for the inmost in due time become the outmost,—and our first thought is rendered back to us by the trumpets of the Last Judgment."[83] The silence of the whale is philosophically considered here, not as a response to the unbearable connection of philosophy to politics but as a representation of the unknown ordinary in wildness from which both politics and philosophy emerge.

Ishmael then presents his complaint and enlists his readers in the attempt to read the whale:

> Physiognomy, like every other human science, is but a passing fable. If then, Sir William Jones, who read in thirty languages, could not read the simplest peasant's face in its profounder and more subtle meanings, how may unlettered Ishmael hope to read the awful Chaldee of the Sperm Whale's brow? I put that brow before you. Read it if you can.[84]

The impenetrability of the whale's brow, the impossibility of reading it (as opposed to Emerson's suggestion that to study nature is to know oneself)[85] is proportionally as great as the attempt to read the human brow. (The mystical brow, Melville notes, is a used as a seal to signify God.) Placed on the scale of the human, the brow of the whale is reckoned as an infinity multiplied, a sphinx, as Melville/Ishmael puts it. And yet that brow is not simply a mask or cover for the skull that encases the brain but a gross disguise of it. "The brain is at least twenty feet away from his apparent forehead in life; it is hidden away behind its vast outworks, like the innermost citadel within the amplified fortifications of Quebec."[86] The unknown mask that Ahab must strike through is an impenetrable mass of junk and sperm. What features lie just beneath such a pasteboard? Here Melville's assessment of the captain could not be harsher: Ahab must be a fool!

Opposed to physiognomy is phrenology, and here Melville/Ishmael suggests that the most obvious reading of the skull of the whale, that the depressions on its top suggest a lack of self-esteem and no veneration, may be mistaken, since the skull needs to be re-evaluated in another, much larger context:

> Now, I consider that the phrenologists have omitted an important thing in not pushing their investigations from the cerebellum through the spinal canal. For I believe that much of a man's character will be found betokened in

his backbone. I would rather feel your spine than your skull, whoever you are. . . . Under all of these circumstances, would it be unreasonable to survey and map out the whale's spine phrenologically? For, viewed in this light, the wonderful comparative smallness of the brain proper is more than compensated by the wonderful comparative magnitude of the spinal cord.[87]

This spinal-phrenological reading of the whale culminates in an appreciation of the whale's hump, which arises from the spinal cord, and which is read by Ishmael/Melville as the "organ of firmness or indominableness of the whale." Thus Melville redistributes the reading of the whale, from the exterior of the brow, to the skull and the brain inside, to the spine which extends to the tail of this "fish."

This vast complexity of the whale's visage presents us with the impossibility of encountering the whale face to face so as to read it, to know it as we presume to know each other. Its very existence chides our presumption to know the other. The whale is not human in this sense and so allows us to reflect on how we constitute our humanity by centering it on the human face, to the neglect of the remainder of the body. The center is a pure, abstract conceptualization that finds its substance of expression in a kind of "faciality." Deleuze and Guattari write of this faciality that "the face is the icon proper to the signifying regime, the reterritorialization internal to the system."[88] To confront that which is not subject to strategies of reterritorialization, in their terms, is to begin to think about ways of being outside the systems that contain us. The larger embodiment of the whale may enable us to think better about the horizontal (rhizomatic) linkages available to us in the quest for a democratic equality of substance.

To take the side of the whale is to begin a process of becoming-animal, in Deleuze and Guattari's terms.[89] From their perspective, Ahab's quest for Moby-Dick can be rendered as a quest to connect with what they term "the anomalous" on the way to becoming-animal. They suggest that this quest of becoming-animal is an important element in the history of human being, underestimated or misunderstood almost of necessity by the dominant paths that reason has taken in civilizing the world. But sorcery, a separation from the pack, a haunting of the fringes of village or other societies, continues to be attempted by some exceptional individuals, in order to pursue their exceptional being more fully. Emerson's lesson concerning the meaning of our individual genius tells us that, democratically comprehended, we are *all* exceptional beings, and we *all* need to pursue such quests if we are to pursue our intuition (to be self-tutored) and develop a democratic sensibility. We might reckon the quality of our lives by reckoning the extent to which citizens are able to engage in such alternative pursuits of happiness. In this quest, the American 1848 might meet the American 1968, young Americans in both eras crashing against the wall that breaks their aspirations to authenticity, perhaps missing the other lesson to be learned concerning the character of their aspiration—that behind the unreasoning mask is not the truth they seek.

Deleuze and Guattari are concerned that "the contradiction between the two themes, 'contagion through the animal as pack,' and 'pact with the anomalous as exceptional being,' is progressively fading."[90] This fading renders the politics of an Ahab, in his sorcerer's guise, almost unrecognizable. And yet to fail to recognize such a sorcerer as someone who is striving toward the exceptional is to work toward the destruction of exceptionality.[91] To learn to be exceptional is to initiate a way of being different from others. Sometimes that way is as mad as is trying to conform. But sometimes democracy itself is madness. The whale's escape, his line of flight, is not yet ours. Nonetheless, the whale is our icon of deterritorialization.

From nineteenth century to twentieth is no great leap: eliminate the romantic engine, eliminate the poetry, and we may find that Melville's whaling industry and the method of agricultural production that Heidegger characterized (when he suggested that modern methods of agricultural production and the methods of administering concentration camps are essentially similar) are not so distant from each other as we might wish them to be. The all-too-human horror of technologized warfare and the general infiltration of war technologies throughout everyday life are anticipated in *Moby-Dick*. But even without overdrawing the past into the present, we might think of Melville, still innocent of the fate of politics in the twentieth century, as having based his critique of the American 1848 on a limning of the ambiguity of savagery, on a both destructive and invigorating blurring of distinctions that might be made between cannibals and Christians. In his vision of the oceanic world and in the details of quotidian life on board ship, Melville points up the inadequacies of transcendental categories in their capacity to comfort humans in the face of our desire for order, in the hope we hold for our cherished and yet dreaded mortality.

Melville's resistance to the unfolding of the events of his day found its location in his art. The paradox he lived was painful: the more aesthetically complete his vision, the further away from influencing the course of the events of his day he seemed to move, so that he would end his life in obscure poverty, with many years yet to pass until his figurative resurrection as an icon of American literature. Generalizing from the fate of Melville, we may ask whether there is an efficacious way to intervene through interpretation, whether the project of thinking about the ordinary is itself a futile gesture or a necessary part of the practice of being free.

Here we might pause and think: How lovely the whale! How desirable, and as Melville presents him, how worthy of desire! The whale blocks our view of the authentic, prevents us from realizing a peaceful death, opens us to the playful possibilities of decentered, ethical being. Throughout *Moby-Dick* sperm whales are exhaustively cataloged, archived, examined, dissected, beheaded, eaten (with gusto!), and, in perhaps the most hilariously transgressive passage of Melville's epic, fallen into headfirst and then exited by means of a Caesarean birth underwater.[92] The whale is a self-consuming commodity; the fires of the try-pots that boil his blubber are fed by his blubber. Whale oil lights the lamps of the civilized world so that we might read our fate. (That this light is the product of such barbarity is not lost on Melville but rather is his very point.) How beautiful the whale, how smooth, and, in his strange asymmetry, how mysterious, how unfathomable. To what species of sublimity might we say he belongs?

We ought to be careful. Moby-Dick is a pagan god of annihilation, who visits destruction on those who would dare try to destroy him. His story ends in the sorrow of a fate pre-ordained, the horrible deaths of Ahab and all of his crew (save one orphan). But the omens and portents that unfold through *Moby-Dick* are not the atavistic ghosts of unreason. They are the ghosts of a particular kind of reason turned upon itself. We might pause again (in our boredom) over that extraordinary phrase: Ahab believes in "some unknown, but still reasoning thing."[93] The weight of Melville's response to this proposition in *Moby-Dick* is to show not that reason is haunted by unreason but that any reason contains unreasonable elements, that there is an unknown that will always remain unknown, and that the attempt to overcome the unknown is too often implicated in projects of destruction.

What does Moby-Dick want? We will never find an answer to this question because it is not intended to have one. Moby-Dick, among other things, is a metaphor (and sometimes metonym) for Woman, she who blocks Man's way in his quest for authenticity. This capitalization seems Melville's intention. It is the magnificent failure of Ahab to turn away from his love for Starbuck, who begs him to abandon his quest for the whale, and nonetheless both to accept the weight of his hermaphroditic marriage to his first mate and to go on to his death and the death of all his crew (save the faithful recorder, Ishmael) in the name of one true moment. This love of Ahab for his mate seems to confound the distinctions we might make between the homosocial and the homosexual, even as (or perhaps because) Starbuck's deepest wish is to return to the bosom of his family. Even though Ahab himself has a wife awaiting his safe passage home as well, he will deny this element of himself and fetishize that centrality associated with his vocation as a philosopher, the attempt to know the unknowable. Ahab seeks to complete the project of modernity.

To borrow from some of the most chilling language of manhood of the twentieth century, for Ahab a preemptive strike is what was needed—against the whale, against the lassitude of the quotidian, against the dead hand of life itself. The doer and the deed, the quest for immortality, the teleology of politics as a war machine—in this language of the event, the aspiration to achieve the deed is both confident (undoubted) and deadly. So much of this quest is redolent of manliness that one might, in the face of the demise of those philosophies that purport to reinvigorate the groundless grounds of action, say good riddance to bad rubbish, or at least laugh at the mighty harpoon of Ahab. And yet, in the pathos of manliness we might find a kernel of a truth concerning the character of the event—the white whale of political theory.

Do I mean to suggest that Ahab's problem is ours? At first glance it would not seem so. This century has allowed humankind to take full measure of the disillusionment that accompanies the wake of tragedy, even though too many people seem not to have learned anything from it. If nothing else, the cataclysms of war and genocide constitute events. It may be the inadequacy of various contemporary responses to the overwhelming sense of historical tragedy of human loss, as much as the less certain awe that arises when there seems to be some positive (re)constitution of political life and human gain, that drives theorists to despair—often an aesthetic despair—determined by their inability to provide a full log of the meaning of events.

But among those us whose vocation is determined by a concern to understand the relationship of truth to power, too many, I think, still evade the questions that so tormented and determined Ahab. Too many political theorists seem to aspire to be scientists of justice, formulating questions and answers in response to the demands of various calculuses of communication or formulas for rationalizing behavior. Pretending to articulate neutral principles in the name of non-neutral ends, the tensions they generate in the quest for justice undermine their ends before they begin. Other, even more sophisticated thinkers succumb to the temptation to retreat from addressing issues of power, more or less advancing the idea that there is, in the end, no sense of something that might even be called "politics," relegating all activity below an Ahabian threshold to realm of "mere" life, holding out for some sort of resurrection of "the political."

Contemporary quests for community, solidarity, justice, and freedom in turn seem to disguise a common desire for security in an epoch defined by ambiguity and dissettlement. Movement is the order of the day, migration the common fact of life. We who are homeless, or we who have never been modern, or we who have succeeded in failing to fulfill the incomplete project of modernity, now seem to risk becoming suborned onto the *Pequod*, becoming members of Ahab's secret team—late arrivals who might serve as his diabolical boat crew, and who might help him to force its fateful sinking to the point of prophesying his fate in our own deaths, entangled in the lines trailing the whale. Behind the unreasoning mask we desire reason and we dread the other that may not have a name. This is our terror, and it comes to us in the bodies of those whom we want to do everything with except acknowledge, for fear of becoming abject, like them; for fear of becoming like them. Of course, that other which has no name is also the name that has been given to the Judeo-Christian God; but the white whale may suffice.

Loose Ends

Through our boredom we may come to other places. Thinking like a poet, Ann Lauterbach invokes Giorgio Agamben's idea of a "*topos outopos* (a placeless place, no-place) in which our experience of being-in-the-world is situated."[94] The role of poetry in reference to the experience of the ordinary may be considered as an engine of difference, a way of sorting the truths that come into being, placing them into words for us to consider. For Lauterbach, the struggle of the democratic poet must be to move from annotation to the undefinable moment of new thought, new movement, when what is exposed is not a fixed point but the fleetingness of desire. She asks the question that must be asked of all who labor in the shadow of the fate of modernity: Condemned to our past, are we confined into the future? Where is the wilderness to which we might repair? In this sense, at a time of closing, the struggle of the democratic poet becomes one with that of the democratic philosopher. The ancient rift between the two recedes in importance when facing the need to protect against the grasping power of those who would nail the truth to a mast like the gold doubloon Ahab offers for the first sighting of the white whale.

Behind the unreasoning mask is that of which we do not know. Perhaps it is but another mask. But the quest for a certain knowledge of what lies behind that mask prematurely defines our freedom as an exposure of the authentic truth underlying the supposed facade. What if instead there was, in fact, a philosophy of events that gave permission to other possibilities—an appreciation for dying at the right time, a celebration of the undefinable, a pleasure in the untamed strangeness of ancient truths, and a delight at our sometimes successful, usually incomplete, escapes into anonymity? What we call an event may be too singular to compare to the heroic deeds of manly men, but in this life of endless repetition, those deeds may now constitute a genre and themselves become subject to the forces of ordering. But those things that are new will still come to us from surprising places, sometimes old places, sometimes places not yet imagined. A politics of the ordinary might aspire to encourage the proliferation of surprising places. We might try to catch the whale or even to become whale, but it is likely as well that we might look for signs of ordinary life in the midst of the flotsam and jetsam of our wrecked ships, like the captain of the good ship *Rachel*, hopelessly searching for his own lost son and coming instead on the orphan of the *Pequod*. Ishmael's tale may well be all of ours, orphans all, seeking a common denominator of the ordinary in an age that threatens its effacement.

2

Resignation

Look it up: *exile, spirit in.*
—Ann Lauterbach, "A History Lesson"

Disappointment

When we are bored, we allow ourselves a certain liberty that can take the form of a kind of self-conscious pause. This is a moment of loneliness that sometimes leads us to deep reflections concerning the human condition. Such an experience is democratically available to anyone who is willing and able to move past the distractions offered up as the fruits of the social contract, to resist the way our commodities come to establish themselves as the conditional terms through which we live together. The most democratic claim we may make in this regard is that we might all be bored. But this very general sense of boredom does not necessarily lead us back to each other, and in fact, the way in which we come to be bored just about always involves a withdrawal from the movements of life around us. The limit of what we might learn from boredom may be the limit of loneliness. In turning over the question of who and where we are, the worst fear we may have is we might not be able to return to questions that concern how we live with one another, to explore together what our isolation in the moment may suggest about the terms of living in common. To fail to turn to that question is to know only the mechanical character of liberal democracy—a collective isolation—and not to acknowledge a benign conspiracy that seeks to animate it—a conspiracy in the sense of a breathing together that helps to cultivate a kind of consolation—which we might realize as a practical lesson in thinking about a politics of the ordinary.

In approaching the terms of our lives together, we could begin with imaginative flights of collective happiness and love and try to retrace our path back to primal scenes of polymorphous perversity, joyous occasions of bodily connection and psychic peacefulness, halcyon days. But I suspect starting there, because a return to such a scene seems unprepared unless and until this psychic past is acknowledged as a conditional gift, never reached, always re-membered. The trip to a particular past might enlist us in a distraction from which we might not be able to return, a move akin to the isolation of boredom, analysis interminable. The conditions of social life might be approached instead by first asking about the efforts we are able to make to try to come together, by noting the difficulties of such efforts in achieving their ends, by making connections at the level of our common languages of consent. The questions we might ask thus focus first on our failures to (re)connect, rather than on the pains of our first separations. Connection is a key trope of democracy and often is characterized as in opposition to the fullest realization of self, an Ahab-like will to know the conditions of one's being. So we might begin to think about the connection and disconnection from another place, one shaped by disappointment, in the most ordinary sense we can muster.

Who has never been let down? Who has not known the sadness that comes when one realizes something or someone has failed to meet one's expectations? Who has not felt the pang of regret, the painful sense that something else might have been, that somehow, something else ought to have been and yet will not be? To suffer a diminished faith in others is an experience of disappointment. In the very syllables of the word (on its very surface) the plain register of its meaning appears: *dis appointed*, removed from appointment. The train of expectation is derailed; the appointment is not kept; the meeting is missed; the friend is unable to take a stand when it matters most. We mark our losses over time, forgive and forget, and move on.

Sometimes disappointment deepens, encompasses a such a wide scope that it overmatches our prior expectations, overwhelms our abilities, and threatens to shade into a more general disillusion that would stop us cold. So an ethical task of critical thinking may be to steer us through our disappointment, to prevent it from turning into a permanent disillusionment; to make of our disappointment a plausible beginning rather than a certain ending. The condition of disappointment has been expressed philosophically by Stanley Cavell as leaving us in a place he calls "Nowhere." This Nowhere is not the utopia it may seem to some but appears as though it may be the last refuge for a kind of philosophical thinking. When Cavell suggests that a task of philosophy is to preserve the skeptical argument, it is this Nowhere he is hoping, against hope, to save. "Skepticism is a place, perhaps the central secular place, in which the human wish to deny the condition of human existence is expressed; and so long as the denial is essential to what we think of as the human, skepticism cannot, or must not, be denied."[1]

The place of skepticism is a place of disappointment. To understand this place of disappointment is to become enlisted in a project concerning judgment generally, and more particularly concerning judgments about the terms that underwrite acknowledgment and consent and the conditions under which they might be withdrawn or redrawn. When are we disappointed? That is, when do we lose our appointment and gain a sense of being out of place? What might it mean for us to evaluate occasions of rupture and loss as ordinary experiences of skepticism, circumstantial evidence of an intimate relationship that conditions our lives to a sort of truth?

The displacement that constitutes disappointment is intimately tied to the experience of resignation. The moment of disappointment is the occasion of resignation. It does not matter how happy the occasion of any resignation may be: every resignation is connected to disappointment in that every resignation marks a rupture, a quitting, the ending of something, which places someone Nowhere in respect to where they were before. We might come closer to acknowledging our skepticism (and expressing the state of our resignation) by assessing the condition of our disappointment in or from everyday life. Resignation is the mark of the loss of an appointment. It is an ordinary way that we express our disappointment and mark the time and place of our ongoing denial of our condition. How does resignation operate in the world?

Two Letters

A professor has been denied tenure at a university. She decides to quit her post immediately rather than stay for another, terminal year. She can resign because in her field she is considered a highly valued member of the profession, and because she has at least one offer from another university in hand. She wants to do so immediately because the circumstances surrounding the disposition of her case have led her to believe that she has suffered an injustice in being denied tenure, and because she feels the negative judgment of her case has placed her in an undignified position. She has suffered because of a poor assessment of the value of her work by referees who appear to have corrupted the process of tenure review in their desire to marginalize an intellectual perspective that she has represented and that they despise. So she tells her department chair that she will not be returning in the autumn. He asks her to submit a letter of resignation in order to expedite the paperwork that will be needed to sever her ties to the institution.

After her initial irritation in response to the request—in this situation *why*, after all she has already been through, must she perform such a task?—she turns to the task of writing the letter. As we imagine a scholar might, she ponders what a resignation letter must contain. She faces representational issues, such as letterhead: Does she use the stationery of the place from which she is departing? To whom does she address her resignation? What does she say in the letter itself? At each juncture in her thinking, she realizes more deeply than before that she is enveloped by the demands and needs of a corporate body whose agents have rejected her. She wonders what would happen should she decline to write. Would her silence be a monkey wrench thrown into the machine of rejection, fouling its works? Or would her silence go unnoticed and thus be as problematic as, or even more problematic than, writing a letter? Depressed, saddened, acutely reminded of the interlocking institutions that all denizens of modern life seem to inhabit and that somehow remind us of our abject dependence on them most intensely during our moments of greatest alienation from them, she takes out a blank sheet of paper and types the following:

Dear Professor K:
I resign.

Below the letter she signs her name.

Among other things, this act of writing and signing may be said to be inspired in its simplicity, Wittgensteinian in its poetry. We are operating with two simple words.[2] But a question presents itself: In what world are these words operating?

To raise the question concerning the possibility of operating in a world is to take seriously another notion that forms a background assumption for this professor, one widely shared but more rarely noticed, namely, that somehow we compose our selves through words and that our words, in ways not always fully appreciated, compose worlds of meaning. If we even grudgingly grant this sort of power to the words of a resignation, we will immediately be drawn to note as well that the act of resignation is a discursive act that identifies or marks a place one is departing from. So in reference to the words of this professor we might, at least, raise the question of place, or perhaps even more accurately, *context.* One of the definitions of *context* is "the weaving together of words and sentences."[3] The sense of "weaving" connects this word to its use as a verb and points toward its use as a metaphor for the work of hand and mind together. The parts of a discourse are often characterized as being knitted together to form a coherent whole: if a part of a whole does not relate to the rest, it is said to be "out of context." We act on the words we weave as though the discursive realms of existence they disclose to us constitute a reality on the basis of which we might begin to act in the world.[4] In so doing, we turn this noun, *context*, into a verb, *to context*. This turning is a steady labor of hand and heart.

"I resign." What does this sentence mean? What is the context of the act of resignation? How does the act of resignation context a world?

The professor's letter is one enactment of resignation. It may be useful to see how her resignation compares to another one. Below is a very famous letter of resignation. This letter is written on White House stationary and is addressed to Henry Kissinger, the secretary of state, a high public official (though once a professor himself).

THE WHITE HOUSE
WASHINGTON

August 9, 1974

Dear Mr. Secretary:
 I hereby resign the Office of President of the United States.[5]

The author of this text is Richard Nixon, who signed his name below the body of the letter prepared for him by his chief of staff, Alexander Haig, *sans* title or printed name. If one eliminates the modifiers ("hereby" and "the Office of President of the United States"), which in cruel retrospect might be seen to have served as self-lacerating and self-aggrandizing reminders of a sovereignty lost—in large part because of his dangerous inability to comprehend presidential sovereignty in democratic terms—one finds that the body of Nixon's letter is identical with that of the rejected university professor. But even while it is like the professor's letter in its minimalism and its lack of concession, somehow it seems to have nonetheless conceded much more, by virtue of the importance of the resignation and the highly publicized character of the letter's release to a citizenry. The public character of the letter is signified here not by the body of the letter but by the address of the author and the recipient of the letter.

The common language of the two letters reflects the substantive commonality of the two resignations. We may note that both resignations are actions their authors undertook in the hope that they might contribute to bringing a traumatic experience to a conclusion. Both are attempts to mark the site of a trauma, to contain it, and to remove its effects. The measure of the success or failure of each letter, moreover, lies not in the quality of the letter itself but in the extent to which it can be said that the letter has been received by all concerned parties. These include the persons or institution addressed and the author of the resignation, understood here as the signer of the letter. (While one might argue that the determination of the author of a resignation cannot to be confined to the person who signs the letter but must extend to the agents who may have forced such a step, the resignation itself should be thought of as a distinct act that is not to be confused with the forces that result in its occasion. Moreover, maintaining a clear distinction between those responsible for forcing a resignation and the decision of the resigner to resign is often the goal not only of those who force the resignation but of the resigner as well. This distinction is important to the resigner because if others fail to distinguish the forces that cause the departure of a person from the action of the person who resigns, they fail to acknowledge the agency of the resigner and hence implicitly denigrate his or her authority, provoking yet further attacks on her or his dignity, most often, though not always, by expressions of pity.) The receipt of the letter is crucial to the resignation because it is the moment of communication, the act of transmission of the sign of resignation.

For both professor and president, the letter of resignation becomes a collaborative act, undertaken by the resigner and those who are charged with the duty of accepting the resignation. (For contrast, we briefly note the phenomenon of the resignation that is refused. Sometimes a breach is healed, a potential traumatic breakdown of relationships averted, by the refusal to accept the resignation. It is a small joke of history that Nixon addressed his letter of resignation to Kissinger, who had often used the threat of resignation as an instrument of political infighting during his years as Nixon's national security adviser.)[6] Generally, it seems, it takes at least two parties to enact a resignation. In this sense resignation may be seen as a social action of a special sort, the adaptation of an ancient act to modern conditions of traumatic disruption and dismemberment that can be comprehended as a kind of rupture with or disruption of the status quo, undertaken as a necessity in the face of an unacceptable present condition.

Is there a common act we might label as "the" resignation that would apply to both letters? I have chosen Nixon's letter of resignation as an example because it is so widely and obviously known as a public act. But is his resignation any more public than that of the professor, other than in regard to the size of the public that was touched by it? Here acts of resignation bear upon the constitution of boundaries that distinguish the spaces we designate as public and private. If we were to say that the professor's letter is private and Richard Nixon's is public, then we would have to claim that the professor's resignation might have an effect on her, her family, colleagues in the field, and even beyond, but that the impact will be recorded and contained as a private trauma. Nixon's resignation, moreover, while it may be said to have redounded to posterity, having an impact on all who are citizens of the United States and many who live beyond the borders of the United States, would have been recorded and contained as a public trauma, having no private effect on him or his family or the private lives of those who were touched by it. This claim is implausible, even though we can reasonably intuit that we might make a major distinction concerning the relative impact and importance of the two resignations. What might be called the consequential power of the two acts varies greatly as a result of the *contexts* in which they have occurred, which is a question not only of the relative sizes of public but of the relevant functions of the publics drawn together, which might vary so greatly as to render the meanings of them incommensurable. But can we go further? Can we say that this incommensurable character of the resignations is secured as long as there is clarity about the distinction between public and private, as long as there is no spillover from the one realm into the other, and as long as it remains possible to claim that the role of public citizen is autonomous and separate from the role of private subject?

That is never so. Resignations show that the simple, obvious, and politically valuable distinction between public and private is instead complex, subtle, impure, and politically problematic. In fact, it seems as though public and private resignations are connected in such ways as to render the meanings of distinction between them problematic at the most important moments when we try to bring it to bear on these two acts. The extent to which the gathered public is sensitive to this feeling informs how resignations are received. In this sense, resignation can be understood as an act that gives shape to an important onto-political category, that is, as an act that connects different aspects of human existence to each other, that constitutes public and private spaces through the institutions it helps shape and break down and through the moods it encourages and elicits. Resignation can be understood as an act of traversal, crossing the boundaries between the particular public and private spaces it helps constitute and amend, constituting them through traversal. Indeed, resignation demands that we think about it as a political act that shapes the boundaries of public and private spaces.

In this sense, resignation is close to founding. In an essay on the founding of republics, Bonnie Honig explains the role that performative utterances play in founding political actions.[7] Focusing on the American Declaration of Independence, Honig highlights two powerful interpretations of the famous phrase from the preamble "We hold these truths to be self-evident," one by Hannah Arendt and the other by Jacques Derrida. Reading them with and against each other, she notes that both Arendt and Derrida recognize a paradox to be found in performative utterances. Both theorists suggest that performatives need to be anchored in promises, and both express concern about the paradox that is the entailment of this need to anchor performatives. Arendt worries about how the need to anchor may tempt one to embrace natural law as a foundational anchor. This move would deprive political action of its distinctive character, destroying its autonomy. Paralleling Arendt's concern with natural law, Derrida suggests that one may be tempted to seek to anchor action in an unproblematized subject who is able to speak in the name of something or someone. (This simple subject causes a lot of trouble in modern polities, for instance, because the principle of sovereignty will increasingly be projected onto a power imagined to be secure but that, paradoxically, cannot be made secure, and which instead must become entangled in a sovereign search for freedom *as* security.) But Derrida is not concerned about the autonomy of political action in the same way as is Arendt, who sees performance as expressing the contingency of political action that she cherishes, and who feels that by anchoring an action, one hampers its purity. Instead, Derrida understands the fabulous deferment entailed in promising as a structural feature of language itself. Politically, the anxieties that attend the thoughts accompanying such actions generate an extraordinary energy, as founders seek to anchor their actions in sites they hope, by dint of position, will enable them to escape or overcome this paradox of performance. In this sense, a promise can open a world of possibility when what is promised is world-changing.

The paradox of performatives is visible in founding acts, but it insinuates itself into actions of resignation as well. Resignation mirrors founding. A resignation is a quitting for reasons that must be enunciated in the act of quitting itself. This is not to say that when one resigns, one lists one's reasons, though this is often the case. More important, the very act of resignation speaks its reason gesturally. It is by definition a giving up of something, one's life, one's being, one's soul.[8] It is a re-signing of the initial promise that marks its breaking, a breaking of a seal. It *is* the breaking of a promise, either by the person resigning or by the institution that has forced the resignation. Like the Declaration of Independence, which required the signature of those committing their honor to it even as it enabled the creation of a community of honor, thus fabulously allowing the signing,[9] the resignation letter requires a signature to mark the breaking of the seal or sign of the honorable commitment. The act of resignation signals an intervention, an impossible departure from the institutional entanglements one once accepted as the grounding of a series of relationships. The resignation inverts the fabulous character of the founding act: it is a parting that attempts to achieve its end by an assertion which repeats that of founding, namely, that all that has gone before is to be of no account for the future.

A resignation can be understood as the withdrawal of consent by someone who once entered into a compact with others, someone who had made a mutual agreement with others to be ruled in common. The act of resignation implies that the consent which had been given was not *tacit* but *explicit*; the explicit character of the resignation matches the drama of consent to be found in founding actions.[10] People find their own voices in acts of resignation as a matter of learning to speak for themselves, against the idea that others can continue to speak for them, or even to them, about what matters most in a particular context.[11] The character of a resignation, then, is potently public, a symbolic gathering together of those who had mutually promised by way of a formal address, in order to mark the breaking of the promise. And yet, because this public is being called together at the moment of its dissolution, simultaneously the act of resignation is potently private, dispersing the community of the contract that had been assumed to exist when the contract was being honored. When it is the abdication of an office, a resignation is a return to the most private from the most public, another way of escaping the dictation of the demand of a promise.

A test of honor is invoked when particular acts of resignation are contemplated. The resignation can be thought of as an experimental moment, a testing of the limits of the community that was called into being by the contract. Such a testing, occasioned by an uncertainty as to the status of the particular community established by the contract, is accompanied by an extraordinary collective anxiety. It is not only the person who resigns who is tested. All members of the community or civil society who are implicated in the promise must respond to the resignation. The form the response takes is usually less important than the posture that is taken regarding the fact of resignation and the context in which the resignation occurs.

Perhaps appropriately, the most prominent response to the act of resignation usually is that of the resigner. Nixon's response to his resignation was to show the gathered public his anxiety during the period immediately prior to his resignation. His was an anxiety that was extraordinarily intense, as befitted the unprecedented character of presidential resignation in the particular context of the government that the Constitution of the United States had created. For him, it seemed as though the end of his administration was also the end of constitutional government. He prevaricated, delayed, wept, prayed with Secretary of State Kissinger, invoked the memory of his dead Quaker mother, threatened executive violence, got drunk, wished he were dead, and spoke to portraits of dead predecessors, conjuring them up as ghosts who haunted the 1974 present of the White House. And those dead presidents might best be understood as specters of sovereignty, called up by the trauma of yet another time out of joint.[12]

Aside from the response of Nixon himself, there were many public and personal responses to his resignation. Among those who had always despised him, some were clearly delighted, and others, while relieved that he had resigned, were shaken and distressed, even mournful. Among his supporters, some were defiant and bitter, and others were relieved that he had resigned, shaken and distressed, and mournful. It was from those who displayed the most complex sense of mournfulness, from those who appropriately postured themselves as witnesses to a trauma, that the most enduring response to the Nixon resignation eventually emerged.[13]

Nixon acted out, upon a national stage, a trauma less visibly performed in resignations such as that of the professor. Beyond the opportunities for hyperbolic gesture, especially the common and understandable temptation toward grand gesture in the comedic tradition—"You can't fire me! I quit!"—resignation is an intensely self-reflective gesture, carried out with a sense that the resignation may memorialize the broken promise but that a promise broken always lasts longer than a promise kept. But the fronting of the resignation, the swirling temporal connection between public and private that constitutes the nexus of its traversals, evokes a very complicated set of moods for those who engage in it and are engaged by it. The mourning of resigning is a grieving that is embarrassing—not only because a resignation inscribes the failure of the promise and the possibility that the person who resigns is somehow deficient in an element of her or his self but because the resignation contains an illicit pleasure for the person who resigns that is akin to attending one's own funeral. In committing an act of resignation one is able, like Huck Finn and Tom Sawyer, to be present at the death of an aspect of one's self. To many who watched the final days of the Nixon administration unfold, especially to those who watched on television as he said goodbye to the White House staff, he seemed strangely excited and perversely energized by this misery—in his final performance as president, pulling back from a total breakdown to assess his self-destruction.[14]

Nixon's melodramatic performance may have been the most appropriate existential behavior, given the kind of stupor that the act of resignation provokes. This stupor appears as the clumsy and witlessly affective response to the first act in the larger action of resignation, the moment of decision, which is relived and intensified in the second act of resignation, the moment of departure. What seems to be consistently surprising for those who resign is the complexity and extent of the entanglements they must sever upon this second act of resignation. This severing is powerfully mundane, immediately concerned with the minutiae of work life—the building where one works, the drive to the job, the paperwork one learns to master and subvert, the social rituals that develop among the people one works beside, the cautionary lessons concerning those in power who could help or hinder one's work and conditions of employment, the machinery, the sounds and quiet, the smells, the color of the paint on the walls. Through the background details of quotidian life, we can comprehend a resignation as the signing away of one's access to a familiar place, where, whether one has succeeded or failed to succeed, one has nonetheless lived.

The fatalism that is attached to the term—to be resigned is to accept the fate that has been meted out to one, to concede the signing over of one's soul—is a consequence of the trauma of this impossible severing of entanglements. Because a resignation is a quitting, it is a commitment to the fate of the trauma of severance and an admission of the open and hazardous field of action that enables the resigner to assess her or his new place in or out of the context of that field. As a founding is like a birth, a resignation is like a death, a giving up *on* life that is akin to a giving up *of* life. This claim may seem exaggerated, but a primary use of the word *resign* concerns giving up not simply one's position but one's life. The *Oxford English Dictionary* cites Shakespeare's *Titus Andronicus*: "What should I don this robe and trouble you? / Be chosen with proclamations to-day, / To-morrow yield up rule, resign my life, / And set abroad new business for you all?"[15] In these lines Titus Andronicus attempts to decline the offer of election to the

Roman Senate, a position from which he would be able to help choose the next emperor (and perhaps, it is hinted, attain the emperor's seat himself, though in this bloody play that is not to be). Importantly, to have accepted the office would have been to have resigned his life. Titus says, "Give me a staff of honor for mine age, / But not a sceptre to control the world."[16] In the United States of America in the late twentieth century, such a refusal is a rhetorical tool of the politician, a device for deceiving others into giving what is covertly desired. We might compare Titus Andronicus to the duke of Gloucester, also known as Richard III, as he reluctantly accepts the Crown of England after pretending that he considers himself unworthy of it. If he is to be believed, Richard takes that which he has murdered to reach only out of a sense of obligation: "Will you enforce me to a world of cares? / Call them again, I am not made of stones, / but penetrable to your kind entreaties, / Albeit against my conscience and my soul."[17] If he is to be believed.

Belief in conscience, belief in some sort of ensoulment, is a key here, not only for monarchs but for any sovereign authorities, and not only for sovereign authorities of government but for any individual who is capable of resignation. We may even claim that anyone who is an individual is so by virtue of the fact that he or she has the capacity to resign. The terms of the soul's gains and losses, its convertability, are important for figuring sovereignty in ways that are sometimes unexpected.[18] Because official public life in the United States has historically more often than not contained material advantages gained from office as its most obvious reward, it presents a temptation, less to murder—though many American politicians, especially presidents, have not hesitated at that threshold—than to venality, for those who would accept power.[19] Hence appeals to the myth of Cincinnatus have served as a politician's rhetorical strategy from at least the days of George Washington. This American adaptation of Roman historical myth points to yet another shape resignation may take. The rough judgment of the character of politicians that citizens of a representative democracy are compelled to make very often, and most appropriately, focuses on the sincerity of their resignation *to* office. The politician's disguise of ambition and the attendant public need for vigilance in judgment compose an element of what Alexis de Tocqueville once called "the courtier spirit" of American politics.[20]

But this is not the only way in which resignation to office inflects the meaning of taking public office. To be resigned *to* office is to acknowledge the traumatic force of the departure from the life one otherwise might have been allowed to live, to constitute the realm of political action as separate from the pleasures of quotidian life. In a democracy, that other life remains a latent possibility—a place to return to, if only in the collective imagination of a relevant public. The 1996 American presidential campaign discussions concerning Bob Dole's deep roots in Russell, Kansas, and Bill Clinton's in Hope, Arkansas, are consistent with a deep tradition in American politics. They reflect an insistence that an authentic person must stand before the gathered citizenry, one who has given up a life of private pleasure to hold public office. Public officials are supposed to defer the enjoyment of the fruits of private labors. They are supposed to do so out of a sense of sacrifice, not for the pleasures that may be gained from holding power, and the deepest suspicion we collectively hold against politicians is that they enjoy the pleasures of their offices. The consent of the governed, in all its ambivalence, is matched here by the consent of the governors. This shared sensibility, what in Emersonian parlance might be termed the mood of politics, is often read as cynicism or, at best, stoicism.[21] But it is also a response, perhaps the most appropriate response, to the demands of consent.

Is it reasonable to think that the resignation *to* office is a breaking of a contract? Here the comparison of taking office with the resignation from a position seems to become tendentious. But the supposed incommensurability of the two experiences appears only if we are able to assume that there is no promise comparable to the contract, tacit or explicit, governing private life. Such an assumption would seem to place the constitution of common life exclusively on the side of the public making and breaking of promises. Alternatively, we might take more serious notice of the fact that there is rarely a single point of promise in what we call private life, but rather a network of promises, tacit and explicit, that establishes a context for the constitution and amendment of an imperfectly private life. Then we may be able to say that promises are made and broken every day, in situations that it would be difficult to claim are exclusively public or private in the common sense of the terms. And then we might also ask: How do these private promises and the breaking of them inflect resignations?

We seem to have left the professor to her thoughts at this point. But this is not so. The ability to sign the resignation places her in the same context as Nixon, assuredly with a smaller domain of consequence than he but in possession of an errant sovereignty no less fragile and no less intact, to the extent that both enjoy something that might even be called sovereignty.[22] Her departure from a university entails a publicly noted movement away from a context of action for her, a place of work. She, too, had resigned *to* her life as a professor in committing herself to the vocation of thinking, to a commitment to teach students. That she may have acted with more dignity than did Nixon in the face of her trauma is not really the point (though we are able to know more of Nixon's dignity and its lack because of the glare of publicity that contributes to the presidential aura). The point instead is that the various commitments to office, as modest or grandiose as they may seem, as unnoticed or famous as they might be, can also be known as a common lot in the lives of democratic subjects.

These two resignations—of the professor and the president—suggest lines of departure for a study of the politics of resignation. One can resign to the public or private and in both cases experience significant loss (while sometimes marking surprising gains). In both instances a resignation marks a significant shift between public and private spaces of existence, even as it draws and redraws boundaries between the two spaces. A resignation is an ending that is incomplete. It fulfills the test of a certain difficulty identified with the loss of a world and a finding of oneself.[23] In this sense, resignation opens a window onto a politics of the ordinary.

Confirming Desperation, Fronting Resignation

A resignation can be like a peaceful death, as it often is when it is a voluntary retirement, or when committed to improve one's situation with the goodwill and understanding of those one is leaving behind. But when a resignation is forced, it is a traumatic killing. Whether the killing is homicide or suicide is often hard to tell and depends on who broke the promise, what the promise was, and how, when, where, and why it was broken. The intense and powerful cycles of gossip and innuendo that attend a controversial resignation are a result of this combination of mordancy and prudential interest. In a forced resignation, the evidence of the murderous intent of those who achieved its signing afterward follows all parties involved, its effects fading away only gradually. That the person who resigns so often lingers on in body (except when there is a suicide or a murderous rampage, as sometimes, notoriously, occurs), that he or she may recover somewhere else in the same field of endeavor and reappear in relevant public venues, sometimes creates a new embarrassment for all involved. The person who has resigned does not want to be seen, and those who have forced the person to resign do not want to see her or him. The reaction of those who have forced the resignation is only in part and only occasionally a guilty response by those who have power and have misused it. It is usually an attempt to redistribute responsibility more generally, a denial of power by those who, in the end, don't want to exercise it but are required to do so, and who do so primarily for the institutional rewards that accompany the exercise of authority rather than because of an intrinsic desire to exercise power over others. Stock phrases—"His work had been falling off lately," "She was very good, but this is a very difficult position to hold," "Yes, we had recommended him highly in our last progress report, but we were only trying to encourage him to improve by praising him"—do a particular work for those who remain in charge, serving to rationalize the resignation as a process in which they can convince themselves of being irrelevant participants, to focus attention on the person who has resigned, and to smooth over the traumatic gaps left in the institution as a consequence of that person's departure, thereby helping those in charge to reach their own sense of closure.

Almost all resignations, forced or otherwise, are inflected with a certain passivity; indeed, this sense inheres in the meaning of the word. To be resigned is to accept one's fate. Both those who resign and those who accept a resignation can be led to feel as though events are beyond their control. The act of *accepting* implies such a passivity on the part of those who receive the resignation, as do all the psychological strategies employed to distance the official function of acceptance from the agency of the person or people who accept the resignation. From the point of view of the one who resigns, the act of resignation casts the person into an ambiguous relationship with her or his life. Because the person who resigns finds that he or she cannot be certain of an important range of relationships in which he or she has been enmeshed, because an important context for acting has been ripped apart, other ostensible certainties of life are called into question, so that after a resignation one often becomes cautious in reference to, and withdrawn from, all sorts of dimensions of existence.

Even in the absence of a direct request or demand that one resign—even when one is being encouraged to stay—a person usually resigns because he or she has come to feel there is no other choice: either the alternative has become so attractive that one feels compelled to leave or the conditions of one's situation are so unbearable that one feels forced to leave. More often than not, the intensification of one condition has an impact on the attractiveness of the alternative, so that a new place becomes more attractive to the extent that the old place becomes unattractive. This dynamic contributes to another kind of passivity that enables those who are breaking a promise to feel as though it isn't their hands that are doing the breaking. The person who is leaving, and hence abandoning those who are left behind, is in another perilous situation, in which the bad faith of a broken promise propels him or her out the door. This situation can lead to a different friction, other quarrels, commonly called burning your bridges behind you. Then the resigner tries to overcome his or her own passivity in an act that reiterates the resignation, deepens it. Or the resigner tries to cushion the departure so that he or she may pretend not to have departed but only to have taken leave, gradually withdrawing effort, slowly ceasing to matter in one context as he or she finds himself or herself more deeply enmeshed in another.

Even under these milder conditions, however, resignations are evidence of the fact that there are no clean slates in life. A resignation, which can itself be thought of as an attempt to clean the slate, is never complete and never painless—only more or less so. A happy resigner may ask, "Does the resignation always have to involve the breaking of a promise?"[24] The simple answer is yes. For no matter how gently it is accomplished, no matter how understandable the reasoning that informs it, and no matter how indifferent those who are left behind may be to the departure of the resigner, a resignation marks the fact that a common future, premised on a shared assumption that a set of conditions will persist, is removed by willful action of someone, even as that someone believes the act to be beyond her or his control or will.

And what of those who would engage in an act of resignation except for the fact that they cannot? There are many people—and perhaps a piece of the soul of almost every person—whose various commitments to family, to duty, to those who would in various ways suffer from their departure should they do what they want to do, which is to break the promise they made and quit, impel them to persist in bad positions, with bad bosses and debilitating work, unhappily bearing on. Instead of resigning, they are resigned to not being able to resign. They endure what is otherwise unendurable; they carry on; they resist the trauma of separation by suffering the institutional entanglements that impinge on them. The harassed secretary, the abused line worker, the pressured salesman, the already-tenured professor who faces a frozen job market and hostile colleagues, the parents who stay together for the sake of the children—are they involved in acts of resignation as well? Here we may distinguish between the movement from one silence to another that seems to characterize the condition of those who are already resigned, and the speech of those who commit acts of resignation. The silence of those who are resigned seems to operate as a confirmation of despair, whereas the statement of those who resign is a willful act of defiance. Why do both seem to lead to a similar place? Does a resignation occur in the absence of a statement of it? Is it possible to resign without making a statement? If not, is the condition of being resigned an accurate assessment of the condition of those who are confirmed in their despair? These unsigned resignations may yet have something more to tell us about the conditions of our commitments to ourselves and each other.[25]

Cavell suggests that the condition of the withdrawal of consent is silence, and that the withdrawal into silence does not put oneself out of community but renders one without anything to say. "The alternative to speaking for yourself politically is not: speaking for yourself privately. . . . The alternative is having nothing (political) to say."[26] He deepens this argument:

> We do not know in advance what the content of our mutual acceptance is, how far we may be in agreement. I do not know in advance how deep my agreement with myself is, how far responsibility for the language may run. But if I am to have my own voice in it, I must be speaking for others and allow others to speak for me. . . . The alternative is having nothing to say, being voiceless, not even mute.[27]

Voicelessness may be understood as the condition of those who are resigned to not resigning, who have failed to sign their resignations. This failure to sign, this voicelessness, leads us to a place that is somewhere else.

When Henry David Thoreau in *Walden* famously writes, "The mass of men lead lives of quiet desperation," his reference is to mass, to men, and to acquiescence as much as it is to despair.[28] The set of references he raises at this key juncture in *Walden* shows how his economy of existence might point toward ways of confronting the desperation that attends life when life tends toward a specific kind of meaninglessness, one that is most directly associated in his writings with the gathering of luxurious goods. The realm of luxury is vast and contributes much to the venality of presidents and other politicians but also to the despair of those who are forced to choose them. And this despair is not even the most important shape this quiet desperation takes. What does it matter that politicians are hopelessly corrupt, if that corruption is but the public expression of the desperation of those enslaved by the pursuit of unnecessary goods? Thoreau follows the aforementioned sentence in *Walden* immediately with this one: "What is called resignation is confirmed desperation."[29] Confirmed desperation is a desperation that has been tested and found as a closing experience of life. To be confirmed in despair is to have closed oneself upon oneself. A self so enclosed substitutes consumption for experience and is less than fully alive. Such a self may exercise the right to remain silent in order to cover the shame of despair.

But before whom will this self be ashamed? Thoreau, in his reckoning of every thing he consumes, wants to write in front of this silence, to experiment with another way of being that emerges from the wreckage of confirmed desperation. In this silence and of it, out of loss, he marks a gain. Those who would front the silence of despair are those who would dignify the *demos*. In doing so, Thoreau presents us with yet another way of understanding resignation, a way of moving toward a politics of the ordinary.

To evade a certain kind of desperation is to be Thoreau's task, or what might be called his experiment in waiting. The experience of Walden is a response to and test of the quiet desperation of the mass of men. Cavell, among others (though perhaps most insistently), has noted the importance of the constant intensity of Thoreau's response: "The experiment is the present—to make himself present to each circumstance, at every eventuality; since he is writing, in each significant mark."[30] To write words in the woods is to turn every leaf to see its connection to every other, to context the moment of fronting nature to a society of presence. Marking the present suggests another way of leading life, being present in one's life, not despairing but professing a faith in the possibility of each moment being, against the meaninglessness of luxurious possession, meaningful. Thoreau writes, "I went to the woods because I wished to live deliberately, to front only the essential facts of life, to see if I could not learn what it had to teach, and not, when I came to die, discover that I had not lived. I did not wish to live what was not life, living is so dear; nor did I wish to practise resignation unless it was quite necessary" (*W*, 66). Thoreau here suggests that his experiment in simple living is designed to uncover a certain truth about the world, a sublimity or meanness, access to either or both being available through the right kinds of experience. And while one might think that a discovery of the meanness of the world would leave one resigned, confirmed in one's despair, I believe that Thoreau wants to wager something else: that the practice of resignation out of *necessity* is not the same as its practice out of a sense of *confirmation*. This second path of resignation turns one back from the depth of a silence and stillness that is as far from the terms of consent as one can imaginably get yet not ever beyond the point of no return; it turns one back toward the engagement with a life to which one has permitted oneself to be necessarily resigned. The difference lies in how experience may be comprehended and practiced.

A sense of resignation as confirmed desperation weighs heavily on contemporary denizens of modern institutions. The weight does not derive from the fact that we are more fatefully encumbered by our institutional commitments than was Thoreau (although surely we must sometimes feel as though we are). Our present is one that he would no doubt respect as much as his own. But Thoreau might also insist that we are every bit as available for experimental living as was he, and he could no doubt take ironic pleasure in the notion that some of us impersonate him in his commitments and eccentricities. These impersonations risk ridicule if undertaken with anything less than a commitment to the cultivation of a democratic sensibility. But in taking his measure as our own, we might also acknowledge that the registers by which we try to calculate the successes and failures of our experiments have become both more explicit and exacting, on the one hand, and necessarily more vague and mysterious, on the other, and in so doing have driven us in our commitments further into the fugitive corners of life.

Alternatively, resignation practiced as a momentary suspension of faith, as a silent pause when language, while it does not exactly fail, falters, can (must) be a part of the experience of fronting the essential facts of life. Thoreau's necessary resignation, almost happily embraced, is most deeply his resignation *to* language. Language bears us and our worlds, builds and breaks us, inevitably *re-signs* us to the exigencies of life in every moment when we remember that we speak in words, sentences, and portions. This realization is a formidable burden happily borne by those who wait.[31] It is yet another feeling of resignation that gives us a sense of return, a turning back to that which we may try to repudiate in our traumatic dislocation. Turning is expedited by the very fact of language, its most intimate constitution as a series of signs. The signing and re-signing of objects through language becomes comprehensible as a political contest.[32] As Judith Butler writes, "Through a figure that marks the suspension of our ontological commitments, we seek to account for how the subject comes to be. That this figure is itself a 'turn' is, rhetorically, performatively spectacular; 'turn' translates the Greek sense of 'trope.'"[33] We turn, and re-turn, we sign, and re-sign, and the better part of each of us struggles to become worthy of the democracy we cultivate with and in each other.

Waiting (The Exile of Words)

Every day people resign. But every day we have available to us alternative experiences of resignation, cutting close to the desperation that shapes life. Here, for instance, is an offering from a poet who sees in the act of waiting a way to be-calm oneself, to refuse the act of being who one ought to be, in the unbidden hope of something otherwise.

> What does it mean, now, to *waste time* or to *waste space?* What is the difference between the crowd and the implied non-utility of these invaluable abstractions, or between the crowd (when is a crowd a public?) and waste itself, the excess that is more than, but not useful, not operative, that falls away from pragmatic necessities? Mother says, *"Stop wasting time!"* For those of us who know the deliriums of procrastination, who live in a relentless morass of *wait* that refuses to realize itself in direct action, so that the actions themselves gang up and gather into a mound or heap of *pending*, a *depending*, this question has a strange ring to it, like a summons which is also an alarm, an invitation to exile.[34]

Ann Lauterbach's incantation to *wait* shows waiting as an active opposition to action, an opportunity seized, a way to make the insistent ring of utility strange, to allow for the time and space to converse in the face of the arbitrary ends that hang like deadlines over our lives in common. Like Thoreau, Lauterbach perdures with the confidence of the democratic poet. What she calls the dread of exile that accompanies those who wait might be noted as arising from a state of emergency produced by the fateful intensification of the quiet desperation Thoreau opposed. It arises as a philosophical problem in the work of Wittgenstein, but Wittgenstein could stand in for all who are concerned about freedom in an age marked by the loss of its space. Here a remark by Cavell resonates as both an observation and prophecy: "The threat or fact of exile in Wittgenstein's philosophizing—I mean of course the exile of words—is not limited."[35] We do not know our way about. But in this waiting, in the exile of words, we might think that we find ourselves by founding, by working our words, weaving our texts, and noting the power of our necessary resignation to language.

We do not know our way about. Yet how busy we are! How incapacitated by the need to move, as yet discerning that in stillness lies a danger greater than flight. Those who have counseled stillness may already have been moved to the margins of contemporary life by the reasoning that tells us all to submit to the powers of our age. Even in this sense, being still is an activity, a resistance to a movement that obliterates the ability to think about the conditions of ordinariness. To wait is to express an unbidden faith that the desideration of being can be fulfilled in the fullness of time, that the desiccated forms of life will be rained upon and rebloom. Looking for signs of another commonality that might emerge in another nature, wasting time in this world, we might be devoted to the task of finding in the ordinary a renewable resource for a democracy of those who, unbidden, are willing to wait. This willingness is a powerful one. It is a kind of standing, a positive acknowledgment and enactment of the prayer that where one stands is where one is. Protestant in character, waiting is the risk we must take in order to fight off and embrace the confirmation of our common despair.

Waiting is a kind of silence. Out of silence we return to lead new lives, to come over to the condition of thinking and acting that might mark us as the bearers of something better than what we were before. The commitment of the democratic critic is to the cultivation of tropes, to the poetic sensibility that is the only way to be resigned to the truth of our lives together and apart, without being confirmed in despair.

Thoreau's ontological commitments led him to Walden Pond, encouraged him to plant a field, not for beans to eat, but "for the sake of tropes and expression, to serve as a parable-maker one day" (*W*, 112). His tropes, in turn, may be ours. We might better know our uncertainty as a proof of our commitments, our assertions and dissents, agreements and affirmations, amendments and initiatives, in short our conversations with each other, as alive to the possibility of being fully awake. Our necessary resignations can then be made without too great a sense of regret, so long as we have undertaken to speak carefully, listen fully, and represent our selves honestly. This moment of resignation might be called the romance of the politics of the ordinary. It is a romance as simple as breathing. Inhale, exile, *spirit in*.

3

Compensation

Is it not necessary, for the sake of preserving this tradition, to try even what might prove insufficient?

—Franz Kafka, "In the Penal Colony"

The Scale of Justice/Spare Parts

When we return from resignation to the world of society, we turn to a certain tradition of justice and injustice, though the principles by which people attempt to derive laws from claims of reason often obscure the idea that justice itself may be a tradition. But what does it mean to say that there is a tradition of modern justice? And what are its insufficiencies? Kafka's question might not even be posed in reference to justice but only in reference to punishment, which surely must be something different, even metaphorically. Our most banal and common metaphor of justice is the image of the scale of justice. The temptation to use this image is so strong that few seem able to resist it. The scale of justice suggests a balance, a shapeliness to life, a symmetry in which justice consists of a return to an original position of balance, a position that is veiled but nonetheless there, underneath the (unreasoning?) mask.[1] But the scale also suggests a kind of stasis, the achievement of an order that has as its end the possibility of another end: that of thinking about justice, a project that can be foregone when a balance is achieved and resumed only when things come out of balance. Then the scales would point to the new weight as the problem to be solved, the new passion as the trouble, the new being as the troublemaker.

But maybe it is best not to consider the scale of justice when asking about the tradition of modern justice and its insufficiencies. There is an alternative tradition of thinking about questions of justice, and at least one alternative metaphor. We can be led to these questions not by Kant or Rawls or any of their loyal progeny but, in this instance, by Emerson and Kafka, a

71

couple of troublemakers who are connected by a common response to both of these questions. Both Kafka and Emerson offer us ways to resist the idea of justice as the product of judgment. They do so by finding some of the ways in which justice is always slightly beyond the capacity of judgment to circumscribe it, even as judgment itself is composed of its deferments. They show us ways of being otherwise than we too often are, ways of thinking that might help us evade the path to a way of being that is too fully determined by our endless determination to pursue justice. The resistance they represent to us is something familiar to many of us by now, but its increased importance is a result of its fittingness as a response to a century in which justice has been pursued with a vehemence that has been more intensely destructive of life than ever before. The idea of resistance is made anew when we read the words of Kafka and Emerson. In response to the idea of modern justice as just dessert, Emerson gives us his idea of compensation, and in response to modern justice as law, Kafka gives us a new literature of delay and deferral. Even at the level of style they connect: Kafka is deeply connected to surface, as Emerson is superficially deep. Emerson gives us startling images presented as ideas, and Kafka gives us entire theories presented as images. This balance is one that might be upset if the logic that connected them was closed, but it isn't. Emerson and Kafka open us to infinite questions.

One such idea is held (almost) in common by Emerson and Kafka. The idea of spare parts as it operates in Kafka's "In the Penal Colony" resonates with Emerson's idea of compensation. Kafka's spare parts reflect an inclination toward an Emersonian compensation as a way of thinking about politics and show the potential of compensation as a distinct political theory. There is, in Kafka, a resistance to the idea of politics as justice that is something like a resistance that may be encouraged by Emerson's idea of compensation. A resistance to the idea of politics as the activity of achieving justice by re-balancing scales may be the distinguishing feature of whatever political theory might emerge to endorse the idea of compensation. And any such theory will be familiar to us, not imposed from above but an infrastructural improvisation—a kind of *bricolage*, sort of designed but open, flexible, and mobile.

There is irony in thinking about the idea of compensation as a kind of political theory. When we accept the idea of compensation, we also accept a diminution of the claims that we can make about ameliorating the pain caused by the imposition of force in the world. This sense of diminished possibility is to be distinguished from a simple resignation from the world, but it is often difficult to accept this distinction in the face of the atrocities that we see before us. Like others who want to be good citizens, I still seek to act, to resolve the problems that arise as a consequence of our political way of being. More particularly, as someone who has been inclined to the vocation of political theory, I am tempted, as others similarly situated seem to be, by the desire to seek solutions that we might act upon to ease the ills constitutive of late modernity. But the idea of compensation cautions me against taking action quickly or lightly. It does not suggest that action is in-effectual but rather the opposite—that acts are profoundly possible, though always more or less beyond our control.

For political theorists justice is one of the most important things to think about. But some of us who think of political theory in vocational terms sometimes still feel at odds with the very idea of political theory, even as we continue to need to theorize, in part because of a failure to come to terms with both the ubiquity of the question of justice and the ongoing, highly practical administration of it. The positions available to us to connect to the world of what we know to be political affairs are too confining, sometimes so confining that many of us are tempted to point to those connections themselves as a primary source of our political maladies. Some of us aban-don theory to operate as advocates for one or another position, to enter into the machine of administration itself. Some of us abandon theory in an at-tempt to think about different things, not wanting to be consumed by the pain we are witnessing, in theory and in practice. As theorists, we easily be-come appalled because the practice of politics always seems to be threatened with reduction to a series of unacceptable, mutually exclusive alternatives. These alternatives are unacceptable, regardless of the substantive outcomes they promise, because they demand the sorts of endorsements that are anti-thetical to the possibility of recognizing the harm intrinsic to the judgments we might be compelled to make. The project of judgment sometimes con-demns the objects of its power to pain or death or a diminished quality of life.

Those of us who think of political theory in vocational terms also need at least to try to get over ourselves and recognize that the epochal struggles of theory ought to be more democratically distributed. The claims of great burden that some of us make, especially those of us who are situated to ob-serve the execution of sentences, too easily distract us from acknowledging the luxury of our position. We need to share a bit more of that luxurious burden, which too often is more like a privilege. In this sense, the compen-satory struggles of Kafka and Emerson may help us loosen our grasp on the arbitration of justice that we claim for ourselves and, in so doing, help reduce the unhandsomeness of our condition—an unhandsomeness that deepens as our grasping becomes more desperate.

Emerson's thinking about compensation may show us one way in which we might evade the judgment that reduces all choices to exclusive alternatives and, in so doing, face up to the facts of justice. And yet Emerson presents us with several traps. The ecstasy of his idea of self-reliance, which undergirds his confidence in compensation, also presents us with the temptation to political quiescence. Moreover, self-reliance can be thought of as a godly doctrine, and godliness is vastly hollow at the end of the second millennium. So we must find a way to question the motives of Emerson even as we try to think with him. This is not such a new task.[2] The narrative of Kafka's story offers new guidelines for doing it. Understanding linkages between Emerson and Kafka aids us in coming to terms with the idea of compensation, which in turn may lead us to make sense of how political theory can come to a kind of compensation in Emerson's sense.

Undoubtedly this task is obscure, in that I take as its end learning how to think through a singularly obscure version of contemporary Emersonianism—one I am piecing together as I go along. Is it dangerous or reactionary to think that we might derive lessons about the pain of politics that would better enable us to bear it than we now do, rather than (one more time) to act to overcome it? Maybe. And maybe it is dangerous as well to be less than perfectly clear about my intentions, even to myself. But on this question of intention I feel greater confidence. Unlike those who want everything to be perfectly clear, I am almost happy to take on this task, because I think that the risk of obscurity should always be welcome. Our difficulties more often begin when we are too easily understood.

Kafka's Harrow

The story "In the Penal Colony" is inexhaustible. But that is not quite right, because its indefinite finitude may be presumed, in one sense, simply by its closure as a narrative. It is a story with an ending, after all. But we might still tempted to say that it is inexhaustible because it represents such a range of possibilities that many readers may find themselves exhausted by reading the story. Maybe it is best to say simply that it is a story that is very rich in possibilities. Given its plentitude, we want to think through a version of it in which there is in the foreground a narrative about the breakdown of an apparatus designed to write sentences on the bodies of those convicted of crimes, the plot of the story. This version is in many ways the one most familiar to anyone who has read the story even casually. The familiarity provided by plot, though, as readers of Kafka come to know, is composed of fragments of the familiar reassembled to expose the familiar to the strangeness of experience. To say this more directly, Kafka is an uncanny writer.[3]

The plot is simple, the genre that of crime and punishment. The premise has to do with a form of punishment that is used at a particular penal colony. When a person is convicted of a crime, his sentence is to have a sentence inscribed on his body by a machine specifically designed for the purpose. This sentence is always a death sentence, because the needles that inscribe the sentence dig deeper and deeper into the body until the person dies; but it is also rehabilitative, because the condemned man learns a valuable lesson before he dies, the substance of the sentence that is written on his body. He dies enlightened, realizing, for instance, that is it best to "HONOR THY SUPERIORS." The apparatus, designed and built by the former commandant of the colony, is itself close to perfect, maintained so as to run silently and automatically once it is set in motion. Yet it does have parts that wear out and must be replaced from time to time.

When spare parts are available, the apparatus can continue to function. But when the spare parts are no longer available, can it be said that the apparatus will cease to function? The lack of spare parts cannot be a cause of failure. Spare parts cease to be spare when used. How can the absence of something that is otherwise only in reserve, something not being used, be blamed for the failure of a machine? This incongruity is at the heart of the plot of "In the Penal Colony."

The officer in charge of the execution that is carried out in this story is the last follower of the old commandant. He expresses a deep ambivalence about spare parts, revealed during the course of his explanation of how the apparatus operates, which he presents to the explorer whom he wants to witness the execution. This indecisiveness is to be found in some of the side comments he makes concerning the value of the apparatus to the regime, especially when he harks back to a time when the colony was under the control of the former commandant, and things operated as they were intended. In those days there were crowds at executions and the commandant's ladies did not intrude in decision-making. There was a general appreciation of the aesthetics of the execution among the many inhabitants of the penal colony. They would watch carefully so as to observe the face of the condemned at his moment of enlightenment. But the officer is harking back to days that are gone, and in the present tense he is very concerned about the details of the machinery itself.

In discussing the workings of the machinery, the officer says, "Up till now a few things had still to be set by hand, but from this moment it works all by itself." He then comments, "Things sometimes go wrong, of course; I hope nothing goes wrong today, but we have to allow for the possibility. The machinery should go on working continuously for twelve hours. But if anything goes wrong it will only be some small matter that can be set right at once."[4] Here we are presented with a subtle contradiction that later has larger consequences. If something goes wrong in an automatic mechanism intended to operate continuously for twelve hours, one would need to *reset* the machine before it can start again after it was interrupted. The machinery is akin to a timepiece, in a sense.

This inconsistency is made clear when we see what happens when the apparatus does, in fact, break down. The first part the officer mentions that is worn out and in need of a replacement is a cogwheel in the "Designer," the part of the machine that sets the pattern to be inscribed on the body of the condemned. During the failure of the apparatus, the Designer spews cogwheel after cogwheel out of its lid.

> At that moment he heard a noise above him in the Designer. He looked up. Was that cogwheel going to make trouble after all? But it was something quite different. Slowly the lid of the Designer rose up and clicked wide open. The teeth of a cogwheel showed themselves and rose higher, soon the whole wheel was visible, it was as if some enormous force was squeezing the Designer so that there was no longer room for the wheel, and the wheel moved up till it came to the very edge of the Designer, fell down, rolled along the sand a little on its rim and then lay flat. But a second wheel was already rising after it, followed by many others, large and small and indistinguishably minute, the same thing happened to all of them, at every moment one imagined the Designer must really be empty, but another complex of numerous wheels was already rising into sight, falling down, trundling along the sand and lying flat.[5]

We might well believe that the initial trouble started with that one worn-out wheel, for which there is no spare part. The intricacy of the mechanism, the elaborate synchronization of the various parts (which presumably would make the breaking of a strap the first manifest failure of the machine, that is, the first failure to have an impact on its effectiveness), coupled with the idea that the old commandant who designed the machine was also the author of the total organization of the colony—these details point toward a series of connections that lead back to the failure of a worn part, one that cannot be replaced for lack of a spare. Thus it seems that any minor failure must be disastrous to the entire operation of the apparatus, and that the role of spare parts to the adequate maintenance of the machine cannot be underestimated.

Spare parts also play a pivotal role in enabling us to establish a formula that will allow us to cling to the incommensurate order engendered in the (mal)functioning apparatus. The officer suggests, "This is a very complex machine, it can't be helped that things are breaking or giving way here and there; but one must not thereby allow oneself to be diverted in one's general judgment."[6] Yet, if its parts continue to break down, how can the apparatus itself be said to work? Is it a machine we are being told about, or is it something else? Can we render a general judgment about the machine on the basis of its utility, or is there some other appeal we need to know about? To obtain such knowledge, we must slip into the realm of metaphor. The machine would be a metaphor for the political order itself, and then we need to ask what the standard is that we must employ if we are to determine the efficacy of an order that is always in (slight) disarray. Instead of asking if the machine is working properly, we might ask if there are spare parts available for it. The officer notes, "The resources for maintaining the machine are now very much reduced. Under the former Commandant I had free access to a sum of money set aside entirely for this purpose. There was a store, too, in which spare parts were kept for repairs of all kinds. I confess having been almost prodigal with them."[7] Later, the officer wistfully recalls life in the old regime, when "I got new parts for almost every execution."[8] The general judgment we are asked to make may concern the quality of a regime on the basis of how it underwrites its projects, not on the basis of how it completes them. Spare parts are a form of insurance.

As crucial as spare parts seem to be, though, the breakdown of the apparatus can never be attributed directly to a lack of them. The logic of breakdown is associative, not directly causal. The breakdown of the apparatus is caused not by a lack of spare parts but by the failure of worn-out parts. Any part, no matter how worn, might hold up long enough for the apparatus to fulfill its twelve-hour function. In fact, we never know what causes the breakdown of the apparatus. In a larger sense, we do not know what it is that is breaking down. We may ask what it was that the old commandant had established that was breaking down and plausibly guess many things, at least at the level of symbolic order—patriarchy, bureaucratic order, theocratic rule, a liberal colonial order based on enlightenment.

The role that spare parts play directly addresses the anxiety of the officer. Spare parts themselves are technically useless as long as they remain unused. The point is that their role is to assuage an anxiety through the fact of their availability. (Who would like to drive through a desert without a spare tire?) They are, in fact, very much like insurance policies, in that they underwrite the possibility of acting by minimizing the risk associated with the act. But once installed, once used to replace a worn or broken part, a spare part no longer relieves one of anxiety. It ceases to be a spare. Spare parts thus can be said to exist in the gap between the actual and the potential, deriving their value from the combination of their potential usefulness and their actual nonuse. (I want to suggest that this is a manifestation of the gap between essence and existence, or more properly, existence and essence. But this is to anticipate.)

Perhaps our most important moments of truth are composed of our willful lack of recognition of the futility of bridging gaps between the actual and the potential. Kafka seems to stage such a moment. It results from the failure of a seemingly superfluous part of the apparatus, not a gear or lever but the felt gag that is forced into the mouth of the condemned by the officer. When the old gag is placed in the condemned man's mouth, "in an irresistible access of nausea [he] shut his eyes and vomited."

> "It's all the fault of that Commandant!" cried the officer, senselessly shaking the brass rods in front, "the machine is befouled like a pigsty." With trembling hands he indicated to the explorer what had happened. "Have I not tried for hours at a time to get the Commandant to understand that the prisoner must fast for a whole day before the execution. But our new mild doctrine thinks otherwise. The Commandant's ladies stuff the man with sugar candy before he's led off. He has lived on stinking fish his whole life long and now he has to eat sugar candy! But it could still be possible, I shouldn't have anything to say against it, but why won't they give me a new felt gag, which I have been begging for the last three months. How should a man not feel sick when he takes a felt gag into his mouth which more than a hundred men have already slobbered and gnawed in their dying moments?"[9]

The claim of the officer concerning the treatment of the condemned man is totally at odds with an earlier depiction the officer provided. In the earlier account concerning the condemned man's arrest and sentencing, he makes it clear that he has no concern about the condemned man fasting for a day before the execution of sentence. Moreover, the condemned man is constantly in the custody of the officer from the time of his arrest and hence not accessible to the ladies.[10] So what is happening in this rant?

One reading of this passage would give to the new commandant's ladies the role of feminine resistance to and subversion of male political order. At the psychoanalytical level, they may be seen as the (male) hysterical elements of the officer's fragmented self that rise up in resistance to his phallocentric death drive.[11] I believe the disordered temporality, represented by the coexistence of incommensurate time frames, can also be understood as an example of one of Kafka's special techniques for highlighting the spatial paradox associated with thinking about the gap between the actual and the potential. He is writing this story not as a fable but as a description of the fullness of time itself. Walter Benjamin, one of Kafka's greatest readers, suggests that "what Kafka could see least of all was the *gestus*. . . . Like El Greco, Kafka tears open the sky behind every gesture; but as with El Greco—who was the patron saint of the Expressionists—the gesture remains the decisive thing, the center of the event."[12] Benjamin sees Kafka's work as an attempt to make the spirit of the world concrete by bringing what has been forgotten to the surface. But rather than understand this exercise psychoanalytically, Benjamin argues that it must be understood as "never something purely individual. Everything forgotten mingles with what has been forgotten of the prehistoric world, forms countless, uncertain, changing compounds, yielding a constant flow of new strange products. Oblivion is the container from which the inexhaustible intermediate world in Kafka's stories presses toward the light."[13] This capacity to make the gesture serve as a substitute for narrative explanation give Kafka's work its importance. While the experiences that Kafka describes are highly individualized, he paradoxically limns these experiences in such a way that they can never be *received* by individuals *qua* individuals. As Benjamin notes, "Kafka lives in a *complementary* world."[14] By this phrase Benjamin seems to mean that in establishing through gesture what is usually noted through narrative, Kafka establishes a world of meaning that is not beholden to tradition and enables us to see how tradition itself might appear to us as a sickness.

Kafka's overrich phrase concerning the condemned man's "irresistible access of nausea" uncannily rests on an arcane meaning of the word *access* as a synonym for *outburst*. But it also suggests that the nausea is something he was able to retrieve from a place. It already existed in the oblivion: the contents of the condemned man's stomach move, thanks to the gag, from the dark recesses of his gut to the light that is soon to be a high noon. In contemporary computer jargon, the word *access* has transmuted into a verb meaning to retrieve something from a file, to bring it on-screen or "on line." It is to call forth that which already exists. The officer's insistence that minor disorders (such as vomit on the machine) are of no matter is consistent with the idea that it is the gesture—in this case the nausea—that matters, and not the consequence, the vomit. This gestural understanding of meaning is not inconsistent with an Emersonian view of compensation.[15]

So it is not what is breaking down that is of interest as much as it is the moment when breakdown is imminent. We ought to want to know what the characterization of that moment may mean for the idea of compensation. In Kafka's story, there is a weariness conveyed by the officer under his hysterical enthusiasm. His gestures, his muttering, his spoken asides, his concern to keep things moving, his fretting over the apparatus's condition, his willingness finally to submit himself to the apparatus, his ultimate hope for a return to an old order, do not immediately signal the sort of calm confidence that might be first associated with the idea of compensation as Emerson presents it. And yet the whole still seems to suggest the gestural shape that a desire to elevate compensation to a transcendental value might take. In a time and place such as our late modern united states, when minor moments of farce reveal important elements of the texture of existence and when the overlooked or unobserved returns to haunt the human capacity to act, Kafka's detailed observations of a complementary world are not an imaginary escape from the pain we suffer but an alternative perspective concerning the meaning of present reality from which we might better see the tradition of our judgments. They show us the connections between the representation of an act and the act itself, how the former incompletely completes the latter—never fully or finally, only as a piece of a puzzle that seems to generate new pieces every time we come close to solving it.

Emerson's Crack

Emerson begins his essay on compensation by noting the ubiquity of the subject, a ubiquity that is, for him, a major source of its fascination. His fascination with compensation has to do with more than its appearance in all dimensions of human life; it is a consequence not only of compensation's ubiquity but of its special essence. Emerson suggests that "in it might be shown men a ray of divinity, the present action of the soul of this world, clean from all vestige of tradition, and so the heart of man might be bathed by an inundation of eternal love, conversing with that which he knows was always and always must be, because it really is now."[16] Compensation is here, is now. Emerson suggests that if we learn something about compensa-tion—perhaps only the smallest arc of "the path of the law of compensa-tion"—we might know that we are better than we know we are. We are bet-ter than we know, Emerson asserts, because we adhere to the law of com-pensation. But what is that law?

Emerson contrasts compensation to the popular understanding of jus-tice. He relates how one preacher argues, from the doctrine of the Last Judgment, that the wicked are successful in this life but that just compen-sation might be (should be) rendered to those who are good in the next one. Emerson objects: "The legitimate inference the disciple would draw was—'we are to have *such* a good time as the sinners have now'; or, to push it to the extreme import—'You sin now, we shall sin by and by; we would sin now, if we could; not being successful we expect our revenge to-mor-row.'"[17] This notion "defers to the base estimate of the market of what con-stitutes manly success, instead of confronting and convicting the world from the truth; announcing the presence of the soul; the omnipotence of the will; and so establishing the standard of good and ill, of success and failure."[18] The market misapprehends compensation as a causal mechanism of justice, and justice as a consequence of the human balancing of good and bad.

Emerson understands compensation otherwise: it is intrinsic to nature it-self, everything that is other than that which is human, an element of the dualism that pervades nature whether in its general laws, its specific mecha-nisms, or even in the nature and condition of human beings as a part of na-ture. He writes, "An inevitable dualism bisects nature, so that each thing is a half, and suggests another thing to make it whole; as, spirit, matter; man, woman; odd, even; subjective, objective; in, out; upper, under; motion, rest; yea, nay. . . . Whilst the world is thus dual, so are every one of its parts. The entire system of things gets represented in every particle."[19] Emerson de-scribes this dualism in reference to human affairs in a series of prescient ob-servations concerning the fortunes attendant to political fame and personal genius. But these descriptions are only illustrations of what he would sug-gest is a fundamental fact of life in the universe. "All things are moral," he suggests. "That soul, which within us is a sentiment, outside of us is a law. . . . What we call retribution is the universal necessity by which the whole appears wherever a part appears."[20]

Yet Emerson is at care to note that the wholeness of things constantly is challenged by the inevitably partial responses of human beings to existence.

For him this partiality, this incompleteness, is an aspect of the dualism of body and soul:

> Every act rewards itself, or in other words, integrates itself, in a twofold manner; first in the thing, or in real nature; and secondly in the circumstance, or in apparent nature. Men call the circumstance retribution. The causal retribution is in the thing, and is seen by the soul. The retribution in the circumstance is seen by the understanding; it is inseparable from the thing, but is often spread over a long time, and so does not become distinct until after many years. The specific stripes may follow late for an offense, but they follow because they accompany it. Crime and punishment grow out of one stem. Punishment is a fruit that unsuspected ripens within the flower of the pleasure which concealed it. Cause and effect, means and end, seed and fruit, cannot be severed; for the effect already blooms in the cause, the end preexists in the means, the fruit in the seed.[21]

For Emerson, it is human to resist the wholeness of the soul that underwrites the varying experience of our bodies. We seek to act partially because we cannot do otherwise. We are bodily beings. That is our nature. In our moral strivings in particular, we seek the pleasure of the senses and not the requirements of character. Nonetheless, we will be thwarted in our delusions by the inevitability of a retributive action. "There is a crack in everything God has made," he notes.[22] That sentence accounts for both the resistance of the body to the soul and the inevitable connection of the two. The connection of the two is what makes compensation such a difficult idea. When placed in the context of human being, the doctrine of compensation is remarkable for its toughness, which comes from the harsh indifference of this insight when applied to specific circumstance, to the always partial responses we are capable of mustering to the wholeness of the soul. As Emerson suggests, in nature nothing is given, and all things are sold.[23] But the idea of a crack in everything God has made also suggests that while it is inevitable that we will resist the imposition of wholeness with our bodies, it is also useless that we do so, because our bodies cannot be completely separated from our souls. The crack is not a gap but a fissure, a space of both opening and connection. It is what enables us to see the whole in every part, an encoding of everything in each thing. It is also what prevents us from evading the reaction that attends every action.

The harshness of our knowledge of compensation might lead us to a stoicism or a passive nihilism. Should we simply become indifferent to action, as a consequence of what Emerson himself calls "the indifference of circumstance?"[24] He insists not. As ubiquitous as compensation is in the nature of things, he suggests,

> there is a deeper fact of the soul than compensation, to wit, its own nature. The soul is not a compensation, but a life. The soul *is*. Under all this running sea of circumstance, whose waters ebb and flow with perfect balance, lies the aboriginal abyss of real Being. Essence, or God, is not a relation or a part, but the whole. Being is the vast affirmative, excluding negation, self-balanced, and swallowing up all relations, parts and times within itself.[25]

Emerson wants us to remember that life is a progress, not a station. We thus have ways of measuring our uncertain movement toward better and away from worse. The absolute measure of ourselves is the whole, but such a whole is not available to us. So underlying Emerson's discussion of compensation, and in fact enabling that discussion, is the question of the relation of compensation to the real Being of the soul. And as he puts it, "In the nature of the soul is the compensation for the inequalities of condition."[26]

Emerson understands the soul as constantly quitting its whole system of things, worldly relations hanging loosely to the circumstances of its existence: the soul "becoming as it were a transparent fluid membrane through which the living form is seen, and not, as in most men, an indurated heterogeneous fabric of many dates and of no settled character, in which the man is imprisoned. Then there can be enlargement, and the man of to-day scarcely recognizes the man of yesterday."[27] So the consistency of the soul paradoxically consists of the mutation of character through time. For this reason he suggests that whatever sadness attends the human condition consists of the lack of faith that follows from the exclusive realization of the partial character of individual experience, and not from the greater knowledge of the unity of things in the soul. Our failure to "believe in the riches of the soul, in its proper eternity and omnipotence," leaves us in a horribly uncertain estate. "We cannot stay amid the ruins. Neither will we rely on the new; and so we walk ever with averted eyes, like those monsters who look backwards."[28]

Emerson presents us with ourselves as "organs of the soul."[29] The soul is a great sublimity, or God.[30] But Emerson's limitless vision is limited by his piety, precisely by his inability to get beyond God. He nonetheless leaves us with an Emersonian quest: Is it possible to think of advancement, to observe growth and development, without thinking of a god, even nostalgically? If we need a god to explain the spiritual laws of compensation, do we not also need a law of compensation to aid us as we free ourselves from belief in a god? Can God be considered as but another spare part?

The soul need not be God when it can be light.[31] We might imagine that Emerson without a god is Kafka. We then might begin an inquiry into the terms through which we also could imagine a politics that would attend compensation in this disenchanted era, whatever name we might want to attach to it. A beginning of such a politics might be found in the actions through which we compensate for the lack of God. We might repair to an appreciation of our existence for what it lacks and, in understanding better our lack, be able to note how full (perhaps overfull) it is. Emphasizing its connection to the emergence of modern democracy and calling forth (sometimes more, sometimes less) George Kateb's evocations of democratic individuality,[32] we may provisionally suggest that the death of God is the historical event that gives rise to the possibility of political theory as compensation. This does not mean that political theory comes into play as the activity that ensouls us but rather that it becomes the activity that allows us to imagine our destinies as connected to each other, free of the encumbrances of a metaphysics that demands of us that we understand ourselves as having a common soul. In short, it might enable us to imagine a kind of community otherwise, one compatible with free citizenship.

Limbo

What happens after the condemned man is freed from the apparatus of the penal colony? He stays in the immediate vicinity of the apparatus and, against the wishes of the explorer, witnesses the apparatus's breakdown and the subsequent death of the officer, after the officer submitted himself to the apparatus. The explorer then seeks the help of the soldier and the condemned man to remove the officer from the harrow.

> But the other two could not make up their minds to come; the condemned man actually turned away; the explorer had to go over to them and force them into position at the officer's head. And here, almost against his will, he had to look at the face of the corpse. It was as it had been in life; no sign was visible of the promised redemption; what the others had found in the machine the officer had not found; the lips were firmly pressed together, the eyes were open, with the same expression as in life, the look was calm and convinced, through the forehead went the point of the great iron spike.[33]

"What the others had found in the machine the officer had not found." The spirit that animated the machine is gone.

The condemned man and the soldier follow the explorer to a teahouse, where the explorer seeks out the grave of the old commandant (hidden under a table). The inscription on the gravestone reads:

> Here rests the old Commandant. His adherents, who must be nameless, have dug this grave and set up this stone. There is a prophecy that after a certain number of years the Commandant will rise again and lead his adherents from this house to recover the colony. Have faith and wait![34]

The people at the teahouse smile at the explorer after he reads this inscription, "as if they too had read the inscription, had found it ridiculous and were expecting him to agree with them."[35] The explorer leaves. He is followed by the condemned man and the soldier:

> Probably they wanted to force him at the last minute to take them with him. While he was bargaining below with a ferryman to row him to the steamer, the two of them came headlong down the steps, in silence, for they did not dare to shout. . . . They could have jumped into the boat, but the explorer lifted a heavy knotted rope from the floor boards, threatened them with it and so kept them from attempting to leap.[36]

A probable reading of this final passage from the story suggests that the soldier and the condemned man seek to leave the colony, to regain the voices silenced by their experience. The explorer seeks to prevent their leap (of faith?) by waving a knotted rope (a phallus) at them, casting them back into their heart of darkness, to their pagan ignorance that makes them smile at the prophecy of a resurrection and return of the commandant.

"Probably," writes Kafka; but Kafka is not a probable writer. He is interested in the gesture, not the motive. The soldier and the condemned man may as easily have sought to prevent the explorer's departure. How does one prevent someone from "attempting to leap"? One would know that one had failed only if an attempt was made. In this last sentence we see the logical paradox of spare parts. To know that an attempt to leap is prevented is only to know that no attempt to leap was made, and to assume the rest.

Let us assume otherwise. The condemned man and the soldier may have known that the explorer would resist the good of the immediate, of life in limbo. Maybe they wanted to explain to him what that life is like. It is a life of gestures, pauses, moments of transition—life exactly like our life except for one difference, and that difference is something we will never know. It is life as oblivious, life in oblivion: to repeat Benjamin, "Oblivion is the container from which the inexhaustible intermediate world in Kafka's stories presses toward the light." It is a place where the explorer would lose his voice because he would lose himself, where nothing is purely individual even as each individual shines in an irreparable light.

Giorgio Agamben presents this interpretation in a passage that has as its *raison d'être* an observation about an artist's representation of people in limbo:

> Like the freed convict in Kafka's *Penal Colony*, who has survived the destruction of the machine that was to have executed him, these beings have left the world of guilt and justice behind them: The light that rains down on them is that irreparable light of the dawn following the *novissima dies* of judgment. But the life that begins on earth after the last day is simply human life.[37]

Agamben uses the phrase "irreparable light" and, in so doing, combines Kafka and Emerson. For Emerson, the soul is light; for Kafka, we are still in this world even as our world is as uncertain as the gap between essence and existence shows it to be. The idea of the irreparable, for Agamben, is "that things are thus and thus—that is still in the world. But that this is irreparable, that this *thus* is without remedy, that we can contemplate it as such— this is the only passage outside the world."[38] *Thus*, for Agamben, means (at least) not otherwise. Being otherwise depends on recognizing that the "thus" is not attached to God. (Agamben understands that God must be recognized as the world, understood profanely.) A thus without remedy rejects the profane understanding of the world (the world as God) and gives us a Nietzschean affirmation, a yes in the fullest sense of existence, the world *as thus*. For Agamben, this idea validates the eternal return of the same.[39] He moves even further:

> Seeing something simply in its being thus—irreparable, but for that reason necessary; thus, but not for that reason contingent—is love.
>
> At the point you perceive the irreparability of the world, at that point is transcendence.[40]

The ecstasy of the world made divine through the disconnection of thusness from God constitutes an obscure Emersonianism. Essence and existence are related through the irreparable, which Kafka expresses as the strange temporality that attends a world that is emptying itself of meaning, and which Emerson expresses as the crack in everything God has made. Transcendence is simply human life, in whatever eternality we can make of it.

For Agamben, the negative community that can emerge through the idea of the irreparable is one that will recognize itself in political struggle between the State and the non-State:

> The novelty of the coming politics is that it will no longer be a struggle for the conquest or control of the State, but a struggle between the State and the non-State (humanity), an insurmountable disjunction between whatever singularity and the State organization.[41]

Expressed in terms of American political experience, we might say that this is a struggle between whatever contemporary form self-reliance can take in a world of massification and the force of massification itself. More precisely outlined in George Kateb's Emersonian concerns, "Individualism must battle massification, more and more."[42] The battle occurs not between individuals and groups, exclusively or even predominantly, but in the massification of the individuality given to us through the happenstance of "whatever singularity," in a struggle against the fascism in us all, in the art of learning to live counter to all forms of fascism but especially the fascism inside each one of us in our duly constituted individuality. We might call this the struggle to attain the state of democratic individuality.

In this way political theory as compensation becomes clearer to me, when it is understood as the preparatory study of human existence. We should always be ready to be human, for those times when our humanity fails us (as it so regularly does). Political theory operates as a kind of spare part, a spare humanity. Its practice is the activity—moral, inclusive, philosophical, and general but also ethical, distancing, practical, and specific—of turning away from the centralizing forces of our age, especially the moral forces of guilt and justice, which by dint of their orientation to final judgments are too often the elements of our human failure not to evoke our suspicion. Political theory moves *thusly* when it contributes toward a perception of the partiality of the human project and opens the closed circle by realizing the incompleteness especially of its own project. When done well, it tutors us in the idea of a moment of truth in our concerted actions, fleeting but eternally recurring. And finally, for now, it places that eternality safely out of reach, by making it always irreparable, always incompletely thus. Among other things, it is a compensation for the fact that we will die, someday.

In the Mean Time, Thoreau's Shit

"But we're not dead yet!" we may exclaim to the sad theorist dwelling on the end as he comes to collect our remains.[43] This attempt to think through the activity of compensation is an exercise in death-bound thinking if it remains rooted in the sky of fantasy. Human beings are not only light; we are also earth. And our final contribution to the earth—let us face this most common fact—is basically shit. Henry David Thoreau, while also accounting for lighter things, writes, "The better part of the man is soon plowed into the soil for compost."[44]

Thoreau roots our limbo in the seat of life, writing, "What is a house but a *sedes*, a seat?"[45] At Walden he connects us to the world by way of our seats: our posteriors are connected directly to the most meaningful sites of government. He understands this site of government, Walden, to be adjacent to government when he notes its proximity to the first battlefield of American Revolution, "our only field known to fame," Concord.[46] But he also knows how the site of Walden overcomes the distance of time:

> We are wont to imagine rare and delectable places in some remote and more celestial corner of the system, behind the constellation of Cassiopeia's Chair, far from noise and disturbance. I discovered that my house had its site in such a withdrawn, but forever new and unprofaned, part of the universe.[47]

To compare this site to a celestial corner behind Cassiopeia's Chair (or seat), Thoreau must know that even as this Ethopian queen (mother of Andromeda) was honored with a place in the heavens after her death, "though she attained this honor, yet the Sea-Nymphs, her old enemies, prevailed so far as to cause her to be placed in that part of the heaven near the pole, where every night she is half the time held with her head downward, to give her a lesson in humility."[48] This remote corner is also one of practiced humility, in heaven but looking downward. Cassiopeia thus remains connected, even at the most elevated height, to earth.

Thoreau sees himself as connected to the society of humanity in a similar way, and all humans as being so connected, to the extent that we seek to be human:

> And, by the way, who estimates the value of the crop which nature yields in the still wilder fields unimproved by man? The crop of *English* hay is carefully weighed, the moisture calculated, the silicates and the potash; but in all dells and pond-holes in the woods and pastures and swamps grows a rich and various crop only unreaped by man. Mine was, as it were, the connecting link be-

tween wild and cultivated fields; as some states are civilized, and others half-civilized, and others savage or barbarous, so my field was, though not in a bad sense, a half-cultivated field.[49]

Thoreau cultivates his bean field with his shit, "putting fresh soil about the bean stems."[50] This is his better part, and he wants to know how the cultivation of beans is to be distinguished from the cultivation of ourselves. It cannot. "Why concern ourselves so much about our beans for seed, and not be concerned at all about a new generation of men?" he asks.[51] This is the puzzle of ordinary justice, phrased not as a question of distribution but as a question of cultivation. The project of this concern is never to be pursued exclusively from within the civilized state of life but from a place that forms the connection between the wild and the civilized. This spare humanity, the diurnal product of our bodies (if we are lucky) plowed back into the earth, giving us beans to eat and for tropes, connects the imaginative project of Kafka to the ethical project of Emerson, allowing us the life of decay and dirt that will frustrate all projects rooted exclusively in the sky or in the earth. We meditate with our brains, we illuminate with our eyes, we mediate with our ears and mouths and hands and feet, we ruminate with our stomachs, we procreate with our genitalia, we connect with our skins, we cultivate with our shit. Above us, the heavens, below us the earth. This is the place of human being.

4

Civil Society

You may or may not take an explicit side in some particular conflict, but unless you find some way to show that this society is not yours, it is; your being compromised by its actions expresses the necessity of your being implicated in them. That you nevertheless avoid express participation or express disavowal is what creates that ghost-state of conformity Emerson articulates endlessly, as our being inane, timid, ashamed, skulkers, leaners, apologetic, noncommittal, a gag, a masquerade, pinched in a corner, cowed, cowards, fleeing before a revolution.

—Stanley Cavell, "What Is the Emersonian Event?"

Filthy Civil Society

Cultivation is dirty work. It entails everyday patience and impatience, care and carelessness, conversation, gesture, housecleaning, grocery shopping, taking out the trash, pulling weeds, making dinner, putting kids to bed, trying to listen to a friend when you don't really have it in you, attending to the pain of a loved one. All in all, cultivation is a process of commitment. It involves all the quotidian obligations and routines that require thought at its lower register, often draining thought and frustrating the illusions of a higher ambition, in the hope and sense that this gesture or that chore is what needs to be done now if things are to be made right later. Cultivation also involves play—going to movies together, making that dinner for guests, singing, witty conversation, planning a trip, making occasions, and overcoming that wish to get back to the work of life, one's life work, when one is lucky enough to have a vocation in life. It is difficult to imagine cultivation proceeding if there is not a passion for it and the things that may grow out of it—friendships, poems, families, food and tropes, children, students, a confounded and complicated set of connections and disconnections, playing across all manner of talk and action.

Where and how the passion for cultivation finds its expression has to be a political matter. Compromise pulls us into the drama of consent, but the passages through which we wend our way back to the scene of political contestation are formed by civil society, and civil society in turn is formed by our cultivation of it. How explicit are we to be in our discussion of this cultivation? Repulsed by the dirt of it, wanting desire and the forms of its expression to be pacified, all of us who consent to be governed nonetheless find the messiness and violence that attend cultivation the subjects of our concern. The question of the governance of cultivation, however, brings into sharp relief our faith (or lack of it) in each other's ways of consenting. Stanley Cavell's test—"unless you find some way to show that this society is not yours, it is"[1]—may be used to read all sorts of activities as signs showing that society is being abandoned. This is when the advocates of a more robust civil society call in the police rather than call for revolution, because they want to understand cultivation as pacification, as a means of supporting political order.

To police is to clean. But it also may be useful to remember that policing is associated etymologically with the very idea of a *polis*, or polity. If we consider that politics has so often been defined as that which occurs in the common spaces of the public, what some would call the public sphere, then the connection seems obvious. Policing may be understood as a particular kind of political action that focuses in an exemplary way on tasks of completion, order, and neatness. In that sense, it is to be distinguished from the more unified and transcendent power of what is recognized as sovereign authority. Underwriting sovereign power, policing enables it as it is connected to it. The early modern connections of policing to government, especially in the republican tradition, have to do explicitly with the governance of manners and cleanliness. As a consequence of adequate policing, the messiness of disorder is reordered; things are put into their place, distributed, cared for. Children are fed, garbage is disposed of, trains are made to run on time, traffic is directed.[2]

A comprehensive scheme of organization provides reassurances of predictability of administration of justice, welfare, and the flows of goods, people, and information. This essentially European understanding of police as policy is captured by Sir William Blackstone: "The public police and economy must be understood as the due regulation and domestic order of the kingdom, whereby the individuals of the state, like members of a well-governed family, are bound to conform to the rules of propriety, good neighborhood, and good manners."[3] Through the demands of general welfare and the need to prevent chaos in markets and other public and private spaces, policing is associated with policy. Among others, though with greater force and directness than most, Theodore Lowi has noted that the emergence of a *national* police power in the United States was a consequence of the economic emergency of the Great Depression and the Roosevelt administration's response to it.[4] While grounds for the establishment of such a nationalization were laid in the United States in the nineteenth century, it nonetheless took the force of emergency to establish this power at the level where a national government's interventions could legitimately influence the behavior of individuals. The policies developed during the New Deal established the infrastructure for what Lowi has called the Second Republic of the United States. The New Deal is famous for having saved capitalism from itself, in large part because it re-established conditions of civic order that were threatened by the immiseration of so many citizens during a period of extraordinary economic dislocation. As such, many of its components were constitutive of a police strategy in Blackstone's sense of the term. One might go so far as to suggest that there is by now little to distinguish European from American conceptions of police power. And to the extent that there ever was, one might say that the difference has always had much less to do with the style of police power than with the extent to which the police were allowed to be deployed in civil society. In keeping with Blackstone, we might say that police power enables propriety, good neighborhood, and good manners to prevail. The point Lowi underlines in his work is that the underlying premise of any police action is instrumental, a means toward another end. He endorses this instrumentality as being essential to a liberal state ruled by law.

Once the order of things is established or re-established, then other things can happen. We could even say that policing is that element of political governance that enables us to do other things. To the extent that policing is delegated to servants, janitors, detectives, bureaucrats, teachers, college presidents, William Bennett, and other administrators of order, we might be able to claim that the rest of us are free to do other things. Policing thus understood could be an underpinning of freedom. But that is true only if we fail to ask an important question: *Who* is left to do other things, and *what* is to be done? In a liberal democratic society this double question places the idea of policing under suspicion, because to the extent that a society is policed, there is that much less possibility of the flowering of spontaneous imagination and dissenting consciousnesses that are the inconstant but essential inspirations of democratic energy. Indeed, the instrumentality of policing is always apparently at odds with the ends of freedom, when freedom is understood not simply as lack of coercion or as achieving security but as a way of being that depends on the cultivation of an imagination that relies in turn on the small violences and boundary violations of impertinence, rudeness, and bad manners; in short, as an imagination that needs to upset order as a means of expressing itself.

Contemporary liberal democracy seems ill suited to prevent the dramatic intensification of the policing of society in recent decades.[5] Many intellectuals of the American Right quietly have claimed that an excess of democracy itself is at the source of the incapacity, because, they argue, American democracy is undisciplined and increasingly unruly. And even as they overtly argue that the emergence of more intense policing is only a response to democratic pressures, the politicians of the Republican and Democratic Parties and their corporate supporters have counted on an increasingly constricted electorate to forge their electoral coalitions. They continue to resist any changes in the system of governance that would challenge the anti-democratic forces underlying electoral politics.[6] An increasingly constricted electorate and an intensification of policing are yoked to a common political strategy that de-emphasizes the participation of the citizenry and treats them instead as subjects in a population. From this perspective (if one is a liberal democrat), the policies that political elites are pursuing are increasingly designed to pacify the citizenry rather than to respond to the will of a popular majority. The very idea of a popular majority is called into question when one comes to understand how majorities are produced through the use of police powers.[7] Above them, engaging in a jockeying for power reminiscent of court society, are competing corporate managers and owners who have discovered that their margins of profitability no longer depend on the cultivation of a large, well-educated, and prosperous class of consumers as much as they once thought. Indeed, it sometimes seems as if the disorganization of world capital is shrinking the size of the relevant consumer market for the strategic purpose of a more efficient delivery of economic goods and maximization of profits.[8] With the abandonment of the costs associated with the cultivation of democratic civilization, cheaper, less discipline-based forms of mass control can begin to emerge.[9] These new kinds of policing play a key role as a substitute for the older, intermediate institutions associated with civil society.

Democracy and Governance

In the United States, Sheldon Wolin notes, a strong distinction historically has been made between government and the state, one that constitutes our common sense as citizens and operates to disable us in recognizing the current powers of the state. Democratic rule has been able to proceed from the assumption that there would be an open and equitable accounting through responsive officials to any incursions into the field of rights. He writes:

> The use of the term "government" rather than "state" is not a question of mere linguistic preferences but the difference between the limited power implications of the one and the more extended power implications of the other. If we say, for example, that "the government has just set standards for controlling drug abuse among government employees," the image evoked is of an agency, such as the Department of Justice, issuing a regulation. It is a very spare image of power, confined and identifiable. But if we say, "The state is now engaged in using the issue of dangerous drugs to impose greater control over the population generally," we are pointing to a more extended entity than "the government" and to a wider purpose, as well as to a more extensive exercise of power. The fact that many corporations and schools, especially athletic programs, have adopted a similar policy has the net effect of unifying governmental and private power to produce a wider and deeper effect than if either had operated singly. It also means that an objective ordinarily denied to governmental power can be achieved. For the Constitution prohibits governmental power from entering into the internal life of schools and private corporations for the purpose of regulating the private morals of students or employees. But because we have been taught to think of governmental action as operating in the public sector and corporations acting in the private sector and of their relationship as adversarial, we remain ignorant of crucial interconnections that are shaping our lives.[10]

Wolin is prescient in his anticipation of, for instance, a 1995 Supreme Court decision that legalized the general use of drug testing of high school student athletes. He also anticipates the more general and deep-seated trend toward criminalizing drug use itself. He notes with great acuity the continued effacement of whatever lines have been drawn in the past between public and private power. As a result of his suspicion that less and less restraint is issuing forth from government officials and from the economic forces that have tempted them into betraying the democratic trust, he calls for the cultivation of a new common sense in American politics, one that will be sensitive to the combinations of private and public power constitutive of what he calls the "megastate."[11]

Wolin sees citizens as being caught between two inviable models of citizenship: one based on direct participation, the other civic republicanism, neither of which is adequately responsive to the demands imposed by the emergence of the megastate, which both floats above us and imposes itself over us. In response to the multiple ways in which this state operates and to the power it has at its command, he suggests that even minimal democratic participation as a form of citizenship in the megastate requires a citizen who is able to negotiate critically through a series of difficult issues. "[The democratization of the politics of the megastate] demands a citizen who can participate intellectually and passionately in the controversies that surround the megastate, such as nuclear weapons, ecological problems, the actions of public men and women, foreign policy, and much else."[12] The task of the citizen is extraordinarily demanding, but the demand is extraordinary because we are required to be *democratic* citizens. What is required of us should be construed not as an impossibility but instead as an ideal against which we may measure our continued capacity to engage in deliberations about the differences through which we are constituted as members of a polity. And he notes that not only knowledge enables us to be democratic participants. Wolin's final comments in this essay provide a hope, if only incompletely sketched, concerning the disruptive power of difference: "The encounter with difference is becoming the most important experience in contemporary America as new populations make their homes here. For difference presents a potential anomaly to the politics of the megastate: it upsets the passivity that is the essential condition of bureaucratic rule and the imaged politics of the mass media."[13]

And yet, in some ways, difference cannot make a difference if the center of democracy is to hold. This worry not only haunts Wolin, who sees the paradox of democracy to be most completely apparent in its "fugitive" existence as an unachievable holism,[14] but is the basis for many interventions designed to localize democracy by means of exclusion and practically realize it by undemocratic means. The paradox is enough to make some of us lose faith in the possibility of democracy at all. It is also what has been exploited by anti-democrats in their attempts to sanctify civil society through rituals of purification.

In his most recent study of the political condition of the United States, Theodore Lowi explains how the agenda enacted by the American Right since the ascendance of Reaganism has been explicitly at war with the possibility of a continued democratic republic.[15] Like Wolin, Lowi sees the attack on multiculturalism to be a key strategy of the anti-democratic forces of the Republican Right, noting especially that the anti-Semitism of some factions of the Republican Right functions for them as a potential blueprint for a strategy of rule. Like Wolin, Lowi argues a need to preserve and fruitfully appreciate differences if there is to be a future for liberalism. Lowi goes so far as to suggest that the inability to cope with difference may be the core weakness of the Republican Party as a political force. He suggests that to the extent that the Republican Right has achieved the hegemonic status that would allow it to become a "Third Republic," or new political regime, in the United States, its ideology has been based in an unsustainable contradiction. "Every ideology is built on a contradiction. Here we have found theirs: *It can govern only if the state and its values are homogeneous.*"[16] Lowi notes that the basic achievement of such a homogeneous state is incompatible with democracy, and that to the extent that democratic forces still operate in the United States, the Republican era may be coming to an end. But like Wolin, he is deeply concerned that there has been a systematic undermining of democratic impulses in the culture that might encourage the continued cultivation of difference. What he embraces as "downright cultural relativism" has become more difficult to defend in the face of the new common sense.[17] For him, such a resistance must be coupled to a rigorously instrumental liberal state. That state must be defended in the face of the moralism of the Republican Right.

Both Lowi and Wolin provide reasons for understanding the contemporary condition of the American republic as reflecting a crisis of the culture as much as a transition in the economy or the institutions of rule. Yet as powerful as their arguments are, neither appreciates as fully as he might the intimate connection of late modern government with what is commonly called culture—what I am calling cultivation—how government operates as a cultural force, and, perhaps more important, how cultivation is enlisted as a governmental power. Wolin's concept of the megastate illuminates how the concerns of security and the demands of empire corrupt the possibility of democratic citizenship. It connects the demands of security at a macro level to biases toward secrecy, exclusion, and authoritarianism operating at the higher levels of the state. But it doesn't enable us to understand how the political activities of democratic citizens are themselves shaped by the demands of security through contemporary policing activities. The arguments that the forces of police use distract us from the cultivation of relationships with each other and organize a civil society in which we become accustomed to identifying freedom with security. Wolin points toward the articulation of difference as a barrier to the more extreme perditions of the megastate without noting how the representations of difference almost completely determine of how difference is understood, both by those who share the dominant political identity and by those who are subjected to inhabiting the position of being different. In a civil society that makes policing its first concern, difference is almost always interpreted as a threat to security.

Similarly, the concept of juridical democracy developed by Lowi in *The End of Liberalism* and rehearsed in *The End of the Republican Era* rests on the achievement of a form of institutional neutrality that is neither achievable nor especially desirable as an antidote to the homogenizing forces that the Republican Right practice. For Lowi, the triumph of this Right in American electoral politics has depended as much on the successful articulation of a cultural imperative to be achieved as it has on the success of any particular policy initiative. In other words, this element of the Republican Party has achieved an almost hegemonic domination of the terms of political discourse.

The failure of this faction to come to complete domination does not mean that the liberal alternative will fill whatever vacuum exists. One procedural liberal response, trying to rebuild faith in instrumentality, an institutional neutrality in the name of a pluralism of communit*ies*, implicitly acknowledges the force of the Republican Right's ability to articulate its imperatives simply by trying to change the subject from ends to means, in a manner that replicates the "me-tooism" of the Eisenhower era. It fails to show a positive articulation of its own, as Lowi recognizes, even when he (nostalgically?) embraces liberal instrumentality over morality.[18] Of course, liberal toleration has never been without its own biases and limits. And it is in regard to the establishment of limits—geographical, demographical, and moral/transgressive—that the question of articulation is especially crucial to an appreciation of how policing unifies and nationalizes the terms of political culture in the absence of any other unifying *telos*.

As a "progressive" substitute for the fundamentalist values of the Republican Right, the call for reinvigorating the institutions of civil society allows communitarian attempts to be precisely that alternative articulation. Communitarians call in the police without generating the same fears that attend the more overt exclusionary arguments of fundamentalists. But once we see how the form of civil society argument *is* the content, we can better understand how communitarian strategies that call for governmental intervention to re-establish or re-enforce "mediating institutions" of "civil society" are actually police matters, and why the most important contemporary communitarian contributions to policy may have been the expansion of the prison system and the destruction of public welfare.

The Civilitarian Strategy

A new kind of policing has emerged in the United States over the past fifteen years. This policing concerns itself explicitly as much with images of order as it does with order's substance, whatever that latter category might be. While the focus of this policing is new, it is rooted in an older sensibility. A key to understanding how the most salient elements of this new policing operates is to attend to the idea of "good manners" that Blackstone includes in his definition of policing. The decline of manners is often considered the mark of a democratic age by those whose elevated status is lowered when shifts in the political economy unsettle the prior order of things.[19] But we might also note how the public perception of the decline in order for the most part has to do with *representations* of disorder, as much as with substantial effects of disorder. Indeed, disorder is largely in the eye of the beholder. Public campaigns against graffiti writers, squeegee cleaners, and aggressive panhandlers, such as the one launched by Mayor Rudolph Guiliani of New York during his first term in office, reflect a presumption on the part of police authorities of a fundamental connection between public displays of incivility and a deeper disorder, and conversely, between orderliness and civility. While many critics argue that the suppression of such activities is based on a causal inversion and that the incivility of working-class and poor people is a result of failures in more basic areas of the modern welfare state, they nonetheless share with the right-wing Republicans the perception that incivility is itself a threat to civil society.

But the evolution of public etiquette is much more complex a matter than conservatives and communitarians seem to appreciate. One way to comprehend the importance of the decline of civility in a social order is to understand how the importance of civility first arose as an issue and from what social practices civility emerged. We may begin by noting that the rise of manners was a key to the emergence of modern civilization in the West, but also that the structure of that civilization was anything but democratic. Norbert Elias suggests as much in his monumental study of the rise of the European ruling class:

During the stage of the court aristocracy, the restraint imposed on inclinations and emotions is based primarily on consideration and respect due to others and above all to social superiors. In the subsequent stage, renunciation and restraint of impulses is compelled far less by particular persons; expressed provisionally and approximately, it is now, more directly than ever before, the less visible and more impersonal compulsions of social interdependence, the division of labor, the market, and competition that impose restraint and control on the impulses and emotions. It is these pressures, and the corresponding manner of explanation and conditioning mentioned above, which makes it appear that socially desirable behavior is voluntarily produced by the individual himself, on his own initiative. . . . In keeping with its different interdependencies, bourgeois society applies stronger restrictions to certain impulses, while in the case of others aristocratic restrictions are simply continued and transformed to suit the changed situation. . . . In both cases, in aristocratic court society as well as in the bourgeois societies of the nineteenth and twentieth centuries, the upper classes are constrained to a particularly high degree.[20]

For Elias, the constraints placed on *those who are to rule* may be understood as the earliest forms of modern policing. These demands are not rooted in the imperatives of an existing state power: in fact, the state itself emerges as a late consequence of the imposition of a social order internal to a particular society. The self-restraint that is the requirement for the emergence of a complex modern social order is the result of an almost organic development in the web of social relationships.

Elias insists that this web can be traced according to a logic that is below the threshold of what many are accustomed to calling rationality. But he also insists that the development of this web cannot therefore be categorized as "irrational." He argues that "the immanent regularities of social figurations are identical neither with regularities of the 'mind,' of individual reasonings, nor with regularities of what we call 'nature,' even though functionally all these different dimensions of reality are indissolubly linked to each other."[21] This "blind" character of the dynamic of human interaction becomes more regularized over the long history of social interactions and thus becomes accessible to planning and to the regulatory interventions of policing bodies.[22] For Elias, the very development of a *depth*—or of what Nietzsche would call conscience, what Freud would term the unconscious—emerges as a consequence of the thickening web of human relations that are at least in part regularized through the emergence of manners. "The web of actions grows so complex and extensive, the effort required to behave 'correctly' within it becomes so great, that beside the individual's conscious self-control an automatic, blindly functioning apparatus of self-control is firmly established."[23] Manners thus operate as a technique for establishing the conditions of civility that will prevail in a hierarchical society.

Manners are akin to language. The web grows larger than anyone can account for; the consequences become a second nature to us (sometimes confusing us, subject to ambiguity); and yet the play of manners is undoubtedly created by us over time, subject to genealogical investigation and an opening up to uncertainty—to the very kinds of acknowledgment that the rituals governing them may be designed to overcome. But manners are much more limited as a means of communication. They are designed to channel communication upward, to prevent certain communication flows and valorize others. This civility is achieved at the cost of candor and the suppression of grievance, at least, and almost inevitably represses the possibility of democratic participation.

We might draw the conclusion that a decline in manners is a direct indicator of the decline of civil society, and that the rise of democracy is synonymous with the rise of bad manners. Elias himself seems to endorse such a reading, concluding his massive study with an argument for the further development of civilization:

> Only when the tensions between and within states have been mastered is there a chance that the regulation of men's affects and conduct in their relations with each other can be confined to those instructions and prohibitions that are necessary in order to keep up the high level of functional differentiation and interdependence without which even the present levels of civilized conduct in men's co-existence with each other could not be maintained, let alone surpassed. Only then is there a chance, too, that the common pattern of self-control expected of men can be confined to those restraints which are necessary in order that men can live with each other and with themselves with a high chance of enjoyment and a low chance of fear—be it of others, be it of themselves. Only with the tensions and conflicts between men can those within men become milder and less damaging to their chances of enjoyment. Then it need no longer be the exception, then it may even be the rule that an individual person can attain the optimal balance between his imperative drives claiming satisfaction and fulfillment and the constraints imposed upon them . . . that condition to which one so often refers with big words such as "happiness" and "freedom."[24]

The scale of civilization moves progressively toward peace through the increased integration of individuals into the larger social fabric. The multiplicity of social contacts spreads wider and wider. Eventually, we are all, in a sense, stuck together by the glue of reciprocal courtesies.

But Elias's vision of civilization is partial, in several senses. The call for self-control Elias announces as his conclusion looks a lot like an ascetic ideal that leaves the activity of democratic political deliberation and argumentation with no place to be. We may wonder to what extent Elias can equate his sardonic understanding of the big words *freedom* and *happiness* with the high degree of sublimation implied by the balance he describes. Second, Elias's civilization depends on a highly gendered and intensely class-based bodily ideal. Indeed, the lineage he traces, from knight to courtier, from nobility to bourgeoisie, is exclusively gendered male. Moreover, the male described in detail is one who exists always already within a hierarchy of power, the effects of which become distributed through the rest of social body by means of the spreading network of contacts that result in and, alternatively, are caused by the gradual intensification of a division of labor that rests upon and presses down on those who are the last to be made civil, or civilized—namely, women, poor and unskilled men, and slaves. Finally, the equation of "civilized" with a particular image of respectability rests upon the continued existence of certain "tensions" between men—those that concern the boundaries of the divisions of labor in society and that constrain their interactions by making it socially unacceptable to challenge the order of things—and means that, by definition, any questioning of that division is uncivilized.

One way in which respectability functions as a means of governance has been addressed by Iris Young. She notes:

> Respectability consists in conforming to norms that repress sexuality, bodily functions, and emotional expressions. It is linked to an idea of order: the respectable person is chaste, modest, does not express lustful desires, passion, spontaneity, or exuberance, is frugal, clean, gently spoken, and well mannered. The orderliness of respectability means things are under control, everything is in its place, not crossing the borders.[25]

Young connects these codes of respectability with the differentiation of public and private in bourgeois society. She argues, "The codes of bourgeois respectability made masculinity and femininity mutually exclusive and yet complementary opposites."[26] For Young, the very system of respectability is a denial of difference in the service of domination by a particular gender and class. The system of respectability operates at the level of the body itself. Even when women, black people, and others who are marked as others comport themselves according to the terms of respectability, they are "chained to their bodily being."[27] Hence the possibility of a public representation of oneself as respectable that is not infiltrated by private markers of race and gender that betray one's self-confidence varies according to the code of respectability that dominates in a given political order.

To identify a decline of civility in public discourse with the breakdown of civil society is itself to engage in a political strategy that excludes and marginalizes subordinate groups through the device of respectability. In reporting on the insistence on civility by the advocates for civil society, Benjamin DeMott has provided a powerful critique of what he has called "the civilitarian impulse" as it operates in communitarian political discourse.[28] For DeMott, the call for civility is basically a call for silence in the face of a systematic depredation of democracy. Those who call for civility often pick as examples of uncivil behavior the protests and unseemly behavior of relatively disenfranchised social groups. DeMott describes how Randall Kennedy and Victor Navasky were marginalized at a conference on civility held at Yale precisely when they tried to point out that groups who were being accused of incivility—especially African Americans—were, in protests, engaging in important civilizing acts. Accused by Gertrude Himmelfarb of behaving with incivility, Kennedy responded that "if you're in an argument with a thug, there are things much more important than civility."[29] This argument was apparently not convincing to the assembled civilitarians. DeMott explains:

> But they who define the issues win the debate. The subject at Yale was the decline of civility, not of fairness, justice or decency among the privileged. And that definition of the subject certified that the problem under consideration had to do with inferiors, not superiors; no tie was made between it and disrespect for the leader classes stemming from the thuggish leader-class beliefs and behavior. Kennedy didn't press on with his case. The vision of the "civility problem" as, at its core, one of bottom-dog manners rather than top-dog morals underwent no sustained examination.[30]

Respectability is seen as the key in this argument.

This use of respectability can be found throughout the work of many communitarians. For instance, throughout her recent study of the status of democracy in the contemporary era, Jean Elshtain focuses on what she terms the "dispositions" of people as the primary indicator of their ability to maintain democracy. The list of dispositions is familiar: the ability to work with people different than oneself toward a shared end, to hold strong convictions and yet be able to compromise, to hold a sense of individuality and a commitment to civic goods that extends beyond the personal.[31] Elshtain suggests that these are important underpinnings of democratic culture, and she worries that they are eroding, in large part as a consequence of a decline in civility. All these qualities can be traced back to the manners that people learn in the course of growing up and depend on developing a sense of pub-' lic restraint that relies on knowing a private sphere where one may be free from compromise and cooperative subordinations of self.

Elshtain suggests that the achievement of this kind of civility is generally that of avoiding resentment:

> We are in danger of losing democratic civil society. It is that simple and that dangerous, springing, as it does, not from a generous openness to sharp disagreement—democratic feistiness—but from a cynical and resentful closing off of others. . . . The long history of the human race suggests that resentment breeds resentment; hatred fuels hatred; isolation feeds paranoia; cynicism stokes mistrust; and fear generates flight from neighborliness, largeheartedness, and the patience necessary to perdure.[32]

But from the perspective of those who are on the bottom of a stratified society, resentment is an entirely appropriate response to the use of manners by those on top to construct a general "we" without consulting those who may not want to be their friends and neighbors, having been injured by them in the past, who think that the move to a general "we" is being made out of a sense of condescension or who suspect that those who are issuing the call to be more trusting of others simply want to disarm them while retaining their position of advantage.

There is no final way of judging the good faith or bad faith of those who issue calls for civility. But we can note how Elshtain's rhetoric operates here. Those who agree with her understanding of the respectable way to disagree are feisty: those who don't are resentful, paranoid, mistrustful, unneighborly, small-hearted, impatient, and lacking the qualities of patience needed to perdure.

Elshtain is highly critical of those who engage in the effacement of the public/private distinction in order to engage in what she calls the "politics of displacement," a politics that undermines "authentic democratic possibilities." In her analysis, there are two trajectories such a politics takes:

> In the first, everything private—from one's sexual practices to blaming one's parents for one's lack of "self-esteem"—becomes grist for the public mill. In the second, everything public—from the grounds on which politicians are

judged to health policies to gun regulations—is privatized and played out in a psychodrama on a grand scale, that is, we fret as much about a politician's sexual life as about his foreign policy; or we favor insured health care only if it pays for our own guaranteed comfort, described as medical needs or even aesthetic wants, and oppose it if it does not; or we see in firearm regulation only an assault, no doubt limited and imperfect, on our identity as gun-toting vigilantes, rather than as a way to try to control slaughter in our streets without eroding the rights of hunters and others.[33]

While this description contains exaggerations, and while it conflates economic self-interest with identity, it nonetheless contains a clear and powerful argument for sustaining strong distinctions between public and private knowledges of the particularities of individuals' lives, especially so that individuals won't identify their own interest with the general public interest. Indeed, on this point Elshtain joins some of the most powerful theorists of identity politics, who analyze how adherence to particular strong identifications can operate as a form of violence against others.[34]

But the examples that Elshtain uses to illustrate the problem are taken almost exclusively from strategies of people whose identities have been stigmatized by those whose position is in what she calls the "center." The identity politics of those who are stigmatized is often reactive, almost predictably a response to their stigmatization and oppression. Elshtain's major examples of damaging identity politics are taken from the arenas of feminist politics, the gay rights movement, and the politics of multicultural education.[35] These are interesting and contentious areas of political argument these days, but in all these arenas, the predominant strategies of advocates have to do with being able to speak and represent themselves fully, honestly, and shamelessly in a culture that is resistant to accepting their presence. Indeed, in the face of the oppression that some of these people face in the daily lives, it is remarkable, though rarely remarked, that they do not express greater paranoia and resentment.

In her analysis of the politics of displacement, Elshtain concentrates on the strongest advocates of balkanizing political strategies within these identity movements, those who make absolutist assertions of identity that disparage and attack those who do not share that identity; those who would, if they could, silence others. And it is true that balkanization, the assertion of a purity of identity, is in fact the most dangerous symptom of an identity politics that has abandoned the possibility of plurality and hybridity.

While those of us who are committed to a democratic polity need to be clear in our opposition to such anti-democratic gestures, there is a serious question to be asked about why the balkanizing practices of marginalized and oppressed groups are considered more threatening to democracy than the balkanizing strategies of other identity groups who have much more effective power. I am referring to powerful groups about which Elshtain herself is, to my knowledge, silent. The most effective practitioners of identity politics in contemporary American politics are the members of the Christian Coalition, and the most violent participants in American politics are those who have been engaging in the bombing of abortion clinics and shooting of abortion providers in recent years. That they have escaped major and sustained criticism by Elshtain for their relentless attempts to subvert democracy is puzzling.[36] These forces of the Republican Right have been joined by an important cadre of intellectuals in recent years, some of whom, in the face of Supreme Court decisions that have not gone as far as they would like in limiting abortion rights and encouraging Christian values, have darkly suggested that the government of the country itself is illegitimate and may justly be resisted.[37]

More important, however, the focus on the identity politics of subordinate groups obscures what is perhaps the most important identity group of all: what C. Wright Mills once called the power elite.[38] Strategic boundary-crossings of the public/private distinction are the bread and butter of the members of this most significant and central political identity group in the United States, and the ranks of these actors are composed of powerful white men.[39] Whether their boundary-crossings consist of continued and quiet support for the oldest of all affirmative action programs, namely, the legacy admission policies of elite colleges and universities; the initiation and completion of business deals in the exclusive venues of private clubs; casual meetings of CEOs with members of powerful congressional committees to influence the outcome of legislation; or a multitude of other intimate contacts that occur in formats and spaces strongly reminiscent of the court society described by Elias, the members of this group are practiced at the art of silence concerning even the fact that they exist as a group. The effect they have on democratic discourse is significant, in that they conceal the highly disproportionate power they wield in determining the shape of the political economy of the United States.

This identity group remains largely unpoliced. The lifestyles of most of its members are deeply informed by the codes of respectability that Iris Young describes. But this does not mean that as a group they are *substantively* more moral than any of the rest of us, and a case might be made that, in many ways, individuals in this group are more at risk to engage in the sorts of activities that our conservative public moralists condemn as moral deprivations—drug use, sexual infidelity, the frequenting of prostitutes, fraud, theft, lying, hypocrisy, gluttony, corruption, and sloth, to name a few of them—than are those of us who are of less-elevated stations, and who are hence not in the presence of so many temptations as often, to as great a degree, or with the leisure time to pursue them. That the members of this group are not imprisoned as often as poor people may be reduced to the fact that they enjoy a great privacy privilege that accompanies wealth, on the one hand, and that when (rarely) they are arrested, they are represented much more competently than are the rest of us, by dint of their wealth.

The interesting demographical difference between this identity group and those of us of less-elevated station may help us understand that the cultivation of respectability is not identical to the inculcation of moral values but is instead the public face of a police code that relies on a public/private distinction in order to do its political-cultural work. This code is more easily violated without sanction by those who can afford the increasingly high price of privacy and is less easily violated without sanction by those who cannot. The moral crisis of democracy thus could indeed be said to consist of abandonment of the respectable elite of their responsibility to be respectable, if one were to accept the idea that respectability is the code of civil society.[40] Another way of putting this matter is to suggest that once the gap between rich and poor becomes large enough, it becomes more difficult for hypocrisy to be accepted as a form of politeness, and the veil of respectability begins to tatter.

Such an argument, however, may place more responsibility for the status of civil society on the shoulders of the elites than they are capable of bearing without becoming decadent. Indeed, the desire of any particular group to identify itself as central to a democratic society may be a strong signal of its sense of increased vulnerability. After all, it seems clear that the emergence of any particular elite is the inevitable consequence of the conjunction of economic and other cultural forces that are always outside that group's control, even though the claim is almost always made by partisans that the achievements are a sign of favor—from God, from family—or of intrinsic individual quality.[41] Perhaps it is only as they begin to slip in their position that the members of a group begin recognize the precarious character of what had before seemed to them to be ordained.

The false sense of privilege, however, has historically been at odds with the idea of democracy as a social system of merit. The promise of democracy, especially in its American incarnation, has never been that of achieving a respectable civil society that would preserve civil hierarchies, but rather that of achieving the conditions under which individuals would be able to express themselves fully and go as far in life as their talents would take them—that is, Thomas Jefferson's meritocracy. Such an ideology has always been at variance with the development and decline of particular elites throughout American history. Importantly, though, it is precisely when an elite is in decline that it most clearly shows itself to be at variance with the ideology of democratic merit. Paradoxically, this is also when it most needs to represent itself as central to the continued good health of society.

So underlying Elshtain's anxiety about democracy, an anxiety she shares with many others, is the concern that plurality cannot exist without institutions that hold people in common by setting limits on the extent to which and the forms through which plurality can be expressed. This delimiting condition reflects the position of an elite in decline. From the perspective of such an elite, the maintenance of a center can be accomplished only through the continued nurturing of the values of that elite as central to the culture, understood by its representatives in terms that identify the legitimacy of various groups in reference to how far they deviate from the central norm they espouse. William Galston, a communitarian who served as an adviser to President Bill Clinton during his first term in office, has put it bluntly: "In the very act of sustaining diversity, liberal unity circumscribes diversity. It could not be otherwise. No form of human life can be perfectly or equally hospitable to every human orientation."[42] Galston underlines the sense that democracy itself is challenged by expressions of diversity that somehow go too far (usually by challenging what the accuser would see as a vital civil underpinning or "intermediate institution" supportive of democratic society). This sensibility has resulted in contemporary attempts to use legislation and administration to engage in the practical drawing of lines concerning what is *respectable* and what is not—more or less overtly in regard to religious belief, sexual expression, forms of intoxication, and the social organization of child-rearing, and covertly in terms of gender, ethnic, and racial identities.

In the absence of explicitly hierarchical codes of respectability developed in the courtier societies of monarchies, the courtier spirit in the United States adheres to those perceived as being the most powerful, which in a democratic polity means those who are closest to conforming with what is perceived as being the norm, closest to the "center." For Tocqueville, that group is the majority, and there is a tradition in the United States of courtier behavior by politicians to those who constitute their majority.[43]

Because courtier spirit is so strongly submissive to the authority it identifies with, and because the authority of the American democracy is increasingly associated with small but effective electoral and social coalitions, the corruption of politicians takes on a particularly vile tone as they struggle to protect the narrowing constituencies who constitute their base of support, and who operate as effective majorities.[44]

This general background may help us understand why police power is of increasing importance, and why the major communitarian policy initiative to meet with greatest success during the Clinton administration's first term in office was the federal crime bill, designed to increase the extent of national police power in its most direct form.[45] Police power in contemporary U.S. policy operates to reconstruct and re-enforce civil society by intensifying the criminalization of unrespectable behavior. The emergence of the importance of this domain of policy is the consequence not of increased social disorder but of increased disrespect for and disaffection with the style of rule imposed over the democratic movements that the reactive center has increasingly demonized. These are groups that imaginatively create and sustain identities in cultural assertions designed both to raise the consciousnesses of those who share in common certain experiences and situations and to question the character of a center that at best can only issue an invitation to them to assimilate and at worst would repress them. The members of these movements have taken seriously the promise of pluralization entailed in the recasting of American society as pluralist in the wake of the civil rights movements of the post–World War II era.[46] In the opposite direction, in the wake of the decline and fall of the cold war, both the imperative to respond to the demands for social pluralism and the need to reorganize the political economy of country have taken the general formula of a battle for the future of American civilization, as framed by the most important leader of the Republican Right, the former Speaker of the House of Representatives Newt Gingrich. That the communitarian movement is unable to distinguish itself from this formulation indicates how its understanding of civil society depends on the association of civil society with respectable—that is, normal—behavior.

Policing Community

The emergence of community policing as a major policy initiative in the decades of the 1990s is indicative of this trend. The idea of community policing is that by having police officers intensify their interactions with the neighborhoods they patrol, they will win the hearts and minds of the people they are monitoring. Community policing refers to an entire ensemble of strategies of crime prevention that involve the residents of neighborhoods in surveillance activities. These programs include neighborhood watch programs that count on citizen participation in the surveillance of public spaces; street patrols; police accountability to the community being policed; the decentralization of police command; and an overall orientation of policing away from response to specific incidences of crime and toward a problem-solving approach to crime.[47] Through regularized and non–crisis situation interactions with the people they are monitoring, police are to be transformed "from what has been described as 'an army of occupation' into an accepted, unremarkable, and institutionalized part of the community."[48] Thus police will develop a sense of a political base among the citizens of a neighborhood, or at least among a particular segment of the citizenry.

In an analysis of the effects of community policing in a democratic society, Jerome Skolnick and David Bayley write:

> [Police] become better acquainted with community so that they can anticipate, and possibly prevent, crime and order problems from arising. They assist in organizing crime-prevention programs like Neighborhood Watch, develop dependable sources of local information, and encourage cooperation in crime solving. The police also meet a more diverse cross-section of the populace, especially respectable, noncriminal people who welcome and support the police uncritically.[49]

Police usually have their most meaningful public interactions with people who are under arrest or suspicion of crimes. By expanding their contacts to the "respectable, noncriminal people who welcome and support the police uncritically," they would gain a different perspective on the meaning of their work. But what perspective would that be? The function of respectability as a norm operates to distance police from understanding the motivations that underlie most of the crime they combat and to intensify their allegiance to the respectable citizenry they are to protect. By increasing the web of interactions with those whom they identify as being the respectable, they will be doing no more than reinforcing the divisions already present in the neighborhoods they patrol or, should the neighborhood be especially distressed, will find no one whom they would be able to identify as respectable.

In fact, community policing would serve to detach the police from any sort of sympathetic understanding of those whom they must try to arrest and prevent from committing crimes. In this sense, community policing is part of a larger political strategy of conservatives. William Connolly notes how William Bennett worried that police in inner cities have been becoming too much like social scientists: "Talking to some chiefs was like talking to some of the school superintendents I had encountered while Secretary of Education. . . . They spoke of deep social problems, alienation and illiteracy. They sounded as they wished to sound, like contemporary social scientists. . . . They, too, had become theoreticians of society's woes."[50] William Connolly explains how this comment (and others) operates within a clearly delineated political strategy:

> Bennett's political strategy is to draw members of the white working and middle classes, street cops, suburban dwellers, veterans, the military, conservative politicians, conservative religious believers, and working black urban dwellers plagued by street drugs and violence into a bellicose cultural coalition, a coalition mobilized and animated through hostilities to university intellectuals, liberal journalists and politicians, moderate school administrators, poor black residents of the inner city, illicit drug users, drug dealers, welfare recipients, philosophical police chiefs and convicted felons. . . . The lines of demarcation are clean: the "American people" value America; the amoral elements de-value it.[51]

Community policing could operate to mobilize Bennett's coalition of the bellicose into a vigilante group. The risk of vigilantism arises as the police come to identify personally with those they protect and is considered to be a primary danger of the use of the community policing model.[52]

Alternatively, in the absence of a clear constituency of respectable citizens, the police would need to mobilize, or even create, such a constituency. As perceived by the more enthusiastic proponents of community policing, the police are to act as a sort of urban Peace Corps, bringing the benefits of American democracy to the natives of urban ghettos. At the conclusion of a lengthy survey of community policing, Mark Harrison Moore waxes enthusiastic about the mission of community policing as a solution to the problems of drug use, random violence, and urban rioting:

> If there are any areas in which the strategies of problem solving and community policing are likely to be most needed, it is dealing with these particular problems. Surely, an important part of dealing with drugs is learning how to mobilize communities to resist drug dealing. Surely, an important part of

dealing with random violence is dealing with rational and irrational fears. Surely, an important part of controlling riots is having networks of relationships that reach deeply into ethnic communities.[53]

This vision, while more inclusive than the one that demonizes those who deviate from the norm of respectability, understands participation as something that police agents mobilize.

This active intervention of police officers, shaping the subjectivities of those who are to be the objects of their discretionary power, makes them full participants in police power in its broadest sense. The transformation of police from an essentially reactive power to a proactive force signifies their blending into and potential coordination with the contemporary roles of other governmental agents, such as educators and welfare bureaucrats.[54] But while police are being given legal sanction to behave more and more like social workers, social workers are being given legal sanction to behave more and more like police—marginalizing the poor, establishing punitive conditions for the receipt of welfare in the establishment and implementation of administrative rules, and placing the responsibility for the shortcomings of a political economy predicated on structural unemployment on those who are unemployed. In short, the emergence of community policing is a result of the need to re-create the conditions of respectability that will allow the respectable to be reassured in their identities. The relevant question, however, is how far appeals to respectability can go to sustain intensifying levels of inequality in what still is formally a representative democracy.

Drug and Other Wars

In a recent study of the relationship of race to crime and punishment, Michael Tonry notes that the policies pursued by the Reagan administration starting in the mid-1980s, the development of a war against drugs, were predicated not on an increased use of drugs (drug use, especially cocaine use, was beginning to decline) but on the desire to cash in on increased public intolerance of drug use. Policymakers knew the draconian sentencing laws and policies would have a disparate impact on minorities yet chose to pursue those strategies anyway.[55] In large part as a consequence of the policies encouraged by the War on Drugs (though other laws were established before this war, most notably the mandatory minimum laws established in New York by Governor Nelson Rockefeller in the 1970s), minorities have been arrested and imprisoned for violation of drug laws between five and six times as frequently as white people since the mid-1980s.[56] This arrest rate is the result not of a disparity in drug use among racial groups (surveys indicate that use of illegal drugs is approximately the same among African Americans, whites, and Latinos)[57] but of the fact that it is much easier to engage the war against the poorest and least able to defend themselves; the social disorganization of poor neighborhoods makes it easier for police to infiltrate them, the public character of street life in poor neighborhoods makes it easier to make arrests, and police are concerned with rates of arrest, which encourages them to go to neighborhoods where there is likely to be less organized resistance to their sweeps.[58]

But Tonry also notes a larger reason for targeting minorities in the drug wars:

> Given what we know about past periods of intolerance of drug use and the tendencies to scapegoat minority groups, and that disadvantaged urban blacks are the archetypal users of crack cocaine—and therefore the principal possessors, sellers, and low-level distributors—anyone who knew the history of American drug policy could have foreseen that this war on drugs would target and mostly engage young disadvantaged members of minority groups as the enemy. It has.[59]

For Tonry, the launching of the War on Drugs was the result of politicians catching up to the sentiment that began to prevail in white communities as the excesses of drug use, primarily cocaine, in the white community took their toll during the 1980s. In this sense, he notes the moral/pedagogical purposes of the war as one devoted to saving the white children of America from the sins of their parents. But he also notes, "The problem with the rationale of the War on Drugs as an exercise in moral education is that it destroyed the lives of young, principally minority young people in order to reinforce existing norms of young, mostly majority people. Put crudely, if explicitly, the lives of black and Hispanic ghetto kids were destroyed in order to reinforce white kids' norms against drug use."[60]

Here the theme of educating into civility comes into stark play. Nothing is more valuable, and nothing more constantly sought by moral pedagogues, than negative moral objects in the task of educating the young into respectability. In a normalizing society, one that seeks to maintain social control by reinforcing and establishing mass norms of behavior that are based in the politics of social deviation and coupled to the politics of moralism, the search for negative examples is accomplished by the criminalization of deviant practices. In the United States, the vehicle of drug laws that contain harsh criminal penalties has served this purpose well. And as an ancillary effect, the administration of these laws has created the conditions within minority communities that can lead to an entire series of associated demonizations. By targeting between one-quarter and one-half of African American and Latino men between the ages of eighteen and forty for removal from the ranks of civil society and placement in the criminal punishment system, the conservative politicians and policy advisers who have advocated and implemented these policies have also been able to weaken severely the infrastructure of the stable family that most of them argue (paradoxically? or hypocritically?) is so necessary to the perpetuation of civil society. They are thus able to demonize more conveniently the young unwed or single mothers in the poor community and to further racialize the identity of a series of unrespectable outcasts from civil society. They also present a warning to all other socially deviant groups, that they too are susceptible to being made objects of instruction to young normal people in their education into respectability.

The War on Drugs has thus been a paradigmatic instance of the contemporary policing of community. The expansion of such efforts in recent years can be seen as part of the ongoing cycle of prohibition and relaxation of codes governing the morality of civil society. But because the very scale of such efforts is unprecedented, because the project to criminalize has touched so many already marked people, because the most important element of this project by those who have engaged in it has been the representation of their efforts in such a way as to gain strategic political advantage over those who hesitate to demonize as quickly or as thoroughly. Moreover, because the new attempt by communitarians to attach civil society to codes of respectability has been made at a moment when some are engaged in using respectability as a tool for validating the existence of social inequality, the danger to democracy that the expansion of police power along the dimension of regulating civil society poses is deep.

At the conclusion of a book-length meditation on the use of drugs in contemporary society, David Lenson calls for a truce in the War on Drugs, an end to the silence that is wrought by slogans such as "Just Say No." He urges the beginning of a period of questions concerning the "why" of drugs, not simply as symptoms of social decay or moral degeneracy (or alternatively, as liberating strategies) but instead as compensations for the shortcomings of a social life organized around the unequal deprivation of social goods and, optimistically, as expressions of life that have been invalidated and delegitimated by the demands of a culture focused too exclusively on consumption and its associated engines of desire. He writes:

> What I see in drug use is a series of reactions to a spiritual disease, the way quail fly in all directions if you toss a stone at them. And this disease is the result of living too long in a world ruled by desire. Seeing no opportunity for political dissent, a certain percentage of the population is seeking change through dissent of consciousness. America's three hundred thousand drug inmates are *prisoners of consciousness*. Whatever solution is found to "the drug problem" must offer reconciliation and reintegration to these dissenters. Diversities, including diversities of consciousness, are valuable only if the diverse parties are eventually to be included in the same community. Otherwise the celebration of difference becomes a new segregation.[61]

Lenson sees drug users as the primary scapegoats of a political regime organized around consumerism. Respectability is the key ideological trope employed by those who seek to dominate a central political order in the face of pluralizations that threaten their near monopoly concerning the meaning of civility. In his willingness to provide voice for this group of dissenters, Lenson risks the moral condemnation of those who see the polity as being organized on the basis of communities that must impose limits on diversity. By focusing on the *question* of drugs, Lenson exposes yet another dimension of the political-cultural struggle that afflicts the United States at this time, that concerning the governance of consciousness. He is as concerned to ask critical questions about the limitations of *straight* consciousness as a hegemonic ideal as he is to ask about the meaning of the diverse consciousnesses associated with various kinds of intoxication. In that inquiry, he both outlines a domain of political regulation and provides an allegory of the opposition between a nationalism composed of exclusion and a polity composed of democratic citizens.

To take but one example: Bill Clinton. Lenson suggests that Clinton's denial of his experimentation with drugs operated in the domain of political culture as an answer to perhaps the most serious, yet unarticulated, question of the 1992 presidential election: "Can anyone of Clinton's generation, whose best moral instincts once drove them outside conventional politics and the law, be capable of administering that polity and law twenty years later?"[62] Lenson understands Clinton's evasions concerning his own illegal activities and his condemnations of contemporary drug users to be a surrender to the Bennetts of the world, an exercise in the logic of exclusion. As such, it connects us to the more general struggle that must be attempted to rearticulate a politics of diversity and plurality. Lenson actually seems to hold hope that there may, in fact, be political leaders who could administer a polity and yet remember what it means to follow their best moral instincts. He senses that it may be possible to begin to talk clearly and openly about alternatives to the rigid moralities of respectability that dominate political discourse.

In this sense, Lenson casts a different light on the subsequent crisis in the Clinton presidency over his lies regarding what used to be called licentious behavior, his sexual affair with Monica Lewinsky. Here policing extends to the family. The extramarital relationship of Clinton presents an opportunity not only to chastise him for his supposed sexual immorality but to humiliate Hillary Rodham Clinton for representing herself as a strong and equal partner in marriage. The two choices presented in the press as responses to her reaction to his public acknowledgment of a sexual liaison were that she was an unwitting victim of her husband or a cynical political partner. Yet there are alternative explanations concerning her relationship with her husband that are not even considered. What would the reaction be if she and her husband were to announce that she approved of his extramarital affair, that she didn't mind that he enjoyed himself in a physical relationship with another woman, that she was secure in her love of him, that he loved her, and that she herself occasionally enjoyed sexual relations with people other than her husband? Here the struggle is to bring to public discussion the possibilities of alternative ways of being in the world. Of course, the cost of representing the center in the presidency is that any moves one might make, say, to end the persecution of gay soldiers or to relax the prosecution of drug users will be met with a ferocious protest by those who believe they are witnessing the crumbling of all value in the improvisations of experimenters.

The Clinton sex scandal's denouement may have reflected a serious shift toward a greater toleration for alternative consciousnesses on the part of that spongy referent, the American public. But it is unlikely that there will be any corresponding shift by the Republican Right regarding their claim that civil society itself depends on further policing of alternative behaviors and attitudes by Lenson's dissenting consciousness. Too much is at stake in terms of their own self-identity for those who are committed to the civilitarian strategy. So instead of demonizing those who they think are risking the health of the civil society, as William Bennett does, the compassionate conservatives of the next generation, such as Governor George Bush of Texas, are more likely to employ a rhetoric of reconciliation and reintegration, in a parody of Lenson's heartfelt plea. It doesn't matter much. Bush will be forced to conclude that prisons are the places where that reintegration must take place. In that deeper sense, he is in agreement with Clinton *and* Bennett, representative of larger consensus, still formed against those who would openly discuss the possibilities of alternative ways of thinking and being in the late modern age.

Connolly outlines elements of that larger struggle in his own thoughts about the drug wars. Concerned to think about how to overcome the nationalism that puts into play the ideal of a nation of regular individuals and that launches a war that multiplies potential enemies with every new discovery of a deviation from regularity, Connolly suggests not only addressing the culture wars but also thinking about how to support pluralistic culture so as to provide the underpinnings for a democratic state in such a way that the state would, in turn, support the plurality that enables it. Connolly's version of civil society is thus quite different from that presented by communitarians who see themselves supporting a nation, not a state. Identifying himself with liberals, deconstructionists, and postmodernists, he writes:

> This is the abstract spirituality I place in competition with the abstract sense of the nation. To overcome the charge that we are either amoral (liberal idealists of the neutral state) or agents of cultural fragmentation (deconstructionists and post-modernists) it will be necessary to show how the effective performance of a pluralist, democratic state requires turning against the massive schemes of social engineering upon which pursuit of the nation is based. How democratic action in concert through the state is a product of creative coalitions coming together from diverse places, animated by multiple moral sources, united by the paradoxical presumption that none of them can claim to correspond in its being to the spirit of a nation.[63]

He identifies the nation as the spiritual force underwritten by civil society. Just as the nation must be brought into competition with a democratic state, so too must the monitors of civil society be challenged, in their presumption to speak of the proper limits of democratic participation, by insubordinations and dissenting states of consciousness that would demonstrate, in the most expansive sense of the term, how we might be free to think about being other than as we are.

The fear of any good citizen thus may be not that there is too much turbulence but that there is too little. The most dominant political-cultural forces in the United States at this time are intent and focused on reducing the levels of turbulence in civil society, not to assure fuller participation and greater social equality but "to preserve and protect" their own privilege. The democratic imagination, however, is not to be too easily suppressed, though it would be better were it not harassed so persistently and insidiously. Our danger and hope lie in recalling that, as Michel Foucault once said, "in civilizations without boats, dreams dry up, espionage takes the place of adventure, and the police take the place of pirates."[64] In response to the polemics of moral nationalism, we might present an attractive alternative: choosing pirates over police, adventure over espionage, and dreams over the dogma of respectability.

5

Toy Stories

The nonchalance of boys who are sure of a dinner, and would disdain as much as a lord to do or say aught to conciliate one, is the healthy attitude of human nature. A boy is in the parlour what the pit is in the playhouse, independent, irresponsible, looking out from his corner on such people and facts as pass by, he tries and sentences them on their merits, in the swift, summary way of boys, as good, bad, interesting, silly, eloquent, troublesome. He cumbers himself never about consequences, about interests: he gives an independent, genuine verdict. You must court him: he does not court you. But the man, as it were, is clapped into jail by his consciousness.

—Ralph Waldo Emerson, "Self-Reliance"

White Men in Charge (Male Subjectivities at the Center)

Let us make a reasonable assumption: I'm a white man in charge. After all, as I write this chapter I am a full professor at one of the elite colleges in the United States. I teach about American politics to young people who are either the privileged children of very privileged people or who, on the basis of merit and luck, are becoming privileged people. I enjoy my own privileges based on my whiteness, maleness, in chargeness. I project whatever social confidence I enjoy in large part on the basis of unspoken assumptions about how I can posture as a gendered male in a male-dominated college environment. I do not bear the burdens that come with the everyday humiliations and slights suffered by my African American male colleagues, for instance, or the disadvantage of my female colleagues and female students, who even now some alumni feel should not be here; not to mention some of my female African American colleagues, Latino and Latina colleagues, and Asian American colleagues of various genders and sensibilities. This year, I am even the chair of my department. (Some luck of the draw.) Of course, when I am in the presence of some other white men in charge, say, members of the board of trustees of my college, I don't feel nearly so powerful, nearly so white, nearly so manly, nearly so in charge as I imagine they must feel. And I can imagine that some of them may feel the same way at times, when divested of their corporate presidencies, when tricked out of some of their big wads of cash. But still . . .

So I am a white man in charge. Within what symbolic order do we white men in charge find our selves? Already we know that this is far too general a question, especially if one assumes that the very identity "white men in charge" is an ideological construction that can and must be resisted by means of a straightforward repudiation of its terms of existence. Some of those engaged in the contemporary war of words over the status of the group of people known as "white men in charge" have come to realize that us guys are no longer as easily in charge if the terms of *whiteness* and *maleness* are successfully destabilized to such an extent that we have to struggle with the constitution of their identity as much as the rest of us do. From a position outside this unquestioned identity of "white man in charge"—perhaps it could be called a "strategic essentialist" position, to the extent that it accepts the premise that what is at stake in struggles for power in contemporary world civilizations is the cultivation of identities through the successful simulation of their essential (that is, definitional) qualities—any discussion of us guys ought to be comprehended in the first instance as a political maneuver designed to reinforce implicitly (the essential unity of the hegemonic identity) what is being challenged explicitly (that very identity's hegemonic status). The trick of developing and deploying such epistemological instruments of cultural warfare is in making the everyday enactment of doubt over identity plausible and desirable to those who stand to benefit from either embracing identities of power or, more often, simply remaining silent in the face of attack, letting the attack reinforce the power of their secured identity, even allowing themselves to be wounded in their attachments.

One major problem facing the translation of this insight into the rhetoric of contemporary public debates is that, for the most part, those who have adhered to the strategy of strategic essentialism are compelled in the end to focus on the most essential identity in play, that which lies at the heart of the structures of power of a particular regime. This would seem to be so because this identity is also the one most likely to become hegemonic. To put the matter another way, one might think of William Bennett, former drug czar and defender of the "values of Western civilization," and other cultural conservatives like him as the most successful strategic essentialists of all. This danger is but one of many of the potential traps of identity politics that have been subject to so much concerned theoretical speculation in recent years.[1]

But there is more to worry about than the trap of hegemonic identities when thinking about the problems of identity posed by white men in charge. We also need to be attentive to the particularities of what might be called the representative constructions of us guys; that is, we need to ask: What particular men go into making the man?[2] In thinking about this question, it may be useful to recognize that various dissimulations of the politicized sexuality of this man are always already underway, even as the idea of a "center" within which the staging of that sexuality and its deployment as a hegemonic form continues to hold sway in the dominant political culture.[3] (In fact, to suggest the center *will* not hold usually means that it *is* holding in the meantime, and the meantime often persists for quite a while.) What is the case in regard to the politics of gender also seems to apply to race and class. None of these categories, however, can simply be added onto each other. Instead, it may be better to try to recognize that the representation of any pure ideological object is always partial, open, incomplete. Focus on one element always obscures others. But this inevitable paradox of focus does not mean that the object represented does not present a truth-ful portrait of its own existence, however partial and incomplete it might be. Truthfulness is always trickier than that.

Maybe the practical problems of identity are more widely shared than some strategic essentialists assume them to be. If so, a more explicit recognition of something called the white man in charge as a distinct ideological object may be coming about, and not coincidentally, precisely at the moment when it becomes possible to interrogate the identity of that imagined man *as* an identity, that is, when the conditions that allowed the white man in charge to exist relatively unchallenged are beginning to change. Identity is always connected in complicated ways to the political order within which it emerges and which it in turn reproduces. And while the logical connections between identity and its place in a hegemonic order are located in the formal recognition that the fantasmic is all around us, even as it operates as an intrusion on our understanding of reality, a minimal precondition for the enactment of the logic of identity must be a recognition that it cannot simply proceed as the *formal* exchange of equivalences between the fantasmic and the real. Because identity is always dependent on a mutual declaration of difference, it may more accurately be comprehended as composed (even in its most fundamental articulations) of the circulation of partial and incomplete signifiers that enable, in their partiality—or their messiness—

the immanent possibility of new positivities and oppositions.[4] The play of positivities and oppositions that concerns us here goes by the shorthand of American political culture.

Cultural histories of the American man that take into account his existence as a specific identity have begun to appear in recent years.[5] They enter an older genre that, while less focused on rendering the theme of manhood explicit, took manhood as a core problem of political and social ethics. What the newer books try to tell us (retrospectively) concerns the formation of a racialized (white), class-determined (bourgeois), and gender-marked (heterosexual male) subjectivity at the center of American political culture. What the older books tried to tell their white bourgeois male readers was how to be what they were. (While many will not be surprised that such a core identity can be historically distilled as a white, bourgeois, heterosexual identity, to make this identity an explicit object of analysis is itself a sign that, by becoming distinguishable as an identity, it is no longer as invulnerable to questioning as it once was. To echo Foucault's observation concerning visibility, identity is a trap.)

The emergence of a central modern American male identity, several historians suggest, is so intimately connected to the development of commercial culture around the middle of the nineteenth century as to be inseparable from it. Michael Kimmel especially emphasizes the attachment of the American man to commerce. He notes that the neologism "self-made man" first appeared in 1832, in a speech by Henry Clay defending protective tariffs: "Almost every manufactory known to me is in the hands of enterprising, self-made men, who have whatever wealth they possess by patient and diligent labor."[6] For Kimmel, it goes without saying that this self-made man is white, even as he notices that the self-made man rises from poverty to assume a position in society. Kimmel *does* explicitly observe that the self-made man comes about as a consequence of a more rigorous sexual division of labor in the home.[7] The appearance of the self-made man, in other words, depended on the disappearance of women into the bourgeois interior of home.

Kimmel's self-made man shuffles off stage toward the end of the nineteenth century as the forces of industrial capitalism take over, and the growth of corporate power gives rise to what David Reisman has labeled the "other-directed" person.[8] But that which goes by the name of the self-made man established a particular way of being that has affected the style of American male self-representation down to the present. In its composition, this style relies upon a fantasmic appropriation of a core identity that seeks to control contingency as much through a renunciation of mastery as through its assertion. In opposition to the Southern model of violent individualism, which became, through several transmutations, the model of an abject masculinity,[9] this model, Yankee in its references, industrial in its assertions, and silencing of women and minorities, came to assume hegemonic status in the United States.

This core American masculine identity, despite the proliferation of many local variations, presents a powerful common temptation to the realization of what Slavoj Žižek calls the *sinthome*.[10] For Žižek, Lacan invents the neologism of the *sinthome* as a way of explaining the persistence of a symptom in the wake of analysis:

> What we must bear in mind here is the radical ontological status of the symptom: symptom, conceived as *sinthome*, is literally our only substance, the only positive support of our being, the only point that gives consistency to the subject. In other words, symptom is the way we—the subjects—"avoid madness," the way we "choose something (the symptom-formation) instead of nothing (radical psychotic autism, the destruction of the symbolic universe)" through the binding of our enjoyment to a certain signifying, symbolic formation which assures a minimum of consistency to our being-in-the-world.
>
> If the symptom in this radical dimension is unbound, it means literally "the end of the world"—the only alternative to the symptom is nothing: pure autism, a psychic suicide, surrender to the death drive, even to the total destruction of the symbolic universe. That is why the final Lacanian definition of the end of the psychoanalytic process is *identification with the symptom*.[11]

Žižek goes on to note that the symptom is both outside discourse, outside the "social bond network," and a positive condition of it. This understanding of the symptom explains why Lacan was able to state that woman is a symptom of man. But he then reframes this formula in light of the positive assertion of substance of the symptom: "If woman does not exist, man is perhaps simply a woman who thinks that she does exist."[12] Thus Žižek states in absolutist terms the condition that is specifically enacted in an impure form by American men. The something we choose over nothing, our symptom—aloneness—risks, in its radicality, becoming the *sinthome*—loneliness. Lonely men, self-made, are cast out of the home and have to invent *themselves* as women. Why are they outcasts? Because they have repudiated womanliness in an attempt to be, autonomously. The idea that man is a woman who thinks she exists can be thought of as a good description of the way in which the grounding of the American man within a corporate order of being occurs.

The white man in charge is the leader of all the children and asexually reproduces through the repetitions of his voice and the power of his will. Žižek tells us there are no women in the world. But by the same token, it is every bit as likely that there are no men either.

The Divided Man

Being alone is the hallmark of the self-made man. He comes from nowhere, lacks social position, creates his material world out of his own will. Being alone is also, and not coincidentally, the starting point of Ralph Waldo Emerson's philosophy. Emerson's idea of self-reliance is premised on an ontological priority of the self over others.[13] And Emerson's genius is such that he may be understood as a common touchstone of American culture. As George Kateb has suggested, "Emerson is the American Shakespeare. His power of articulation is so great, so uninhibited, that he gives voice to almost all the general thoughts and recurrent sentiments that have since arisen in American culture."[14]

But Emerson also expresses the divided subject of American manhood in perhaps its most radical way. "An inevitable dualism bisects nature, so that each thing is a half, and suggests another thing to make it whole. . . . Whilst the world is dual, so is every one of its parts," he writes.[15] This dualism is clearly, if complicatedly, gendered. Emerson embraces a spiritual hermaphrodism:

> In fact, in the spiritual world we change sexes every moment. You love the worth in me; then I am your husband: but it is not me, but the worth, that fixes the love; and that worth is a drop of the ocean of worth that is beyond me. Meantime, I adore the greater worth of another, and so become his wife. He aspires to a higher worth in another spirit, and is wife or receiver of that influence.[16]

Kateb, who has brought to light this Emersonian valorization of hermaphrodism, notes the bias of the hermaphroditic ideal, its privileging of the role of men. But Kateb also considers more important the privileging of what he terms mental self-reliance over active self-reliance.[17] And in the realm of the mental, he argues, Emerson makes possible both an elevated sense of self-worth and an overcoming of limits for all.

Indeed, the hermaphrodism that Emerson idealizes is itself a mental hermaphrodism. Kateb writes:

> Identification with the superior proceeds from incorporation; the receiver's active love converts the receiver, otherwise passive, into the equal of the superior and thereby abolishes envy. This is not identifying with the aggressor. Rather it is pleasure in thinking that although one does not share privileges, they exist in the world and enhance it. In abandoning resentment, one loses sight of one's lack. To use gendered language, the feminine thus becomes masculine, or overcomes it.[18]

Kateb asserts that Emerson believes everyone is more or less a hermaphrodite. In this assertion, Emerson not only follows the lines of Aristophanes' story of the pairing of feminine and masculine elements to compose a whole self (as memorably staged in Plato's *Symposium*) but anticipates Žižek's appropriation of Lacan's understanding of woman as being the symptom of man. As the Lacanian symptom operates outside social discourse, so too does the Emersonian hermaphroditic operate symptomatically, as a binding of pleasure outside the social that gives shape to it. As an explicit idealization, the Emersonian hermaphrodite differs from the Lacanian *sinthome* by being a fantasy once removed—a *telos* of ultimate reconciliation available mentally, as a part of the rich inner life of the Emersonian subject, but blocked in the world of active self-reliance.[19]

The ideal of the Emersonian hermaphroditic is designed to show men how to become womanly in their active lives. This womanliness has nothing to do with female subjectivity, and in that Emerson and Lacan seem to be brothers under the skin. Hermaphrodism, while loosening the bounds of gender in some ways, is finally a method of incorporation, one that succeeds without necessarily having an impact on the terms through which the corporate social entity is reproduced. Indeed, because self-reliance is in large part a method for learning how to be alone, hermaphrodism may not be its most important active phase. In its most dominant active phase, its practice, Emersonian hermaphrodism may show how being alone risks loneliness, in that without an accompanying bisexuality, the hermaphrodite is not merely irrevocably split but guaranteed an eternal incompletion, in that the mental comes to exist in a (theoretical) balance even as the body is not. To put it more bluntly, instead of engaging in bisexual relations, the Emersonian hermaphrodite fucks himself.

Emerson muses, "Was it Boscovich who found out that bodies never come in contact? Well, souls never touch their objects."[20] Everyone is untouchable or untouched by others. Coming to terms with this fundamental fact of isolation drives Emerson to his most ecstatic philosophical posture. We will yet realize ourselves, we will come to be, oh yes, we will! is the self-confident cry of the confidence man. The deeper we go, however, the closer we come to the realization that the pathos of this quest is only a part of it. The very thought of this chance to realize ourselves can lead us forward to what is already there:

> But every insight from this realm of thought is felt as initial, and promises a sequel. I do not make it; I arrive there, and behold what was there already. I make! O no! I clap my hands in infantine joy and amazement, before the first opening to me of this august magnificence, old with the love and homage of innumerable ages, young with the life of life, the sunbright Mecca of the desert.[21]

This is the realization of the unity of self-reliant thinking, what Emerson calls "its transformation of genius into practical power."[22]

But for those who would rely on the earlier split in Emerson, based on the Neoplatonism expressed in his earliest thought, a distinction can still be traced between mental and active self-reliance. Then Emerson shows how mental self-reliance enables one to endure, to have the consolations of solitude, to be aware of the beauty of the world. Its attenuated relationship to active self-reliance, however, constantly threatens mental self-reliance with the possibility of reducing to solipsism, narcissism, and affected grievance against the outside world—in short, the general condition of the American white male in charge during a period of downsizing. This comment may be no more than an obscure way of suggesting that when it is set loose in the social field of American culture as the corporate order of its possible expression shifts, self-reliance can evolve into either submissive individualism or reactive rage. We may come to be "clapped into jail by [our] consciousness."

Christopher Newfield underlines this submissive element of self-reliance with great directness and force. For Newfield (though he does not exactly use this language), the bulk of the Emersonian edifice is built on a peculiar binding of enjoyment that we might apprehend as the symptom of submissive individualism. Newfield locates this binding first in the assertion of the doctrine of consent: "The sovereign subject of representative democracy and the sovereign son of the oedipal scenario both acquire a delegated yet fully possessible power by consenting to a law which derives circuitously from themselves. Emerson's work exemplifies the gratifications on both sides of this combination."[23] The "possessible power" of citizen and son, it may be noted, is a power that exists as the Lacanian (or perhaps more appropriately, Žižekian) symptom. Newfield emphasizes that the means for achieving this state of completion is incorporation. He thus shows how Emersonian individualism has come to operate in a social field of corporate capitalism as a way of turning men away from the active precisely to ensure their social acquiescence. For him, the radicality of Emersonian's individualism is frustrated by the fact that the potentially equal inner uniqueness of all individuals operates as a substitute for substantive equality in the public realm.[24]

Newfield seems to suggest that the early, most vital Emerson was, in his neoplatonism, enough of a monist to guide his interlocutors to inner freedom and outer submission. In this sense Emerson's monism operated as a doctrine of reassurance, not agitation.[25] He established for American men a means to overcome our lack through an act of renunciation, rather than through an active struggle to seize power so as to establish democratic conditions. This renunciation applies across class. The quest for solidarity must remain, in the corporate liberal imagination, an empathetic acknowledgment of common pain that ignores the circumstances of power to the extent that each person is *himself* an inner ocean.[26]

American men, when we become corporate liberals, displace our desire for equality into highly privatized searches for pleasure. Our various placements within (or without, but always in reference to) the hierarchical corporate order determine the extent to which each of us achieves the minimal autonomy necessary to become an individual more or less integrated into that order; but paradoxically, the more fully integrated into the corporate order we become, the further away from autonomy we are likely to be. This danger, more militantly expressed by Thoreau than Emerson, is nonetheless an important cautionary moment in Emerson's thought, best captured in the closed economy of existence he presents in his essay "Compensation." The pathos of our reduced circumstance leads to both the most telling comedy and violence of our time, products of our failure to become self-reliant. Newfield's lament seems to be that Emerson, knowing what he knew, was nonetheless unable (or unwilling) to present us with a means of *actively* opposing the integrative order that establishes the terms of American manhood to this day. (It is less clear what Newfield's alternative to the corporate order is, but this is of less importance than one might initially think.)[27] As our alternative to mental self-reliance, we are presented with the option of a peculiarly incomplete life, a life of fragmented parts; but unlike the nonidentity presented as a kind of individuality by Deleuze and Guattari, the corporate individual is nostalgic for wholeness, for completion.[28] If we cannot achieve it by imagining ourselves as complete and integrated actors, imagining the ideal woman who would become the complement to our ideal man, the alternative has been to focus our lives on death as the integrative ideal. This latter ideal underlies and empowers the idea of fraternity in America.[29]

It is easier to comprehend these alternatives now because the contemporary situation is not that of a corporate society requiring submission to a disciplinary order to be efficacious. It seems to be becoming clearer that a consumption-based order over time becomes a postdisciplinary one.[30] We are currently experiencing the likelihood that an important phase in the history of the corporate organization of life is ending. The downsizing of the American economy represents one important element of this shift: work is becoming less important as a means of acquiring identity even as the demands of productivity intensify its importance as a sign of personal value. This situation presents the current order of masculinity—which has, since its emergence in the nineteenth century, been implicated in the corporate order—with the simultaneously frightening and exhilarating possibility of becoming obsolescent. The most frightening elements of this transition are being addressed in discussions of the rise of resentment and cynicism among the most central category of American men—those who are white, "middle-class," and heterosexual in orientation—and of the renewed possibility of the marginalization of all "others" internal to the body politic.[31] The more exhilarating element of this renegotiation occurs in the generation of the possibilities of fresh subjective arrangements. What will our new symptom/symptoms be? How will it/they emerge? What impurities will it/they engender? The now failing attempts on the part of the central male subjectivities of the corporate order to negotiate for themselves new identities presents us with the danger of the emergence and solidification of older fundamental identities, but the issuance of new ways of thinking about and acting on nonfundamental politics may help us ameliorate those dangers.

Infinite Insecurity

Charles Ives was an insurance salesman at the turn of the twentieth century who established a technique for "measuring the prospect"—a formula for determining the amount of life insurance a person should carry—that became the standard of the life insurance industry.[32] As a result of the application of that formula in New York City, he became a very wealthy businessman. Ives believed that life insurance was an extension of the social evolution, the heart of a new civilizing process, organized altruism, which would expand the secure horizons of human endeavor.[33] Insurance was to relieve the burden on middle-class families of caring for extended generations, simplifying and reducing the multigenerational family before Social Security came into existence. Ives dreamed of a wholeness of life, a great anonymous community of the human, in which, he believed, as his biographer writes, "the divine law of averages would ensure that the majority would tend to make the right decisions. Society, evolving along with nature, moves always toward greater democracy, greater cooperation, greater unity within its inevitable diversity."[34]

Ives, as many know, was also a great American composer of music, perhaps the most influential experimental composer in American history. He believed in the universal appeal of music, writing at one point that it "will develop possibilities inconceivable now—a language so transcendent its heights and depths will be common to all mankind."[35] The power of his music, though, was to be ignored and denigrated throughout most of his life. It was only through the financial sponsorship he himself provided that much of it was performed at all, until very late in his life. And after a severe heart attack in 1920 at the age of forty-six (he lived from 1874 to 1954), Ives did not produce works as ambitious, as large, and as powerful as what he had written before. Indeed, he produced little more.

Ives was a man of great generosity of spirit, who argued that the work he did as an insurance salesman advanced the human prospect in tandem with his music. A perfect example of the corporate man, he had a great faith in the progressive spirit that would see the United States rise to ever greater levels of prosperity during his life—even though the Great Depression, which ensued after his retirement from active work, was a test of that optimism. Yet there was a limit to Ives's generosity. He was a raging homophobe. Ives constantly accused any musician and any musical work that he thought less than completely realized as being emasculated and feminine. He would attack those who didn't like his music as "pansies" and "ta tas."[36]

One of the major supporters and promoters of Ives as a serious musical force was a modernist composer, Henry Cowell, who was steadfast in his loyalty to Ives through periods when Ives's reputation was virtually nonexistent and who did much to keep Ives's work in the public eye, especially from the late 1920s through the early 1930s. In 1936, Cowell was arrested in California for sodomy and corrupting the morals of a minor. Eventually sentenced to fifteen years of prison (he was released after serving four), Cowell was totally shunned by Ives in this moment of crisis. Ives was in fragile health at the time of the news—he suffered from diabetes as well as heart trouble—but his reaction was consistent with his long-held views concerning weakness and effeminacy. Harmony Ives, his wife, writing to a friend, described Ives's reaction:

> In the mail with your letter was one from Henry addressed to me which contained a letter to be given Charlie if I saw fit. It was a strange letter—admitting his commission of the offense but no *suggestion* of contrition—there was in fact, a spirit of bravado it seemed to me—his "spirit was undaunted" (stock phrase) & he is "absolutely contented." Is he contented with *himself* do you suppose? Anyway, I told Charlie & he & I feel just as you do. A thing more abhorrent to Charlie's nature couldn't be found. We think these things are too much condoned. He will never willingly, see Henry again—he *can't*. . . . The shock used him up & he hasn't had a long breath since I told him but he will get used to it. . . . He said characteristically "I thought he was a man he's nothing but a g— d— sap!"[37]

Ives shunned Cowell, not writing to him. Harmony Ives, who handled much of Ives's correspondence, returned letters from Cowell unopened, though Ives quietly supported efforts to have Cowell released from prison, even writing to the parole board in Cowell's support. There was a "happy ending" to this story, however. In September 1941, Cowell sent a letter to Harmony informing her of his impending marriage, to a woman named Sidney Robertson (perhaps an overdetermined name). They reunited in person in April 1942. "But never again would Henry presume, as he had just before the disaster, to begin his letters 'Dear Charlie.'"[38]

What might one make of this? How is the meaning of being a man so closely associated with the avoidance of femininity, and how is femininity associated with homosexual desire? Kim Townsend offers an appropriately complex analysis of the status of manhood and the panic that afflicted those who were taught a particular kind of manhood at Harvard during generally the same period that Ives attended Yale. Becoming a man meant learning to overcome nervousness, to be tough, to project power, to be "well proportioned, strong, poised; to be capable of persevering, and though self-contained, capable of functioning with others, and if need be, of leading them."[39] It was during this period, from the 1880s through the 1920s, that an earlier, more gentlemanly ideal gave way to the ideal of manhood in order to fulfill the need for corporate and military leaders in the century of American empire. Other characteristics became suspect. George Santayana, for instance, was to suffer at Harvard for lacking in manly qualities. As Townsend puts it, Santayana (and supposedly, less famously documented Harvardians of the same bent) suffered not so much for what he *was* as for what he wasn't. "He was not manly, not what William James and others had worked so hard to be, not what they represented to their students."[40]

This turn of identity emphasizes a strong shell of power and a deeply private interior. John Wikse describes this condition as "the ethos of self-possession. . . . The more a man is able to take it, the more his life becomes his own, the more he becomes his own man. Being dependent on no one, he can be rejected by no one."[41] For such a man, the presence of other men who do not manifest such self-possession can be unnerving. Townsend notes, referring to Santayana and Henry James (whom Teddy Roosevelt called a "miserable little snob"), "They were not manly presences. They made Harvard men nervous."[42] These days, a lot of men in corporate positions are nervous, and most of them have never been near Harvard or Yale. But to the extent that "Harvard is the ideal of America," as Governor Curtis Guild told those assembled at the 1908 commencement[43]—that is, to the extent that elite institutions of higher learning shaped the cultural meaning of manliness—the consequences of addressing this bounded masculinity continue to be felt.

Ives, double-bound by his desire to be a musician—a suspect activity to begin with, from the perspective of manly men—and his genius as an insurance salesman who saw in the redistribution of risk the opportunity for a greater security for all—do risk takers really need insurance?—had only one outlet through which he could shore up his manly identity: by denouncing whatever signs of unmanly weakness he could discern in others. Of course, this mindset harmed him. (Could it not harm his music?)[44] Being reduced in dimension to one's manly character certainly presents one with a limited palette from which to realize one's practical power. At the height of American empire, this limited, narrow, constricted vision of the core identity of American manhood would be set up for a fall. But this image of manhood predominated in American culture until Vietnam, at least, spreading like a stain (from Harvard and Yale?) throughout the structures of social life, reinforced by war and economic expansion.

But something has happened to that ideal in recent decades. It is obsolescent. Civil rights, feminism, and gay rights are all markers of the shift that has come about. How have we memorialized this shift? I took my kids to see a Disney movie a couple years ago, and what we saw was a renunciation of manliness. Pat Robertson may be right: the folks at Disney may indeed be teaching us how to raise our kids gay.[45]

Falling with Style

One of the largest-grossing movies in the United States released during 1995 was Disney Studio's *Toy Story*. *Variety* reports a domestic gross of $189 million for the movie by the week of April 15th, 1996, and a worldwide gross of close to $300 million. Visually dazzling in its innovative use of new computer graphic technology, *Toy Story* tells the tale of the anthropomorphic toys of a young boy who is getting ready to move from one community to another. These toys love Andy, but they also have a very active community of their own. They are led by Woody, a talking cowboy doll (voice by Tom Hanks) who is Andy's favorite toy. All is well for the toys at Andy's house, and all is well for Andy (even though Andy seems to have no father)—that is, until Andy has a birthday. The old toys, it turns out, are always anxious on holidays, because they worry that Andy will get new toys that will replace them. They fear they will become obsolete, even as they hope that new toys will arrive that might supplement them. Mr. Potato Head (Don Rickles) is especially anxious about the possible arrival of a Mrs. Potato Head.[46] Their main concern is Andy's continued attachment to them. Their concern is articulated in corporate submissive terms: Woody, when explaining the ethos of the toys, says, "It doesn't matter how much we're played with, it just matters that we're here for Andy when he needs us."

The toys form a hierarchical society. Those who are most privileged are those who most closely resemble human beings. These include Woody, Buzz, Mr. Potato Head, and Bo Peep. Animals are next in the hierarchical order—the pig, the Slinky dog, the dinosaur. The inanimate toys, such as the Etch-a-Sketch, are lower still, even though through the miracles of animation they are given a quasi individuality. Off to the side, enjoying their own autonomous military hierarchy, are the little green toy soldiers, although they are clearly under civilian control.

What Woody especially fears happens: Andy receives a Buzz Lightyear doll (Tim Allen). Buzz immediately challenges Woody for the leadership of the group by impressing all the toys with his attachments (wings, flashing lights, a voice system that is superior to Woody's) and his supreme confidence that *he is real*. Even Miss Bo-Peep (Annie Potts), the only gendered woman among the "normal" toys, finds him attractive. Woody finds Buzz most irritating for his denial of his "toyness."

In the course of few days, Buzz displaces Woody in Andy's affections. The western motif of Andy's bedroom is transformed into a space motif; cowboy sheets are replaced with Buzz Lightyear sheets, a cowboy lunch box is replaced by a Buzz Lightyear one. The final insult is when Andy takes Buzz, instead of Woody, to bed with him. Woody is relegated to the toy box for the night, with all the other, less favored but somehow more content toys. The sequence of scenes that illustrates Woody's fall from favor has as its background music a song written for the film by Randy Newman, titled "Strange Things Are Happening to Me."[47]

Woody attempts to regain his leadership from Buzz, but a key attempt to humiliate Buzz by knocking him behind a dresser (thereby getting him out of the way so that Andy will take Woody with him to a fast-food restaurant) results in Buzz's disastrous fall from Andy's bedroom window to the ground outside the house. The other toys think Woody deliberately pushed Buzz, so Woody has no choice but to try to rescue him. This rescue involves a trip by Buzz and Woody to a Pizza Planet franchise restaurant (a sort of Chuck E. Cheese theme restaurant) in order to try to reunite with Andy. At the restaurant they are captured by Sid, Andy's sadistic next door neighbor (The name Sid may well be an homage to the Sex Pistols' Sid Vicious.) Sid is abusive to his sister, sometimes taking her dolls away from her and mutilating them. Indeed, Sid is especially feared by Andy's toys because he loves to take toys apart and reassemble them.

Woody and Buzz have some of their most important encounters in Sid's house with the mutant toys assembled by Sid. Initially they think the mutants are like Sid, seeking only to dismember them. But the truth is that the mutants very much resemble what Toni Morrison has called "disturbing nurses."[48] They want only to repair Buzz and to help Woody. They put back an arm of Buzz's that had broken off in a fall. They participate in a rescue attempt that Woody organizes, confronting Sid and overcoming his regime of cruelty, enabling Buzz and Woody the opportunity to make their final escape back to Andy in the nick of time, before his family moves to another neighborhood.

The thematic heart of this film, and the major plot device, is an allegory about white-collar unemployment. The toys live in constant fear that they will be thrown away or put into storage, no longer loved by Andy. Buzz lives out the script of the white-collar manager who sustains himself with the belief that his skills are indispensable, that he is unique.[49] Three moments in the plot are of great emblematic importance for the enactment of this allegory. Two bracket the story: (1) when Woody and Buzz first meet and (2) when they are, at the final moment, trying to catch up to the moving truck that is taking Andy away from them. In the first scene, Buzz, having claimed to be able to fly, executes a series of tumbles that make it appear *as though* he can fly. Woody knows better. "That wasn't flying," he says, "That was falling with style." Woody is trying to shatter the confidence that is Buzz's most important feature as a character, to disillusion him so that he will fall into place. At the time, of course, Buzz blissfully ignores Woody's arguments as cynical and pessimistic. In the later scene, Buzz has a rocket attached to his back (a complicated result of Sid's sadism: Sid is planning to execute Buzz's catchy motto "To infinity and beyond!" by shooting him into the sky attached to a Roman candle). Woody lights the rocket so that they both can fly to the moving truck. Woody exclaims to Buzz, "You're flying!" and Buzz responds, "This isn't flying, this is falling with style!"

What accounts for the end of Buzz's delusion? While trying to escape from Sid's house, he sees an advertisement on television for . . . the Buzz Lightyear doll. In shocked disbelief, he tries to fly by jumping off a banister, falls to the floor of Sid's entry hall, and breaks off his left arm. Severely depressed by the realization that he is indeed "just a useless toy," Buzz is brought to his senses by Woody in the emotional climax of the film. "Over in that house is a kid who thinks you are the greatest because you're *his* toy," Woody tells Buzz.[50] Woody and Buzz become friends and subsequently cooperate with each other to effect their own rescue. The final scene implies that Woody is once again the leader.

The voices of Tom Hanks and Tim Allen reinforce this setting of the world back in order. Tim Allen's star persona is invested in being a passive observer of the world around him, an entitled white male who is always slightly screwing things up. He emerged as a star as a consequence of his role in a hit television show, *Home Improvement,* the serial plot of which centers on gender differences between men and women in an era when men are becoming more and more superfluous in the political economy of the home. Tom Hanks, who is better known, is an everyman hero—a latter-day James Stewart—when playing an idiot savant, when playing a widower, when playing an astronaut in trouble, even when playing a person with AIDS. (Hanks's first starring role was in a TV sitcom called *Bosom Buddies*, which was about male cross-dressing. In fact, one might claim that Hanks has made a career out of bringing to the center male subjectivities at the margin. That Hanks has symbolized the Emersonian hermaphroditic may account for his status as the most popular "serious" actor in Hollywood.)

The third important moment in the enactment of the white-collar male allegory has to do with the realization that Sid's mutant toys are not bad guys but good guys. They surround Buzz and Woody after Woody has rescued Buzz from being a guest at Sid's little sister Hannah's tea party. (Buzz is feminized at that party, in a way directly reminiscent of James Stewart's feminization in *The Man Who Shot Liberty Valence*. In *Toy Story* the feminization is intended to signify the traumatic disability of the newly redundant toy, or as the advertisement calls him, the action figure, while in *The Man Who Shot Liberty Valence*, Stewart's apron signifies the feminine character of the law, as opposed to John Wayne's masculine gun.) It turns out that the mutant toys are interested only in repairing Buzz's arm.[51] They also aid Woody in the final confrontation with Sid—they violate the most important taboo of toys, that of showing a child that you are a sentient, animated being, in order to straighten Sid out.[52] They surround Sid, and Woody gives another speech about taking good care of your toys. Shaken, Sid agrees to be good.

In *Toy Story*, the anxiety over structural unemployment becomes an anxiety over the constitution of identity. While at the most explicit level the film recuperates the corporate order—Woody and Buzz are reunited with Andy, order to the bedroom is restored—at another level, that which reaches to the form of film animation itself, it is not until Buzz embraces his inauthenticity as his reality principle that the re-establishment of order can take place.[53] This is an inversion of the Emersonian pedagogy that would urge each person to recognize his uniqueness. Buzz is able to act once he comes to know and accept that he is not unique. He thus presents the majority reading of *Toy Story*, the necessity of passivity and nonthinking in a postcorporate normalizing order of being. *Toy Story* is relentlessly white, relentlessly straight, and relentlessly male.[54] At its most explicit level it smooths over all differences. It claims that if one submits to the corporate order, one will achieve peace and commodious living.[55] In its anti-authenticity, *Toy Story* is authentically Hobbesian.

If a man's price is his worth, then the worth of a mass-produced person, who achieves his authentic moment only upon realizing his inauthenticity, is a vision of the body politic with the head finally cut off—but not exactly as I think Foucault might have hoped. Indeed, it is at this point that one may need to part company with Foucault, who in his late work repairs to an understanding of the care of the self articulated in bodily, not in cyborgian, terms. But this observation is not completely accurate. In his detailed history of disciplinary society, Foucault analyzed the tight hold that political economy has had on the production of self in a manner that deepens the observation of the early Marx. Foucault pursued the connections between identity and economy in terms that expose the production of subjectivity as a realm indistinguishable from other elements of political economy. Our souls are produced not only by the ways in which we produce but by the ways in which we consume, and we consume even our owned identities. Indeed, it was on the rituals of truth that Foucault was to focus our attention. *Toy Story* is precisely such a ritual, a meditation on the authenticity of the inauthentic, told through means of cartoon animation, a medium that announces its own inauthenticity in every frame of film.

The majority reading of *Toy Story* would thus situate it as a parable in learning to accept one's diminished circumstance in a postproductive corporate order or risk being thrown out of the New Enclosure, excluded from the remnants of civility in a postcivil order.[56] But in a minority reading, *Toy Story* may also be read as a machine that generates difference, encourages pluralizations, and points toward the abolition of self-reliant masculinity. I wish to dwell briefly on the mutant toys, because their abject status—their assembled, partial, fragmentary, far-beyond-simple hermaphroditic monstrosity—combined with their benign intent, suggests that such a minority reading of *Toy Story* is also possible. How do you make a body without organs? Sid, as the inverse of Andy, is the *deus ex machina* who creates toys that are alternatives to the commercial products advertised on TV, mainly mutant babies. His house is a mess (though interestingly, he has two parents and Andy seems to have only one).[57] He has a younger sister who fights with him. Andy's younger brother is a beatific baby, a pre-toddler, pre-gendered, perfectly typical. Sid is in a full-scale subversive rebellion against the consumer order. Andy fetishizes what he sees on TV and receives it unmarked, unchanged. Sid acquires his toys by picking them out of a twenty-five-cent vending bin at the local fast-food restaurant. Andy's gifts are chosen for him. One imagines Sid, if he succeeds in being employed in future years, as either a computer hacker or a drug dealer, or perhaps a combination of the two. One imagines Andy as an intern at Morgan Guaranty. Of course, Sid is also a slave master. The mutants he creates (à la Dr. Frankenstein) engage in a slave rebellion against him, even as Andy's toys endlessly seek to curry favor with Andy. Sid is brought into a democratic moral order by his very own creations, as they engage in their own moment of the politics of enactment. One might envision Sid as either a political activist or as a terrorist. (Sid's dog, named Scud, surely is meant to convey a terrorist, if not anti-Arab racist, connotation.)

But in the end, it is important to note that Sid and Andy are secondary characters in this movie, generic children, one good and one bad. Far more important are the toys. It is, after all, their story. Andy's toys. Sid's toys.

Sid's toys are evocative of an emergent category in film, introduced most vividly in George Miller's *Mad Max* films and in Ridley Scott's *Blade Runner* and domesticated in a variety of science fiction films since—the friendly mutants. Mutants are decidedly cyborgian in form, not monsters in the classical sense of the term.[58] In their happenstance appearance, their borrowed bodily presentation, their consumer familiarity, they provide us with a note of reassurance. Paradoxically, they can remind us of a fragment of a meditation by Patricia Williams, about a white woman who sued a sperm bank because the daughter she bore as a result of artificial insemination was black:

> What will she buy with the money? Into what exactly will this compensation be transformed? . . . I think that in some very central way, this child is the icon of our entire civilization. The pure child, the philosopher's child, the impossible union of elements, forged in a crucible of torment, rattling the bars of the model prison, to wit, the schoolyards and the quiet streets of small "safe" American towns; the black daughter's very integration at the heart of her duality. Trapped in racial circumstance; a little Frankenstein of ingredients, intolerable, fearsome even to its creator, this monster child's racial hermaphroditism, the unpropertied guerrilla birth of herself, like a condensation, a rain of isolated social confrontations, like a prayer without an answer. Like the birth of a daughter, O Misfortune.[59]

Williams recasts the bodily existence of the miscegenate child in cyborgian terms, making her a mutant by reminding us of the field of constructed space into which she is to be thrust, a body out of order and yet negotiating her way through the suburbs of America. Sid is a fictional reworking of the guerrilla warfare fancifully imagined by Williams (in which young white men and young black men cooperate to smuggle black sperm into white sperm banks). He combines Williams's vision of genetic subversion with Donna Haraway's cyborg manifesto,[60] reworking his toys. Sid brings back to the realm of the social the fantasy that might allow us to rethink our symptom. The mutant toys of *Toy Story* are the "others" left behind as the gang of "normal" toys moves onward and upward, probably to a house in a better suburb far away from the likes of Sid. But in leaving, these toys (and their putative owners) display the brittle improbability of their own happenstance existence. The center will not hold, or at least there will be life after the departures of the store-bought toys.

In *Toy Story*, the potential for such a racial fragmentation is minimal. Here I know I am reading the movie too wistfully (as in wistful thinking). But if the racial subtext needs to be coaxed from the film, the dissolution of manliness and the opening to gay desire is rendered transparent. At the 1996 Academy Award ceremonies, Jim Carrey provided the clearest evidence of the widespread recognition of this, using Buzz Lightyear and Woody dolls hilariously to reenact a scene from the 1969 film *Midnight Cowboy*, which at the time controversially suggested a homosexual love between Rizzo (Dustin Hoffman) and Cowboy (John Voight).

Other Masculinities

Toy Story was produced by Disney Studios using computer animation technology developed by Stephen Jobs's Pixar Animation Studios. *Business Week* reports, "Only 27 animators were used, as opposed to the seventy or so who worked on *Pocahontas*. Animators make $100,000 or more per year, so Disney saved $10 million on the film."[61] The simulacrum of *Toy Story* closed before the movie ever opened. Participating in the very event it reports on and celebrates, the Disney Corporation hides in the light. This is not a new strategy, of course, but it is certainly bold. As the rumbles of discontent from a disenfranchised white-collar class of business executives grow, it is difficult to know what lesson *Toy Story* will be made to tell in the future.

Toy Story appears as but one more moment in the era of a transition in the meaning of masculinity in the United States of America. And it is not the only, or even the most artful, expression of the loss of power to be found in the most recent popular representations of the man in charge, the corporate man.[62] The old order of corporate being, in which a masculinity that needs to be associated with the ideology of the self-made man is waning, may be said to be losing its final residual force. This order may simply be recycled in more direct assertions of power, as men in charge seek new footholds. Indeed, one important view of recent American history tells a tale that brushes against the grain of the argument I present here and relates a reassertion of American masculinity, a renewed power of the man in charge, as embodied in the angry male, the militia movement, and the Republican ascendancy in American national government. But these visible signs of power are not necessarily what they seem to be. They could well be the signs of the death rattle of a style of being masculine that is radically inappropriate to the late modern condition.

If this is the case, then the old style of being a man may be open to new enactments and deliberate stylizations. Buzz's recognition of his happenstance existence does not necessarily alleviate him of responsibility—though it might, if he were to think a little bit longer, relieve him of responsibility to Andy. What does it mean to think about a masculine ethos that embraces inauthenticity; that understands it is itself a shattered version of a former self; that might slowly, painfully learn the power of an abjection that neither rages against its own monstrosity nor withdraws in humiliation and fear from further insult and loss, but instead enjoys dissolution for the opportunities of pleasure and alternative enactments it may present?

The appeal of *Toy Story* might then be found more in its enunciation of the dissembling of the old order than in its construction of a new one. Of course, what is saddest about this movie is that its central danger is still posed by the threat of the minority other; that its motive force is white flight; that the relief of its central characters, Buzz and Woody, is a result of the fact that they haven't been left behind by those who moved, presumably further out to the suburbs. I find that conclusion the least plausible element of this fantasy. It resituates *Toy Story* as yet another western, in which the cowboy—in this case, Woody—is able to ride into the sunset. But there are no places left to run. The era of masculinity, the era of the dominance of the manly man, may be drawing to a close, even in some of our most pleasant fictions.

6

Aliens

It will become *all* one thing, or *all* the other.
—Abraham Lincoln, "House Divided" speech

The King's Two Bodies

In his monumental study of the medieval monarchy, Ernst Kantorowitz introduces modern readers to the politico-theological concept of the King's Two Bodies. Kantorowitz refers his readers to Edmund Plowden's *Reports*, in which Plowden remarked of a case predating the reign of Queen Elizabeth concerning the authority of the monarchy:

> For the King has in him two Bodies, *viz.*, a Body natural, and a Body politic. His Body natural (if it be considered in itself) is a Body mortal, subject to all infirmities that come by Nature or Accident, to the Imbecility of Infancy or old Age, and to the like Defects that happen to the natural Bodies of other People. But his Body politic is a Body that cannot be seen or handled, consisting of Policy and Government, and constituted for the Direction of the People, and the Management of the public weal, and this Body is utterly devoid of Infancy, and old Age, and other natural Defects and Imbecilities, which the Body natural is subject to, and for this Cause, what the King does in his Body politic, cannot be invalidated or frustrated by any Disability of his natural Body.[1]

This dualism of the king having two real bodies, one visible and one invisible, provided sovereign authority a means by which it might stabilize its representation before the public, as that public was coming into being as the constituency of the emergent state. The gathering of authority into the hands of the king was a way to signify the unity of the people. The unity of the king's two bodies was to be a living symbol of the body politic at a moment of transition, when an epistemological crisis concerning the extent and limit of God's domain over earthly matters was coming to the fore of earthly concern.

But this doctrine also described an ontological condition of the human body of which the king was to be an exceptional representative. It gestured toward the Cartesian splitting off of mind (or soul) from body that has haunted us in the modern era. This moment, in all its peculiarity, is the moment of the birth of sovereignty and of the modern subject. The emergence of the nation-state itself hinged on the birth and continual rebirth of sovereignty out of the instabilities of this representative power. The organizational power of this abstracted community is introduced into the history of politics by way of a new knowledge of corporeality that was inexplicable through earlier representations of God and God's inspiriting forcefulness.[2]

Following Kantorowitz, some contemporary political thinkers have sought to understand how the principle of the King's Two Bodies might explain certain important continuities between medieval and modern political experiences. Perhaps most famously, Michel Foucault refers to the doctrine of the King's Two Bodies (and Kantorowitz's reading of it) to raise a key question about the political status of the modern subject. In *Discipline and Punish* he asks, "If the surplus power possessed by the king gives rise to the duplication of his body, has not the surplus power exercised on the subjected body of the condemned man given rise to another type of duplication? That of a 'non-corporal,' a 'soul,' as Mably called it."[3] In Foucault's work, this modern soul is the prison of the body. The inverted power of the King's Two Bodies finds renewed expression in the conjoining of discipline to a new sovereign right. This new sovereignty, born of the era of disciplinary society, migrates from the king to the liberal individual.[4] For Foucault, the double character of modern political subjectivity—a rights-bearing citizen and a subjugated, docile subject—is constituted in some of its most important details as an echo of this earlier sovereign dualism. In reference to the contemporary manifestation of this dualism, Foucault at one point suggests that a continued emphasis on sovereign right in modern polities obscures the power of normalization that underlies disciplinary civilization.[5] "We need to cut off the King's head: in political theory that has still to be done," he wrote.[6] Processes of a normalizing power continue apace, while modern subjects are distracted by the spectacle of sovereignty played out as the contest of competing rights and the clash of states.[7]

These forces become increasingly explicitly thematized and decoupled from the institutions of modern states at the end of the disciplinary era. What might be called postdisciplinary society emerges as a result of the failure of sovereign right to sustain its legitimacy as a principle of the state, at the same time that governmentality is becoming increasingly ubiquitous. But sovereignty does not, in this era, simply disappear. It migrates to the institutions most likely to sustain its fictive reality. We might now see expressions of sovereignty as the face of the representative institutions of corporate life, since this is where the greatest concentrations of power now may be found.[8] Since, in a late capitalist politico-economic order, commodification has extended outward and downward into the infrastructures of everyday life, the spirit of the body immortal may appear in the most obvious artifacts of commercial culture—television, music, popular movies. In fact, the most potent claims about the meaningful exercise of presidential power at the end of the twentieth century concern the capacity of presidents and wanna-be presidents to perform well—that is, to perform credibly as presidents—on television. It is news to no one that presidents are now icons of popular culture. Here is where we might look for whatever signs of life the principle of the King's Two Bodies may still exhibit.

Michael Rogin has convincingly argued that the politico-theological principle underlying the doctrine of the King's Two Bodies survived its transfer to the American body politic and continually makes its appearance in our political culture, as a combination of Constitution worship and a vigorous and expansive understanding (by presidents of the United States) of the importance of presidential leadership. For him, the danger that attends the deployment of this powerful metaphor is that the identity of the king was so often absorbed into the immortal realm, giving "transcendent importance to the person" holding office and wrapping their all-too-human decisions in a fog of theocratic inevitability.[9] As the dramaturgy of this representative power is played out on the stage of American politics, the Constitution has represented the enduring and immortal body of law, while the president himself has served as the mortal agent—all too human—of the sovereign power of law. Complicating this modern incarnation of the metaphorical dualism of mortality/immortality is the transformed role played by theological belief in the secular system of Enlightenment political institutions. Whereas the doctrine of the King's Two Bodies both reinforced and depended on a faith in the Christian concept of God, the secular translation of that faith by way of the coupling of constitutional rule to presidential leadership depends on a different mechanism. How does the president (mortal) legitimize (sanctify) the (immortal) constitution?

To answer this question, Rogin focuses on three episodes of presidential sacrifice: when Abraham Lincoln, Woodrow Wilson, and Richard Nixon, each in his turn, seemed called on to give up his (mortal) body in an effort to preserve the Constitution. In each instance of presidential sacrifice he examines, Rogin finds that the sacrifice of the president is synonymous with his transgression of the constitutional role of the president. As Nixon claimed of Lincoln, "Actions which would otherwise be unconstitutional, could become lawful if undertaken for the purpose of preserving the constitution and the nation."[10] Rogin writes:

> The White House, for all three, turned body mortal into body spiritual and conferred the power to create and destroy. Would they, in punishment for their lawless ambition, die the unsanctified tyrant's death? Would they be stripped of their royal bodies, or redemptively sacrificing their mortal lives, would they regenerate the body politic?[11]

In answering his own question, Rogin seems to suggest that the historical evolution of the American presidency makes it increasingly less likely that any president can successfully engage in such acts of self-sacrifice. The crisis of representation attending the late modern state generally, but especially the United States, makes the attempt at even a symbolic sacrifice by a president appear a cynical act of opportunism. Only those who can embrace the presidency as a fictive office, on the model of Ronald Reagan, might be able to secure some sense of the old sovereignty, appropriately as a simulation of the Hobbesian sovereign. The practice of presidential sacrifice is in decline, from this perspective, because it is no longer necessary to sacrifice that which is so transparently already dead.

We might supplement this account of the decline of presidential sacrifice by thinking about the fate of the office of the American president in the era in which the rise of Reaganesque strategies of subvention have occurred. This would mean taking seriously the idea advanced by another student of the American presidency, Stephen Skowronek, concerning what he calls "the waning of political time."[12] For Skowronek, political time expresses a persistent cycle one may detect in presidential governance associated with the uniquely disruptive role of presidential elections, in which successive presidents find themselves alternatively reconstructing previous regimes of power, articulating and expanding the preexisting commitments of a regime, or preempting the commitments of the prior regime without reconstructing its most important assumptions of rule. The waning of political time suggests that the impact of presidential disruption is increasingly limited as the structures through which presidents govern become more autonomous, that is, less susceptible to presidential manipulation or control, with the passing of history and the accruing of bureaucratic power.[13] This historical development, in which, for Skowronek, secular time overcomes political time, leads to the potential dominance of a politics of preemption, as new presidents tend to become trapped by the commitments of the last reconstructive regime and at best must manipulate the dominant (and usually inert) opposition to change. Generally, preemptive presidents interrupt previously established regimes. "Intruding into an ongoing polity as an alien force, they interrupt a still vital political discourse and try to preempt its agenda by playing upon the political divisions within the establishment that affiliated presidents instinctively seek to assuage."[14] Lacking the political mandate and the institutional freedom to repudiate the commitments of a prior regime and unwilling to endorse those commitments, preemptive presidents are always testing the limits of their authority to depart from the earlier regime and always risk plunging into constitutional crisis.

Skowronek places both Wilson and Nixon on his list of preemptive presidents, an inclusion that suggests a connection between Rogin's understanding of failed presidential sacrifice and the politics of preemption. This connection has to do with the failure of these presidents to gather the warrants for their actions that take the country into untested constitutional ground. Wilson miscalculated his own ability to convince the American public over the heads of the Senate that he should be president of the world. Nixon, knowing that he could never get warrants for his acts, acted covertly and illegally. But both, to paraphrase Nixon paraphrasing Lincoln, were unable to make what was unlawful lawful. When they acted, they found that their actions were not sufficient to break down the strictures that had developed over the course of secular time.

One twentieth-century president succeeded in the exercise of preemption: Dwight Eisenhower. Bill Clinton may also be a preemptive president, but whether he is a success or a failure remains to be seen.[15] Of course, Skowronek's argument goes further than suggesting that these specific presidents engage in a politics of preemption. With the waning of political time, *all* presidents become preemptive, because no president can break through the developed institutions of power that block the effective exercise of their disruptive authority. While presidential candidates may represent themselves as outsiders, upon assuming office, they become what they ran against. A successful preemptive president in the waning of political time is someone who must be a pragmatist, a deliberative compromiser. A failure is one who succumbs to the temptation to use power without warrant, to engage in "clandestine tactics," and ultimately falls into disgrace as a consequence.[16]

Precisely because they are forced to be pragmatists to avoid disgrace and failure, post-Reagan preemptive presidents must become adept at techniques of representing a sovereignty that is no longer necessarily there. The sorts of incremental policies that they are likely to be able to enact do not give them a good script to highlight leadership. Domestically, they are constrained by the bond markets and a ravaged bureaucracy. In foreign affairs, still always the most dangerous arena of presidential power, the next phase of market integration, globalized capitalism, further fetters meaningful presidential action. War by the means the United States has available is increasingly inefficient. To represent sovereignty, as Ronald Reagan showed, involves acting *like* a president more than it does acting *as* a president. Those who succeed at the "acting like" function are more likely to win election and remain high enough in the polls to be protected from congressional or special prosecutorial subversion. This technique of presidential impersonation would seem to have its limits: it generally favors those who act the most *presidential.* Acting presidential is a very difficult thing to do, sometimes especially when one *is* the president. This is because the style of being president (acting *like* a president) has for so long been decoupled from the substance of presidential decision-making (acting *as* a president) as to deprive those who hold the office of any secure guidelines on how to conduct themselves in office.

Rogin describes how Ronald Reagan took his cues on how to act like a president from the various film roles he inhabited during his acting career. Two presidencies later, it may be that there is a general failure in the capacity of presidents to act *as* presidents, rooted in the demand that they act *like* presidents. This failure of presidents is not simply an institutional failure. It is a mark of a crisis in representation that has precipitated what several critical theorists are taking to calling the pathological public sphere, a mass subjectivity that increasingly depends on a uniform identification by political subjects with a univocal public sphere. The failure of American presidents to negotiate adequately a way to represent the sovereign body of the people has led to a rise of the phenomenon of the celebrity as president and the president as celebrity, "who rules through a politics of identification-as-projection."[17] In short, the contemporary presidential temptation is to reinhabit the immortal body of the king through the means given him by the society of the spectacle—in short, to rearticulate, in post-Christian terms, the political theology of the King's Two Bodies, but not necessarily through the worship of the Constitution or the activity of strong presidential leadership. The Constitution becomes increasingly anachronistic in this vision of presidential power (a playground for constitutional amendments proposed by members of Congress), and presidential power is only a means toward the end of creating representations of the president that make him look like he is powerful.

In this context, popular cultural representations of presidents become a direct source of information concerning presidential power. The president's link to the people is prepared by their understanding of how presidents act *like* presidents, and the cultural *lingua franca* where this understanding is developed is that of movies and television shows. In the politico-economic order of late capitalism, commodification extends outward and downward into the infrastructures of everyday life, and so we might say that the spirit of the body immortal appears in the most obvious artifacts. Yet at the same time, the culture that is confabulated out of the materials of commodification in the mass representative formats of television, music, and popular movies (among others) provides countertexts about the meaning of citizenship, taking up objects and representations in their everyday appearance, providing a potentially rich critical archive that we might analyze in terms of how it expresses and reinterprets, reinforces and undermines, the force of sovereignty. Lauren Berlant has discussed such a critical project in reference to how it forms a "counterpolitics of the silly object," allowing us to think through how the force of nationalism, for instance, persists in the face of its illogics and violences.[18] We can think about the representation of presidential sovereignty through the lens of commercial film simply because popular films represent and intensify citizens' understandings of this aspect of political power, even as they make a weaker claim to the "authoritative"—that is, most self-legitimizing—understandings of the mechanisms through which presidential sovereignty is expressed. This way of reading the intertextuality of film and presidential sovereignty is consistent with the most basic political beliefs of the citizenry, a point most fully realized when we think about the founding of the polity not on a basis of blood or land but on representation itself. This sheer textuality of American self-understanding has constituted us as a republic of signs, as Anne Norton has brilliantly noted.[19]

In the context of spectacle, acting like a president has a warrior aspect these days. Whether it be Michael Douglas in *The American President* (1995), who launches an attack on Libya before going out on a date, or

Harrison Ford in *Air Force One* (1997), throwing Russian terrorists off his airplane to protect his wife and daughter, the combination of alpha male and father protector, operating beyond explicitly enunciated political ideology, guides the decision-making of these presidents. Against this backdrop, we may ask about the fate of yet another American president, President Whitmore, who was depicted, in the summer of 1996 in movie theaters everywhere, as the last president of the United States. His career, traced in the movie *Independence Day*, may be said specifically to illustrate the barriers to the successful employment of presidential sacrifice in an era of perpetually preemptive politics. More generally, *Independence Day* may be most profoundly understood as a reflection on the crisis of American national politics that is precipitated by the decline in confidence in our system of representation generally, a reflection that provides us with an allegory of the latest attempt to cut off the head of the king—this time to destroy the immortal body of the king, perhaps only to restore it after the end of an age of disenchantment.

Normal People

Independence Day is most explicitly an alien invasion movie. In fact, it may become the most successful alien invasion movie of all time. But as Jodi Dean remarks, "The big alien movies marked rather than ushered in the cultural prominence of the alien in the nineties."[20] Dean suggests that the "breakout" of the UFO subculture into the more general arena of popular culture representation is the result of a shift in political context. The end of the cold war marked the conclusion of the critical function of UFO studies as skeptics of a U.S. national security state. The transfer of that skepticism to a more general concern with the fugitive character of truth is the restive claim of ufologists. She writes:

> The fugitivity of truth is now a problem for all of us. It no longer plays itself out in the marginal discourses of popular (or academic) culture. The confusions, hesitations, and potentially horrific possibilities of the UFO discourse are just a concentrated version of the facts and pseudo-facts of life at the millennium. The alien icon accesses our anxieties around the fugitivity of postmodern truth; it marks the disequilibrium we face at the dissipation of distinctions between truth and falsity, fantasy and reality, original and copy. Put more strongly, the prominence of the alien in postmodern American culture marks the widespread public conviction that previously clear and just lan-

guages and logics, discourses and procedures, are now alien, now inseparable from their alien other.[21]

In the context of this anxiety, there will be attempts to recuperate, to develop what William Corlett has termed "discourses of reassurance," designed to rebuild "common sense" around reconfigured notions of traditional truth.[22] Indeed, what we see in the most commercially successful movies that address unsettling controversies welling from the margins of the popular are precisely such recuperative moves. But these moves are rarely unambiguous, and it is possible to investigate what may be called the minority voices present in some of the most reactively reassuring films of all.[23]

As an alien movie, *Independence Day* (hereafter referred to as ID4) may, at its simplest level, be seen to transfer onto an alien other the extraordinary anxieties associated with the loss of an external, demonized enemy. The uniting of the world in opposition to the evil aliens is an obvious substitution for the cold war enemy of the Soviet Union—a restored national purpose for the United States, as it leads the (free?) world in counterattacking the alien force and defeating it. The pleasure of ID4, from this perspective, is not dissimilar to the pleasures of watching Sylvester Stallone in the *Rambo* movies, except that in this case we are not refighting a war that we putatively lost but definitively celebrating victory in a war that never was properly concluded. ID4, in this sense, is the valedictory for the cold war.

At another level, the alien other can be understood as the displacement of the anxieties of the denizens of consumer capital at the moment when the ecological consequences of our actions are no longer obscured by the priorities of fighting the cold war. This motif is suggested by the quotidian environmentalism of one of the film's heroes, David, played by the ubiquitous Jewish scientist/blockbuster-movie/nerd Jeff Goldblum, who moves from saving the planet by recycling aluminum cans to saving the planet by infecting the alien mother ship in outer space with a computer virus and depositing a thermonuclear bomb deep inside it. Goldblum is the first to realize that the aliens do not come in peace, but his alarm is infectious—the gradually (over a period of a few hours) dawning realization on the part of one and all that the aliens are here simply to consume all the resources of the planet, and then moving on, becomes a way of signaling both their evil and their power. As President Whitmore (Bill Pullman) notes, "They're like locusts."

By engaging in such acts as nuking Houston, Texas, the defenders of (Mother) Earth become better environmentalists. This theme resonates deeply as a referent, because it serves as a mechanism for yet another displacement and recuperation. The aliens in ID4 bear a family resemblance to the Europeans who originally descended on the New World, destroying everything, not even acknowledging the sentience of those whom they were killing, to say nothing of their lack of appreciation for the life of "harmony with nature" enjoyed by the aboriginal tribes of the Americas. The superior technology of the Europeans is matched by that of the aliens. Yet the eventual realization by the natives that the Europeans were, like them, also human, also vulnerable, is paralleled by the knowledge gained by Earth's natives—once President Whitmore learns that Area 51 is for real—that the aliens are as weak as human beings (if mightily telepathic and intellectually off the charts in terms of Richard Murray's most important measure, that of IQ; of course, being smart is no guarantee of success, especially in American popular culture).

In romanticizing native sensibilities, ID4 shares a surprising affinity with Disney's 1995 cartoon release *Pocahontas*, which explicitly presents a sentimental view of Native Americans in order to displace anxieties concerning the impact of rapacious capitalism on the environment. In both cases, of course, there is no follow-through on the critique. *Pocahontas's* Governor Radcliffe, in his quest for gold, is safely buried by history and cultural foreignness. In ID4, once the aliens are destroyed, life can go on. (And the congratulatory cigar smoked by David and Captain Stephen Hiller after returning from their successful mission seems to indicate something more: that with its horrible cities destroyed, the inhabitants of Earth might go on as they did *before* the hole in the ozone appeared, that is, with no further concern for such things as cancer, secondhand smoke, or other pollutants. The alien invasion weeded our garden for us.) And while one might note that both films share the dominant Hollywood casting of capitalists as bad guys, the critique of capitalism goes no further than to suggest that there are some bad capitalists "out there." Indeed, the visual organization of the alien mother ship seems to suggest something the contrary—that the ravaging consumers of planets might not be capitalists at all, but communists. Whatever. The main point here is that those of us who consume movies are not implicated in such nastiness. *We* are just normal folks.

This theme of normalcy is perhaps the most enduring contribution of Hollywood movies to American self-identity. In most popular films, the normal is devoid of historical events, specific dates, sometimes even seasons (especially in films shot in California) and specific locale. Normalcy is represented as under siege in ID4. While at the most explicit level, this normalcy is subordinate to existence itself—as President Whitmore says in his speech before the final battle, "We are fighting for our right to exist"—it turns out that the conditions of existence represented in ID4 are, of necessity, the conditions of *familiar* existence, that is, suburban or even ex-urban existence. (Paired to the destruction of cities, one may recall the army of RVs that descends on Area 51. This scene might be understood iconographically as the most important symbol of postapocalyptic American community—the Wally Benham Society [Jetstream trailer] writ large.)[24]

In contemporary movies, much of the representative burden of normalcy is carried out through casting. Increasingly, producers look toward broadcast television stars to accomplish this effect.[25] Star persona for the 1996 summer hit movies, especially *Twister* and ID4, is put into the service of rendering the characters in the movies generically familiar. Helen Hunt of NBC's marriage comedy *Mad about You* stars in *Twister*. And the real star of ID4 is another (former) NBC comedy star, the *Fresh Prince of Bel-Air*, Will Smith. Indeed, like its predecessors in the related genre of disaster movies (if not sci-fi), the ensemble cast of ID4 is full of familiar faces from television. Such casting is used sometimes to ironic effect (as in the casting of Brent Spiner, Mr. Data from *Star Trek: The Next Generation*, as Doctor Okin, the slightly addled chief research scientist in the secret base in Area 51 that holds the alien ship and the bodies of dead aliens). But for the most part, it bathes the movie in a sense of the familiar—as, for example, in the casting of *Taxi*'s Judd Hirsh as Jeff Goldblum's father.

One might make too much of casting in this sense, and one could argue that the roles of President Whitmore (Bill Pullman) and the first lady (Mary McDonnell) counter this claim. But one may also note that neither of these roles was filled by a first-rank movie star (at the time), but rather by people best known then for playing supporting roles in large movies or idiosyncratic leads in smaller ones. I believe this second-rank casting was attempted because the star power of a first-rank movie actor would have undercut the intense sense of normalcy the film's director, Roland Emmerich, wanted to establish as his way of signifying American democracy. Had Michael Douglas, for instance (who *is* cast as a president in Rob Reiner's 1995 *The American President*), inhabited the role of President Whitmore, his iconographic status as a movie star would have rendered the important actions that Bill Pullman–as–president takes—flying a fighter, hugging his daughter—less plausible. The point here is that even the president of the United States is (or must be perceived as) a normal man.

Why? The short answer is that it has always been the case that presidents must be perceived as ordinary men engaged in extraordinary actions. This is the Americanization of the theme of the King's Two Bodies, perhaps most successfully displayed in the movie *Dave* (1993), Ivan Reitman's meditation on the theme of the symbolic power of the presidency. The long answer, one that explains why presidential sacrifice gives way to what might be called citizen sacrifice in ID4, is what the remainder of this chapter explores.

The Declining Significance of the American People

If one were to think of ID4 in genre terms not simply as an alien invasion movie but as a small yet special subgenre that we could call the alien invasion/presidential sacrifice subgenre, one might be able to locate its politics with a little more precision. Prominent in such a subgenre would be the movies *The Day the Earth Stood Still, The Invasion of the Body Snatchers* (1978 remake), *Alien, JFK,* and *Nixon.* Each of these movies shares in and/or develops certain dualisms that parallel the dualism of the King's Two Bodies. Each movie resolves or renders problematic the sacrifice needed to restore a representative order in the face of the crisis brought on by a failure in the dualism.

Early on in ID4 another film is quoted, the 1950s classic *The Day the Earth Stood Still* (Robert Wise). *The Day the Earth Stood Still* involves an alien who succeeds in convincing one of Earth's leading scientists to gather the smartest men and women from all the nations of the earth (primarily scientists, of course) in front of the newly landed alien spacecraft, so that they may hear and learn how an oversized mechanical man, Gort, is to become the new sovereign power over the earth. Gort will succeed in his quest because he is capable of threatening Earth's total destruction if there is no peaceful resolution of interstate conflict. The appearance of the alien is a consequence of an interplanetary civilization's collective decision concerning the state of affairs of Earth. Advancing technical abilities by the earthlings make it likely that they will someday soon explore the larger universe inhabited by the alien superiors. For the sake of everyone, it is important that they learn to control themselves. Nuclear power is not for the immature. The earthlings need to grow up.

Gort is no medieval king but rather the embodiment of Hobbes's less religiously inspired and more familiarly modern principle of an overawing power, the power of the sword. Being a machine, his immortality is not metaphysical but physical, derived from his indestructibility. Controlled by aliens who live in an interplanetary federation, he is both the empirical repudiation of the Christian version of immortality, a theological worldview that is not capacious enough to include intelligent life from other planets, and an implicit rebuke to the doctrine of the exercise of unilateral power, which in the 1950s, as now, was a popular stance among Republican politicians. Gort implements a policy of mutually assured destruction only of those who fail to live peacefully. Those who repudiate force are protected by his power.

The alien visitor who brings Gort to Earth comes quickly to understand that the real power on Earth in the relevant matter of ending war is not the American president. The first authority the alien attempts to contact is, in fact, the American president. His flying saucer lands on the Mall, between the Capitol and the Washington Monument, and the alien is captured and interviewed by a top aide to the president. The alien asks that the president gather all the leaders of the world to Washington, to hear what he has to say to all of them. Even after trying, the president fails. The president's aide conveys this message, clearly indicating that it is beyond the president's powers to gather all nations together. It is then that the alien realizes he must try another path and engages in an end run around the politician, in a sense engaging in a politics of preemption.

At the climax of the *The Day the Earth Stood Still*, the alien visitor and Gort confront a group of the best and brightest scientists in the world, assembled on the Mall in Washington, D.C., to inform them of the plan of a confederation of galaxies. Chiding these scientists for having allowed the nuclear arms race to proceed so far, the alien explains how Gort is to be left on Earth to operate as part of an interplanetary police force, automatically destroying Earth if the people fail to end the arms race. He says, "The universe grows smaller every day, and the threat of aggression by anyone can no longer be tolerated. There must be security for all or no one is secure. Now this does not mean giving up any freedom, except the freedom to act irresponsibly. Your ancestors knew this when they made laws to govern themselves, and hired policemen to enforce them. We of the other planets have long accepted this principle." Evoking the principle of the police moves the function of authority from the realm of transcendent representation to that of practical force. It does not matter whether we believe in Gort's legitimacy—his power is not a consequence of our acceptance of it. What we accept is to be governed by an overawing power. We accept the facticity of this power because the only other choice is annihilation.

The Day the Earth Stood Still is an Eisenhower-era movie—Eisenhower himself was a preemptive president, trapped by the commitments of the New Deal, on the one hand, and by the national security state that emerged in the Truman administration, on the other. His impotent presence hovers over this film. Indeed, the "money shot" in *The Day the Earth Stood Still* is a series of scenes in which all traffic in Washington is stopped dead by the force of an alien ray. These still streets define a Washington, D.C., that is itself paralyzed by the bipolarities of the cold war.

Throughout *The Day the Earth Stood Still*, however, the most frequent scenes of streets are of streets at night, with people either being driven in cabs through sparely trafficked avenues or walking on deserted sidewalks (either to or from the boarding house where the alien is staying, among the citizenry). Empty streets are a powerful signifier in sci-fi movies, usually designed to emphasize the spooky or conspiratorial elements at work just off-screen (of course, empty streets are also cheap to shoot, a consideration given that many of these films were at best B features; one thinks here of George Romero's 1968 *Night of the Living Dead*) or, in the aftermath of apocalypse, as a sign of devastation.

The Invasion of the Body Snatchers (1978 remake, directed by Philip Kaufman, of the 1956 Don Siegel film) provides us with many such streets, punctuated by hordes of pod people getting ready to be shipped out to other cities. These pod people gather at secret locations. Rather than being imposing foreign machines, they exactly replicate the bodies of those whom they are replacing. In this movie, Donald Sutherland is the key government representative, a San Francisco Department of Health restaurant inspector. He comes to discover that people are being turned into plants, their surface normalcy hiding the horror within. In 1978 this critique of the normal was directed at Jimmy Carter, a technocrat who linked success in office to successful manipulation of bureaucracy. During his administration, Jimmy Carter was to offer a scolding to the American people in the form of a domestic summit that would result in a speech discussing *malaise*. Something is wrong, but we don't know what it is.

Hiding under the surface of the normal are plots, conspiracies. The conspiratorial mode is one that is indefinite in domain, and conspiracy theories offer us a reassurance of certainty in the absence of faith. In Oliver Stone's *JFK* (1992), Sutherland is cast as Mr. X, the insider who knows and who can encourage Jim Garrison in his search for the truth of the death of John F. Kennedy. This modern regicide, captured on the famous Zapruder film, opened before the American public as its first video spectacle *avante la lettre*. Stone, by using Sutherland in this role, signified through casting the connection between assassination conspiracy and alien conspiracy. For Stone, the entire political landscape since Kennedy's assassination can be traced back to this act, not only because the conspiratorial allows such a retroactive repiecing of history but because the unique social trauma the assassination caused virtually demanded such a resort to conspiratorial explanation.

Underneath the normal conspiracies operate. What is the greatest conspiracy of all? That of the normal. In fact, the normal contributes to making the truth "fugitive," in Dean's terms. This fugitive character is expressed in film by the alien inside. While in *The Invasion of the Body Snatchers* there is a transfer of subjectivity, a change in personality, beginning with the film *Alien* (1981, directed by Ridley Scott) the alien becomes manifest, the least body of the citizen doubled and controlled by the alien inside. While at first this embodied alien is brutal and animal-like, as the series has advanced it has been given a greater subjectivity, a more malign but more understandable set of motives. And the genre itself has become much more complex; technical advances have allowed there to be even more graphic depictions of the alien inside, as films such as *Species* (1995) demonstrate by making visually explicit the struggle between child and adolescent as the body undergoes metamorphosis over a few seconds.

These transformations represent the presence of evil in film, starting as early as *Nosferatu* (1922). *The Exorcist* (1974), a Watergate scandal film, brought this transformational logic of the alien other to the foreground in dogmatic theological terms. But the use of an underlying, internal bodily struggle as representative of the presence of evil has long been present, a topic of periodic renewal and re-creation in films. The idea operates in contemporary acting craft as a basic means of portraying duplicity and venality. One might observe Ian McKellen in the 1995 remake of *Richard III*. As he accepts the crown "reluctantly," he turns away from the delegation and an inner evil is revealed, but only to the observing audience. Similarly, in Oliver Stone's *Nixon* (1995), Anthony Hopkins (who had recently won an Academy Award for the role of Hannibal Lecter, a sociopathic psychiatrist, in *The Silence of the Lambs* [1991]) Nixon is seen first in shadow—unobserved, brooding, and dark—and then struggling to put on a smile as the spotlight hits him, so that he can accept the Republican nomination for president. I am not, of course, the first person to compare Nixon to

Richard III.[26] My intention here is only to note how the effect of the representation of a two bodies struggling for control has had an impact on how we might view the presidential body.

This struggle plays itself out most obviously in presidential elections, when the competing candidates struggle to make their bodies act more presidential than their opponents'. In the final debate of the 1996 presidential election cycle, Clinton handily won this contest, physically invading Dole's space, glaring at him as Dole looked downward; Dole even stepped out of Clinton's way as Clinton roamed the stage. There is still an internal struggle, and it might be writ large in the body politic, though it seems, in this last election cycle, in a strange paradox that the presidential body was not at stake. Dole's ruined body crashed to the ground, easily symbolizing the failure of his candidacy; but nothing more. Clinton is large—the largest president since Taft—but his is not, despite his easy dominance of Dole's space, an imperial body, like Taft's or Teddy Roosevelt's or even, in its B movie form, Ronald Reagan's. Clinton's body is a soft, marshmallow-man body.

Ivan Reitman, who knows the marshmallow man, having directed *Ghostbusters* (1984), is also the director of *Dave* (1993), the first presidential film to appear during the Clinton presidency. This movie is once again about two bodies—a mean president and an imitator (the president's physical double) who assumes the presidency when the real president has a stroke. The text of *Dave* is extraordinarily rich in its alternating refusals and embraces of presidential power, sending the basic message that anyone can become president, not because it takes great skill but because ordinary people *are* what the office itself is about. The president is not an emperor, simply a personnel manager. What invests him with power is the goodwill of people. In an early scene in the film, when Dave first appears in public as the president, he walks down a long hotel lobby to the applause of the assembled citizens. As he walks between these people he grows in stature and confidence, gathering strength from their sanction, power from a mutual recognition. Before climbing into a limousine, Dave turns back to the crowd and shouts, "God bless you. God bless America!" The crowd erupts in cheers.

Dave brings the presidency back to earth, humanizes the president (much better than *The American President* does), and paradoxically sets up ID4's refusal of presidential sacrifice by unveiling a simulated sacrifice as a completion of its plot. The "real" president is in a coma in a secret basement hospital as the fake president fakes a stroke to provide a suitable closure on his term in office and to assure the succession to a decent vice president. You can't diminish the office more than that.

The sense of an alien invasion as external to the presidential body declines even further in ID4. The alien is fully outside the presidential body in this film. I suggest that the significance of the externalized body is to provide a transition in the principle of sovereignty away from the presidency as a receptacle of the two bodies of sovereignty. In President Whitmore's career path in the three days (from the Last Supper to the Resurrection) after the appearance of the aliens, we see a glimmer of a possibility (no more than that) of a refusal of the iconic alternative to presidential sacrifice, an abandonment of the pre-given terms of mass democracy by the destruction of the masses. This refusal occurs on two fronts. First, the aliens are not secret invaders but blatantly external, and they subvert our satellites only in encoding their destruction orders. Their appearance, though, shatters the Christological cosmology on which the principle of the King's Two Bodies originally rested. Why? Because the existence of alien intelligence signals both the death of God and God's replacement by an alien power, in this case a hostile one. This creates a major crisis in the presidency but also an opportunity to leave the office behind.

This leads to a second refusal. No longer bearing the burden of sovereignty, the president also no longer needs to engage in plausible deniability. Tragically, or conveniently, this lesson is learned too late for the first lady to survive. The first lady dies in this movie *because* she calls the president a liar. Her first words to him and her last contain the accusation. But, we might protest, she is being ironic. Well, yes; precisely. The irony holds the truth that what he is lying about is less consequential than the fact that he lies, and she knows it. Her accusation that he is a liar is ultimately an accusation that he lacks the confidence, the duplicity, to be a good president. As the truth teller, the destroyer of presidential confidence, she must die.

The president is relieved of the need to try to lie, to maintain confidence, when the White House is blown up by an alien death ray. (In a coordinated attack, the aliens destroy Washington, D.C., New York City, and Los Angeles, the political, financial, and cultural capitals of the country. Boston, which could signify the intellectual capital, is, not surprisingly, spared.) Then he is reduced to saying, "God help us all." He briefly, on July 3, early in the day, becomes nostalgic: "In the Gulf War," he says, "we knew what we had to do. It's not that simple anymore." But the movement toward the new solution is at hand. The end of a need to protect by lying—plausible deniability—leads the president to Area 51, the secret site of the dead alien body, the spacecraft, his own rendezvous with destiny. The president fulfills his compact by telepathic conversation with the alien, by an attempt to reinhabit two bodies, through the device of bonding with the alien. The alien uses the body of the scientist to speak, already one mediation away:

> *Alien (Dr. Okin):* Release me! Release me now!
> *President Whitmore:* I know there is much we can learn from each other if we can negotiate a truce. Can there be peace between us?
> *Alien:* No peace.
> *President Whitmore:* What do you want us to do?
> *Alien:* Die. Die!

At this point, the alien tries to kill the president telepathically, and the secret service shoots the alien. The president then says, "I saw his thoughts. I know their plans. Nuke 'em. Let's nuke the bastards."

The rest, as they say, is history. But it is a history not of presidential performance, despite the rallying speech, but of warriors. In a peculiar turn of events, an alcoholic Vietnam veteran, a widower father who neglects his kids and who has long believed that he has been a victim of alien abduction, is recruited for a desperate last attack on an alien ship; he dies as a reborn family man in a kamikaze attack. The attack is made possible by a computer virus that has rendered the alien defenses vulnerable; throughout the world, improvised air forces launch attacks on other ships, and the mother ship in outer space is blown up by a planted nuclear device. The world is united as it falls apart.

There is a peculiar individualism that reigns at the end of the world in this film. We have a species of individualism rendered bare, a postsovereign individual operating as a singularity. There are, however, great problems with such singularities. This postsovereign fight against massification parodies the Emersonian wish for self-reliance, by the most traditional of Hollywood means. The effect is eerie. There is little mourning over the death of millions of citizens, over the destruction of cities, over the loss of our political institutions, and a strange cheeriness energizes the characters as the movie comes to a close. The president communicates with the alien telepathically, but the substance of the communication is one of death, of destruction.

The lesson of such a film may be this: here, at the end of the world, the president should feel free to act like a president all he wants, just as long as he doesn't act as one. The consequences of serious presidential action are apocalyptic. The cheerfulness with which this message is rendered in a movie such as ID4 may insulate us from the horrific lesson of destruction and power at the end of the world, but its deeper message is that the polity a president is to reside over relies on him to act like a president and not as one. We are counting on the sturdiness of that distinction to hold up as we move to the next phase in the continuing process of constitutional amendation.

Epilogue: The Marshmallow Man

How might we read the presidential scandal of the day? Is Clinton acting *like* a president or *as* a president? In 1996, Clinton used his State of the Union message to remind us that the era of big government is over. Paralleling Nixon, the president whom he mirrors in so many ways, who in many ways was the last president of the New Deal era, Clinton may be considered the last president of the Right Republican era. Like Nixon, he is said by his enemies to have disgraced his office, diminished it by trivializing its most spiritual element, the dignity that is its most intangible but important quality.[27] Has Clinton somehow sought to shrink the presidency? If so, in seeking the diminishment of the office, Clinton might be said to have placed his presidency on a death-bound course. The sexual metaphors are blatant. We could ask: What death does Bill Clinton seek in his secret communications with the alien from Brentwood (Monica Lewinsky)? It is, as the French like to say, a little death. Perhaps Clinton's uncanny contribution to the diminishment of the structure of American sovereign power is his enthusiastic willingness to part with his vital fluids rather than preserve them and protect them, as Jack Ripper, the fictional general in Stanley Kubrick's *Dr. Strangelove* (1964), sought to do, to the point of beginning nuclear war. A shrinking presidency was tried before, but Jimmy Carter's timing was bad; and besides, Carter's confession of lust in his heart was sincerely made and felt—he wasn't *acting*. With his big ole' body in his easy way, in his empathetic corporeality, Clinton reverses the Reagan act at its most affective level.

At the climax of the movie *Ghostbusters*, the intrepid heroes are asked to choose the means of their destruction by the ancient Egyptian god of evil. They try to keep their minds blank, but eventually one of them, by accident, thinks of the most comforting image of his childhood—the Stay-Puff marshmallow man—and the final battle between good and evil is staged. This comedy suggests that there is an evil lurking in the sweetest and stickiest of banalities. Bill Clinton is the new marshmallow man, sticky and sweet, trying to rebuild the power of sovereignty, a new King's Two Bodies, through the most banal means possible. If we are fated to be joined with him, we will need to cultivate our senses of humor. Otherwise, we may end up presenting ourselves with new, less benign aliens acting *like* presidents, being tempted, always being tempted, to act *as* presidents.

But humor is in short supply.

7

Wild Things

I caught a glimpse of a woodchuck stealing across my path, and felt a
strange thrill of savage delight, and I was strongly tempted to seize and
devour him raw; not that I was hungry then, except for that wildness
which he represented. . . . I love the wild not less than the good.

— Henry David Thoreau, *Walden*

A Song Is Being Sung

In the spring of 1989, Jean Baudrillard attended a conference at the University of Montana in Missoula that was devoted to a wide-ranging exploration of his work and its cultural implications. After delivering the keynote lecture for the conference, he listened to a response by an American L-A-N-G-U-A-G-E poet and then editor of the *Socialist Review*, Ron Silliman. Silliman allegorized Baudrillard as "the drag queen of theory."[1] Misunderstanding Silliman's comments; or taking the compliment as too little, too late; or deciphering a deep insult that some of us missed; or suffering from an uncharacteristic failure of imagination, for some reason Baudrillard took offense. So on the last night of the conference, he snubbed Silliman by arriving late to a coffeehouse where the poet was giving a reading. (The reading consisted of one long poem about a day in San Francisco; I remember a description of a dumpster and some riders on a bus.)

Silliman's reading was the warm-up act for a performance by a fairly obscure but highly esteemed guitarist/performance artist named Eugene Chadbourne. Chadbourne had at one time been a member of a 1980s pseudo–New Wave, post-punk band called Camper Van Beethoven, whose best known song was "Take the Skinheads Bowling." After Silliman finished, but before Chadbourne began, Baudrillard sat down at a table where several participants in the conference were gathered with students and faculty from the Missoula community, drinking beer and enjoying ourselves. Baudrillard watched with the rest of us as Chadbourne began to play. He sat, placid, bored perhaps. The entertainment unfolded.

Chadbourne's performance was an example of post-punk picturesque at its finest. Overwrought, frenzied, humorous, playful, loud, and silly, he inhabited the role of clown with gusto, moving from old Spike Jones songs with updated lyrics about Barbara Bush and urban conflagration to homages/parodies of rock 'n' roll classics. In keeping with the high silly aesthetic of the performance, toward the end of the set Chadbourne unveiled an unusual instrument—a rusty old garden rake strung with guitar strings and with pickups attached to it, what he called his "electric rake." He began producing noise, feedback, strange chords, odd static. In his seat, Baudrillard smiled slightly. After several minutes in which he produced a whole lot of noise, Chadbourne, a heavyset man who at this point of the evening was sweating profusely, leaped off the stage, which was composed of low risers cobbled together in the tradition of temporary stages in modernist cafeteria utility spaces of student union buildings everywhere, and crawled under it. He barely fit and could not be seen by most of the audience, but some of the listeners were able to infer that he was somehow connecting the rake to the stage, that he was starting to play the stage itself. As this realization spread through the audience, the cheers and applause began and then intensified. There was more noise coming from that audience than there was from Chadbourne's amplifier; almost everyone was up, cheering, whistling, stomping feet, laughing, craning to get a better view, trying figure out what would happen next. Baudrillard continued to sit.

Then, suddenly, a familiar melody emerged from the speakers, simple, primitive, inevitable, based on the most common three-chord progression in rock 'n' roll music. Chadbourne was playing the one, four, five chord progression for either "Wild Thing" or "Louie, Louie" (which until the lyrics are sung are, for most discernable purposes, identical; the words "wild thing" being but two beats, versus the double time of the words "Lou-ie, Lou-ie," then set a singer on a slightly different path). As if with one voice the audience began to sing: "Wild Thing, you make my heart sing, you make everything groovy, Wild Thing." At this moment of audience participatory bliss, a look of uncomprehending panic crossed Baudrillard's face. The theorist (in)famous for his implacable stoicism in the face of the collapse of reality—the person who only two nights before had been urging an audience of Montana ranchers, hippie farmers, black-garbed graduate students, and avant-garde literary theorists to "drive (slowly) to a delirious point of view," in response to what he claimed to believe to be the fact of a world driving us to a delirious state of things—appeared to be resisting the trip to delirium.[2]

It seemed to me then, and it seems to me now, that this look of incomprehension betrayed Baudrillard's studied indifference, that the event somehow overcame his faith in a stoicism that he had imagined could match the depthless nihilism he had prophesied. In observing the enthusiastic response of these (allegedly) postmodern intellectuals, of an audience composed primarily of his assembled admirers, Baudrillard could not discern an answer—a really good answer—to some of the questions he himself had been posing for years about the paths that mutual recognition and attempted acknowledgment of others might take in an era when signals have come to be as important as, if not more important than, signs. The people composing this audience seemed possessed of a knowledge; they seemed somehow to know, with an irresistible intuition, that what was being played was one song instead of another. They anticipated the lyric that was emerging from under that stage—and they sang.

Why do I dwell on this moment? Baudrillard's reputation isn't what it was then, and my worries over his influence on an impressionable mind—namely, mine—have abated. His work doesn't inform most of the arguments I care the most about these days. So there must be other reasons I return to this moment, and this concluding chapter is an attempt to think about those reasons one more time, undoubtedly not the last time.

I am confident about the need to return to this particular thought, because it is implicated in the project of resistance I increasingly identify with the ordinary. In explorations of the ordinary, the question of method seems to engage inevitably the return of thinking to places where we can work through who and how we are in the world. To approach knowing in ways that evade sheer positivity without succumbing to blind faith, to move toward routes of acknowledgment, and to find them in the everyday—these issues might be raised in regard to this event. The questions that are come up at such places—junctures of skepticism—are uncomfortable, or perhaps, in Emerson's parlance, unhandsome. How does one separate oneself from the field of the ordinary that is inevitably a part of one's self? How does one reckon oneself as a self against important claims of identity that allow us to go on in the world and yet imprison us in falsities, on the one hand, and the void or the nothingness that awaits us all, on the other? Underwriting all our concerns about justice, fairness, and freedom, political theorists tend to whistle by the graveyard of meaninglessness and the questions that meaninglessness raises. We make noises about faith; we argue about the extent of rationality in discussions of justice; but underneath too much of our discussions, we are lost souls. With a sense of resignation, many of us become Rawlsians or Habermasians, submitting to church, law, or other powers, hoping that some variation on the Kantian bid for a freedom achieved through surrender might at least assuage the nightmare of nihilism. But when we return to the ordinary, we find that all our pretense has not dispelled the question: Why exist?

Each and every day we return to this question. It is in keeping with the aspirations of the ordinary to do so. And to do so, we have a practice of theorizing available to us. It is not a practice that has been followed by Baudrillard, though he has kept this important question visible and open during a time when it might have been easier not to do so. I have had trouble with Baudrillard's thought in the past; I have thought his provocations to be shallow, unserious in a dead-end kind of way, superficial, but, most important for me, uninspirational, not helping me breathe—in fact, suffocating to my aspirations to think about what it means to lead a democratic life. If one argues that the role of theory is to inspire, to help us breathe, to inspirit us as we turn to the task of thinking and as we turn away from it, then someone like Baudrillard isn't likely to be of much help. But then again, neither is Jürgen Habermas or John Rawls (at least not for me). But Baudrillard's simulated indifference, as far as I can tell, has in the long run not helped the project of inspiration and has done something instead to steer people toward a strange indifference over the very fate of breathing. Worse, his identification as an avatar of postmodernism has made it easier for conservatives of the Left and the Right, those who are invested in the contests of the present hegemony that they share with one another (how many times is the liberalism-communitarianism debate going to be repackaged anyway?), to dismiss what some of the rest of us in the world of thinking find vitally important in popular culture and its expression of ordinary aspirations. So I've had it in for Baudrillard for some time.

But I have a problem. Some of my friends have always thought highly of Baudrillard, in a way that is familiar to me and that makes me admire them. I try to follow a rule of conduct in thinking about thinkers. Once I come to know a contemporary thinker well enough, I try to be steadfast in my regard for that thinker, through the predictable cycles of their reputational rise and fall and reconsideration. Indeed, ill-considered attacks on some of them have often made them more worthy in my mind. My affinities with other writers are usually strengthened if I can note that they exercise this sort of loyalty, not through blind submission to mastery but through a cheerful insistence on the worth of a thought carried by someone. Baudrillard has been a lucky thinker in that regard, because he has had William Chaloupka as a cheerful defender. My friendship with Bill Chaloupka was a large part of why I was in Missoula in the first place. He was hosting this conference, and it seemed that this was one way I was going to get to visit him, then a new friend (and still a friend, not so new).

In retrospect, I can see more clearly the condition of our friendship then. At the time, the maneuvering between the passions of friendship and a sense of responsibility versus my too often mean insistence on criticizing and de-mystifying arguments that seemed deeply wrong to me, especially by deflating what I would judge to be the pretentious claims of those who had become complacent in their thought (in their despair), worked to create some very unhappy scenes and required great tolerance on Bill's part. I knew I sometimes acted like a jerk, so I was in an odd position that evening. I wanted to think about the failings of Baudrillard in a way that wouldn't do the sort of damage to such friendships that I imagined my usual jerkiness might do. Some people might call this a lesson in growing up. But I am not sure what is learned in that kind of growing, especially since it seems to involve a growth into silence.

Do such issues of manners, or what might be called the substantive etiquette of friendship, matter in this larger scheme of intellectual struggle? One might ask more pointedly: Is the truth of things immune from reflections on friendship and performance that might be deflected or muted or heightened or amplified, depending on the passions one carries with one? Political theory is performed by political theorists, after all. We teach each other, we learn from each other, and we hurt each other, even in the strange empire of imagination. Ten years later, I still wonder what is right and what is wrong in this regard.

But I would still make a claim—against my friend Bill, against another friend (who had been trying to warn me against my jerkiness by praising it), against yet other friends gathered that spring evening in the mountains—that Baudrillard failed to be a wild thing that night. Others did not. I want to think about why that might be the case, and why it might be important to approach some errant understanding of what happened that night in Missoula, Montana, to speculate about that unbidden yet determined moment of singing, the expression of a common sense in the face of the always recurring collapse of meaning—especially the one that was supposed to have been occurring sometime around 1989.

Mediated Uncanniness, Elective Affinities

My claim from memory is that the audience knew that the song was "Wild Thing"; that they started singing that song; that the cues given to sing were ambiguous; that they were instead embedded in a complicated set of collective memories that variously informed individual members of the audience as they participated in the comedy staged by Chadbourne. Would it make a difference in my claim if I misremembered, that is, if there were cues directly given to that audience by the performer, if Chadbourne himself had started the singing? Only that I would then refer the question to him—to his own intuition, to what he thought he might know or infer about the audience, to his acknowledgment of their part in his performance, to his role as entertainer, to what he did not know about what he said and sang. Chadbourne would not be standing in for the collective sense of the room but pursuing his historically contingent, loosely situated position as singer. His performance is what that led us to that moment of song, and we were following him, we were following his spontaneity, as he was by then following us in our spontaneity, like Walt Whitman and America. The relationship of the performer to audience plays out this way in improvisation, and Chadbourne was improvising that night.

Why did we sing "Wild Thing" instead of "Louie, Louie"? Why does it matter at all? That one song might have been sung instead of the other and that it could have been "Louie, Louie" as easily as "Wild Thing" might be the case. But the fact is that "Wild Thing" was the song that was sung. Was there a conspiracy operating here; was there a Pynchonian logic to the singing of that song; was something systemic going down that night? How did we, Chadbourne and the rest of us, come to sing this song and not that one?

The explanations are alternative, multiple, and non-exclusive. Here is one. A popular logic of association, a kind of paralogy, was doing its work that evening. Chadbourne began his set with an adaptation of an old Spike Jones song, "Fhhhpp in der Fürher's Face," for which he dressed in drag as Barbara Bush. His earlier performance established an associational clue that prepared the audience to sing "Wild Thing" instead of "Louie, Louie." For while "Louie, Louie" never inspired a popular political parody, in the winter of 1967/68 a satirical cover of the Troggs' hit song "Wild Thing" swept the AM airwaves of the United States, with a comedic imitator of Senator Robert Kennedy performing a stuttering reading of the song in a Kennedy accent, speaking the lyrics over the music. The embedded memory of this earlier song may have triggered associations for at least a couple of people in that audience, and once they began to sing, the rest may have gone along in a happy recognition of the appropriateness of the song as a fitting finish to the evening.

The song "Wild Thing" is an esteemed artifact of rock 'n' roll history. It was written by Chip Taylor and originally recorded by Jordan Christopher and the Wild Ones. In 1966 it was covered by the Troggs and became a major hit, spawning the parody "Wilder Thing (with Senator Bobby)" recorded by the Hardly-Worthit Players, who produced an entire album of such covers, called *Boston Soul* (Philadelphia: Tames-Parkway Records, 1967). "Wild Thing" was also covered later that year at the Monterey Pop Festival, by an until then (relatively) unknown American guitarist and singer living in England named Jimi Hendrix, who, on being recommended to the organizers of the festival by Paul McCartney, returned from exile to give a performance of the song that is now a legendary moment in rock 'n' roll history and is often considered the definitive performance of it.[3] This song, then, may have had deep associations for some members of the audience, who under the influence of beer, nostalgia, and the slightly sweet smell of something either recalled or didn't but nonetheless responded to a provocation and when faced with the music, when faced with this past, when faced with this unexpected scene of happy silliness and a crescendo of joyful noise, offered up the lyric of "Wild Thing," a positive response to music, past, silliness, and noise.

There is yet another, more local reason for the singing of this song. When compared to "Louie, Louie," itself one of the most covered songs in the history of rock 'n' roll music, "Wild Thing" would have a greater appeal to an audience composed of English Ph.D. candidates, political theorists, and cultural studies mavens. Why? Because in the United States the ranks of the humanities professorate are generally composed of people who, as students, have shunned or been shunned by the dominant campus cultures of fraternity life. "Louie, Louie" has been legendarily connected through the most obvious of film iconography to fraternity life in America. The popular comedy of 1978 *National Lampoon's Animal House*, in which a drunken, toga-clad slob, played to perfection by John Belushi, leads his fellow slobs in choruses of the song, is exemplary of a kind of drunken excess that this audience may not have viewed as being resonant with their own (now hidden) utopian aspirations. Indeed, at a base level, the beery associations of "Louie, Louie" with a transcultural politics of misogynistic violence, the cult and culture of the brownshirts,[4] would have been anathema to the deeper aspirations of this crowd of men and women in black. In the contest of Eros versus Thanatos, "Wild Thing" stands for sex and "Louie, Louie" for beer.

Here is another explanation: the lyrics of "Wild Thing" inspired the audience to respond to Baudrillard's injunction to drive slowly to a delirious point of view. Each verse intensifies the feelings the narrator of the song has for his wild thing. He wants, he needs, he loves, in each successive verse, in a slowly building crescendo of desire. Perhaps it was a spontaneous acknowledgment by his disciples and admirers of Baudrillard's better self, the sensibility that guided him some years later to perform a nightclub act in a casino in Nevada. What Baudrillard's sympathetic interlocutors might have hoped he wanted could go by the name of Wild Thing. In the most generous reading of intent, Baudrillard's Wild Thing could be connected, at the only American university with a mountain on its campus, with the democratic experience of (con)fronting nature.

At this point Henry David Thoreau might be offered into conversation. His deeply *serious* resignation from the unnecessary presents at the very least an anticipation and an overcoming of a sensibility of Baudrillardian nihilism.[5] Thoreau insisted that the tropes through which we are invested in ourselves also allow us to return to society, to lead new lives, born again after crises of meaninglessness, making our mark in response to but slightly beyond the skepticism that is engendered by the losses we incur every day. Thoreau's nature, as Jane Bennett has illuminated it, presents the conditions of uncertainty necessary for the development of an art of self appropriate to democratic politics.[6] Thoreau knew wildness well enough to love it, to recognize its depthless indifference to the fate of any one of its representatives, including us and errant woodchucks. He knew this indifference as an essential element of human being. Thoreau would not scorn "Wild Thing" but sing it in his own way. We might ask, in retrospect of the event and inspired by Thoreau, how we are to (con)front nature when we are in the Rocky Mountains, only to discover that nature here is as it is everywhere else, a figment of the imagination that continually has the most profound effects on us because of its unknowable character. We gathered in Missoula—"Baudrillard in the Mountains" was the advertisement, the call for papers, the conference title—to hear a lecture on the death of nature, among other things. Baudrillard delivered, and then, on the final night of the conference, it may be said that Baudrillard took it back, refused to play, refused this unbidden gift. The point of turning had been reached, and Baudrillard turned away.

At very least, the hearty unpredictability, the historically contingent accidents of association that make up the democratic aesthetics of such an event, were on display that night in Missoula, and it may have frightened Baudrillard. Maybe, when faced with such a display of free association, he couldn't *handle* the truth (to paraphrase Jack Nicholson in one of his more delightfully cheesy film roles).[7] If this is so, his next step was at that moment prescribed by his own thinking: seek the comfort of a blank emptiness, evade and avoid the lively and frightening unpredictability of the dance.

As millennium approaches, Baudrillard himself seems a distant memory to many, firmly a part of a decade of speculative theory at its seeming worst, a charlatan who failed to live up to his own public image in the end and disappear. Baudrillard recently performed, wearing a gold lamé jacket, in a Nevada casino.[8] In the face of his terror he still seeks the secret of America (which is yet another example of a wanton courage). But by turning away from the signs of life that are right in front of him, he cannot hear the singing that surrounds him. This deafness is not a result of "foreignness," though foreignness can be the excuse for it. It is not overcome simply by turning up the volume (like an American yelling at a Japanese tourist, believing that by speaking more loudly he will be better understood). Instead, to hear the singing we are required to listen more closely, with a greater care and attention to the nuances of each message that comes to us, the overlay, the implicit tones, the careless play of puns and associations that informs the music of the ordinary.

It could have happened that way, that night in Missoula; and the truth is that we do not know what the final truth is. Can we handle that? "Wild Thing" was sung, not "Louie, Louie." We might call this phenomenon mediated uncanniness. It is hardly the concatenation of coincidence, but it is a category of event becoming subject to intensive explorations in cultural studies, with sometimes powerfully disturbing results.[9] What are we to name the combination of recalled cultural effluvia and reflexive response to unexpected situations, the forums for the staging of events that inform these moments of public life? How are they more than mechanical responses prefigured in the affirmative culture of commodification that seems, in retrospect, to have been the postmodern moment? How do such responses inspire more than mechanical reactions to the style of the moment?

These are questions that might be asked in a politics of the ordinary. The varying explanations for the reception to the song "Wild Thing" I present above suggest that the habitations of language that we construct and that bear us enable us both to negotiate between the ordinary and the event and to reflect on their interplay. Of course, they can do no more than that; but the direction of the suggestion of a politics of the ordinary is toward the wildness of language itself, its strangeness in its familiarity. This wildness, this contingency, this inclination toward what Emerson might have called an intuitive reception, is a part of the play of the ordinary. It is a rededication to the ordinary, akin to what Stanley Cavell refers to as a resistance to the dictation of others, giving it the form of Emersonian self-reliance,[10] and it requires a particular valorization of ordinary experiences, an attempt to emphasize the powers of experience while avoiding the temptation to make experience into a force for normalizing the ordinary.

Democratic Sentences, Democratic Songs

Why shouldn't the representation of everyday life hold our interest as intensely as Thoreau may have wanted to hold that woodchuck in his teeth? What does it mean for the study of politics that so much of what is written about it in scholarly journals is basically unreadable, and hence unread? What is unreadability? Is it a question of difficulty? No, what is problematic in our discussions of politics is the lack of difficulty to be found in most of what is written and thought. For instance: "Policies that provide alternative opportunities for those caught in dysfunctional networks are as important as those that stimulate and encourage positive networks."[11] This sentence seems to mean: "Getting people out of bad situations is as important as putting them in good ones." What stops the author from making this simple observation is not what is usually, and accusatorily, called jargon. Every word ever written is jargon to somebody else. What stops her is instead the need to hide the obvious so as to obscure the difficult insight, namely, that the obvious is not so obvious after all. The relentless positivity of the style of science demands that everything be knowable in a particular way. To ensure that everything is knowable, the science of politics never leaves the firm ground of what is always already known. This is the old problem of behavioralism, and it is revisited in the rational choice theory of the present, which demands of its practitioners only that they not leave the ground of the knowable and the known. What is already known, however, is dead. In this sense, Baudrillard's observation "For ethnology to live, its object must die" is apt, possibly his best aphorism.[12]

The critique of objectivity in the social sciences, which for at least a fragment of the last generation of scholars won its champions a space in which to explore the qualitative substance of arguments, has been largely forgotten by a new generation of thinkers who have lost (or squandered) that space once won, for lack of sensing better what to do with it. To paraphrase Emerson, we have instead succumbed to the temptation to submit to the more prosaic slavery of books. But as Emerson reminds us, "Books are for the scholar's idle times."[13] Of course, there is a trick in this question; for when is the scholar idle? What are the conditions of our idleness? There are moments when we are not thinking, when we are not singing, when we are not writing books for the next generation to read, and when our work is so concerned with knowledge that we fail to acknowledge the limits of what we can say to each other. Can we afford to waste the opportunity that may once again open up for us? Are we ever even to try to realize ourselves philosophically and politically, as democrats? Or must we count our meaningful sentences on the fingers of a single grasping hand and turn away in quiet desperation?

Who in the world of letters is writing the books for the next generation to read? Who is marking the experience of the present? I do not think to look to those who insist on deriving the rules of morality from timeless principles, nor to those who fight endlessly and exhaustively over small differences in the meanings of words, sentences, and paragraphs. Too many scholars are not equipped to do better than regurgitate a partial and illusory past or repeat an endless present. But there are others who try to write criticism that lights fires; who attempt to conjure specters; who seek out the contest of tears; who show us how to make trouble, celebrate minority experiences, and pluralize differences.[14] These scholars, among others, provide us with guides for looking at the present and seeing it not as dead reckonings but as mobile armies of metaphors, mysterious and powerful forces that must be acknowledged. These scholars, among others, suggest that the rigors of vision should not slip into rigidity but that we instead ought to be prepared to be surprised by what we see. All of them, in ways direct and obscure, help us prepare for an engagement with a politics of the ordinary. In their own ways, these scholars, who struggle on the boundary line between what is experienced and what is known, sense that the ordinary does not come cheap, that the claims we make concerning it must be approached with extraordinary delicacy and care, and that the overwhelming sense of loss that could swamp us when we approach its unknowable vastness must be converted to a cheerful engagement and resolution to amend our selves and hence our fortunes. In the face of events, on the one side, and the normalization of vast tracts of life, on the other, the repository of the unknowable and indefinitely open ordinary is an imaginary site where we might dream democratically.

This list of concerns and names is amendable, expandable, and contestable. Like any list, it marks certain kinds of engagements as inspirations for thinking, and in these cases the thinking may prepare us for singing. Such engagements, such thinking that prepares us for singing, may in turn guide us toward yet other ways of writing, inscribing our experiences with the aim of opening some possibilities for an imaginative rethinking of what, for lack of a better term, we still might call the human condition. Rising above and sinking below the threshold of method, this writing turns, always incompletely—blessedly incompletely—toward the possibility of reconnecting currents of poetry and philosophy, making better the love that we might have for both.

We return to the nocturnal by way of the diurnal and greet the sun by being fully awake before it rises. Sometimes that may mean staying up all night in order to say good morning. Wild thing, you make my heart sing.

Notes

NOTES TO THE INTRODUCTION

1. This benchmark is hardly an uncontroverted one, but the historiographical controversy concerning the meaning of happiness among eighteenth-century political thinkers—the Enlightenment optimism concerning its measurability weighed against its potentially ineffable character—echoes the controversies concerning the relationship of the ordinary to political matters contemporarily. On the disputed meaning of the word *happiness* in the Declaration of Independence, see Garry Wills, *Inventing America: Jefferson's Declaration of Independence* (New York: Random House, 1978), 249–255.

2. For a study of this theme, see Stanley Cavell, *Pursuits of Happiness: The Hollywood Comedy of Remarriage* (Cambridge: Harvard University Press, 1981).

3. The relationship of common sense to the ordinary can be pursued through Immanuel Kant's transcendental philosophy. This is a controversial pursuit. For a compelling critique of this common sense, see Gilles Deleuze, *Difference and Repetition*, trans. Paul Patton (New York: Columbia University Press, 1994), 31–37. The sense of the ordinary I pursue here is one that attempts to resist the orthodoxy that results in an image of truth that is upright or straight, the unity of other faculties. I believe there is warrant for a different kind of common sense provided by a particular reading of Emerson, Thoreau, and Cavell, and I hope to demonstrate, rather than argue, this point as this book unfolds.

4. See Austin Sarat and Thomas Kearns, "Editorial Introduction," in *Law in Everyday Life*, ed. Austin Sarat and Thomas Kearns (Ann Arbor: University of Michigan Press, 1993). While commenting on theorizations of the "life-world" that advance the claim that everyday life is somehow pre-theoretical, a backdrop for more thematized elements of life, such as politics, they ask a question that is a good starting point for any discussion of the ordinary: "In the face of these claims one might ask whether any inquiry into everyday life is not, at best, a vain effort to rescue being from becoming, the past from the future" (5). The intimate relationship of what they call everyday life, and what I call the ordinary, to politics is the subject of this book.

5. Here I am troping the ordinary as feminine—as mysterious, hidden, penetrated by other forces, disciplined, fecund, a primal source of renewal and creativity.

Does it matter that I do so self-consciously? As with the question of the feminine itself, the question of intentionality is a becoming subject to explore. Moreover, the tropological character of the ordinary is explicitly a subject of some of those whose writing will inform much of this book, especially Thoreau and Emerson. For a recent exploration of the tropological as an important theme in intentionality, see Judith Butler, *The Psychic Life of Power: Theories in Subjection* (Stanford: Stanford University Press, 1997).

6. Hannah Arendt, *The Human Condition* (Chicago: University of Chicago Press, 1958).

7. See Dana Villa, *Arendt and Heidegger: The Fate of the Political* (Princeton: Princeton University Press, 1996), 206.

8. Gilles Deleuze and Félix Guattari, *A Thousand Plateaus*, trans. Brian Massumi (Minneapolis: University of Minnesota Press, 1987).

9. This phrase is borrowed, on her suggestion, from Jane Bennett.

10. Quite useful as a response to a parallel canonical elitism is Lauren Berlant's response to those who accuse her of cheapening literary analysis by focusing on what she calls "silly" objects, such as episodes of the cartoon show *The Simpsons*. See Lauren Berlant, *The Queen of America Goes to Washington City: Essays on Sex and Citizenship* (Durham: Duke University Press, 1997), 11–15.

11. Allan Bloom, *The Closing of the American Mind* (New York: Simon & Schuster, 1987).

12. See the *Compact Oxford English Dictionary*, new ed. (Oxford: Oxford University Press, 1987), 1446.

13. Max Weber, *Economy and Society*, ed. Gunther Roth and Claus Wittich (Berkeley: University of California Press, 1978). Weber suggests that "sociology seeks to formulate type concepts and generalized uniformities of empirical processes. This distinguishes it from history, which is oriented to the causal analysis and explanation of individual actions, structures, and personalities possessing cultural significance" (19). The use of proof through exemplification suggests that neither the sociological nor the historical is adequate to the discussion of the ordinary. For more discussion of the question of historical analysis, see chapter 1's discussion of Stanley Cavell and Paul Ricoeur.

14. On the idea of being surprised by things, see the seminar following "What Did Derrida Want of Austin?" in Stanley Cavell, *Philosophical Passages: Wittgenstein, Emerson, Austin, Derrida* (Oxford: Blackwell Publishers, 1995), 80–81.

15. The notion of "live metaphor" is deployed usefully by Lauren Berlant in *Queen of America*, 60.

16. See Thomas L. Dumm, *united states* (Ithaca: Cornell University Press, 1994).

17. See Richard Rorty, "The Unpatriotic Left," *New York Times*, February 13, 1994, sec. E, 15. Rorty invokes the memory of Ralph Waldo Emerson, among others, in the name of national patriotism—an invocation I find myself at odds with,

down to his notion that "The American Scholar" is an essay filled with "joyous self-confidence." That reading seems to me extraordinarily misleading. Emerson's self-confidence was attached not to his thoughts on the state or prospects of American scholarship but to the hope that scholarship might amount to something other than what it was. Rorty has recently published a book-length fulmination on the same topic: *Achieving Our Country: Leftist Thought in Twentieth Century America* (Cambridge: Harvard University Press, 1998).

18. See the *Compact Oxford English Dictionary*, 1288.

NOTES TO CHAPTER 1

1. For a more sharply observed sense of this place, see Brenda Bright, "Heart Like a Car," *American Ethnologist* (November 1998). Much of the background information in this section is a result of the experience of my having lived in Chimayo, New Mexico, during the summer of 1990. To see a lowrider from Chimayo, one can visit the Smithsonian Institution's Museum of American History, where a lowrider called Dave's Dream is on permanent display.

2. See Hannah Arendt, *The Human Condition* (Chicago: University of Chicago Press, 1958), chap. 3, "Labor."

3. Gille Deleuze, "Preface to the French Edition," in *Essays, Critical and Clinical*, trans. Daniel W. Smith and Michael A. Greco (Minneapolis: University of Minnesota Press, 1997), lv.

4. Jean-Luc Nancy, *The Sense of the World*, trans. Jeffrey Librett (Minneapolis: University of Minnesota Press, 1997), 14.

5. Primo Levi, *Survival in Auschwitz*, trans. Stuart Woolf, with an afterword by Primo Levi and Philip Roth (New York: Macmillan, 1986; originally published 1958), 76.

6. Thanks to Larry George, who coined this phrase while driving the streets of West Los Angeles, serving as a tour guide during the spring of 1997.

7. William Connolly, *Politics and Ambiguity* (Madison: University of Wisconsin Press, 1987), 149–150.

8. Perhaps this claim is mistaken. I think here of the argument developed by John Berger in the first book of his trilogy, *Into Their Labors*; see *Pig Earth* (New York: Pantheon, 1979). That description of peasant life is at great variance with the frontier experience of families, members of whom often went mad as a consequence of isolation. But the frontier experience is hardly the same as that of a peasantry.

9. Robert D. Richardson, Jr., *Henry Thoreau: A Life of the Mind* (Berkeley: University of California Press, 1986), 389.

10. Such a project follows on a particular interpretation of some of the work of Michel Foucault. See Thomas L. Dumm, *Michel Foucault and the Politics of Freedom* (Newbury Park: Sage Publications, 1996).

11. I am referring to William E. Connolly, *The Ethos of Pluralization* (Minneapolis: University of Minnesota Press, 1995).

12. This insight has been pursued with great clarity and vigor by Anne Norton. See her *Republic of Signs* (Chicago: University of Chicago Press, 1993).

13. For more details on the question of the relationship between democracy and resistance, see Claude LeFort, *Democracy and Political Theory*, trans. David Macey (Minneapolis: University of Minnesota Press, 1988); and Sheldon Wolin, "Fugitive Democracy," in *Democracy and Difference*, ed. Seyla Benhabib (Princeton: Princeton University Press, 1995). The idea of resistance as a form of politics has its most prominent contemporary advocacy in the work of Michel Foucault; see, especially, "Two Lectures," in *Power/Knowledge*, ed. Colin Gordon (New York: Pantheon, 1977).

14. Foucault has convincingly advanced this claim; see *Technologies of the Self: A Seminar with Michel Foucault* (Amherst: University of Massachusetts Press, 1988), 35.

15. James Madison, "Federalist No. 10," in James Madison, Alexander Hamilton, and John Jay, *The Federalist Papers*, ed. Clinton Rossiter (New York: New American Library, 1961), 78: "Liberty is to faction what air is to fire, an aliment without which it instantly expires."

16. See Paul Ricoeur, *Time and Narrative*, trans. Kathleen McLaughlin and David Pellauer (Chicago: University of Chicago Press, 1984).

17. Stanley Cavell, "The Ordinary as the Uneventful," in *Themes out of School: Effects and Causes* (Chicago: University of Chicago Press, 1988; originally published in San Francisco: North Point Press, 1984), 189.

18. Ibid., 191.

19. Ibid., 192–193.

20. See Stanley Cavell, *Conditions Handsome and Unhandsome: The Constitution of Emersonian Perfectionism* (Chicago: University of Chicago Press, 1990), 38–39. Here Cavell notes how the idea of grasping operates in Emerson (and Heidegger) as a metaphor for the kind of thinking that blocks a path to truth. The relationship of thinking to handsomeness follows.

21. Ibid., 39. If this argument sounds like Heidegger, it is because this insight comes from Cavell's reading of Heidegger's *What Is Called Thinking?*

22. Cavell, "The Ordinary as the Uneventful," 193. In his lecture Cavell suggests that this passage is in Emerson's *Nature*. It appears in "The American Scholar." See Ralph Waldo Emerson, *Essays and Lectures*, ed. Joel Porte (New York: Library of America, 1983), 68–69.

23. See, especially, Michel Foucault, *Discipline and Punish: The Birth of the Prison*, trans. Alan Sheridan (New York: Pantheon, 1977).

24. On anonymity, see Michel Foucault, "Maurice Blanchot: The Thought from Outside," in *Foucault/Blanchot* (New York: ZONE Books, 1988). Also see

Alexander Hooke, "The Order of Others: Is Foucault's Anti-Humanism against Human Action?" *Political Theory* 15, 1 (February 1987), 38–60.

25. Foucault, *Discipline and Punish*, 296.

26. Of William Connolly's recent work that undertakes to enunciate a democratic ethos, see, especially, *Identity\Difference: Democratic Negotiations of Political Paradox* (Ithaca: Cornell University Press, 1992); and *Ethos of Pluralization*.

27. On the idea of the new enclosures, see Thomas L. Dumm, *united states* (Ithaca: Cornell University Press, 1994), chap. 4, "Rodney King, or the New Enclosures."

28. I use the term *troubled* in a sense akin to that which Judith Butler suggests in *Gender Trouble: Feminism and the Subversion of Identity* (New York: Routledge, 1990), 1–2.

29. Emerson, "Fate," in *The Conduct of Life*, in *Essays and Lectures*, 962.

30. See Stanley Cavell, "Emerson's Constitutional Amending: Reading 'Fate,'" in *Philosophical Passages: Wittgenstein, Emerson, Austin, Derrida* (Oxford: Blackwell Publishers, 1995), 12–41.

31. Emerson, "Fate," 954; and Cavell, "Emerson's Constitutional Amending," 25. The full passage of Emerson that Cavell is working with here is as follows:

For if Fate is so prevailing, man also is a part of it, and confronts fate with fate. If the Universe have these savage accidents, our atoms are as savage in resistance. We should be crushed by the atmosphere, but for the reaction of the air within the body. A tube made of a film of glass can resist the shock of the ocean, if filled with the same water. If there be omnipotence in the stroke, there is omnipotence of recoil.

32. Emerson, "Fate," 954–955.

33. Ibid., 944.

34. Ibid., 946.

35. Foucault, *Discipline and Punish*, 30.

36. Cavell, "Emerson's Constitutional Amending," 14.

37. Stanley Cavell, *"This New yet Unapproachable America": Lectures after Emerson after Wittgenstein* (Albuquerque: Living Batch Press, 1989), 3.

38. Cornel West, *The American Evasion of Philosophy: A Genealogy of Pragmatism* (Madison: University of Wisconsin Press, 1989), especially 28–35, "Emerson on Personality (and Race)." See also Christopher Newfield, *The Emerson Effect: Individualism and Submission in America* (Chicago: University of Chicago Press, 1996), 187–200.

39. Emerson, "Race," in *English Traits,* in *Essays and Lectures*, 794.

40. One might suggest first that racism is itself only enabled by philosophy, as shocking as this idea may seem. Racism is, after all, a kind of knowledge. Many Enlightenment claims of truth developed out of natural philosophy, as it was once called, and are investigations into the supposed racial characteristics of different

human beings. But in contemporary times, most of those earlier claims having been refuted through the methods of science that gave rise to their prominence in the first place, the associational arguments that scientific racists use rise not from concern about the ordinary but the normal. For an example of contemporary racist philosophy in this degraded Enlightenment tradition, see James Q. Wilson and Richard Herrnstein, *Crime and Human Nature* (New York: Simon & Schuster, 1985). For an analysis of their work and its impact on contemporary racism in the United States, see Dumm, *united states*, chap. 4, "Rodney King, or the New Enclosures."

41. The persistence of institutional attempts to impose inequality needs to be persistently traced. Two recent examples of excellent work in this tracing are Melvin Oliver and Thomas Shapiro, *Black Wealth, White Wealth* (New York: Routledge, 1995), which shows how present governmental policies and their implementation have favored white accumulation of economic resources over and against black accumulation of such resources; and Benjamin DeMott, *The Trouble with Friendship* (New York: Times Books, 1996), which analyzes how racial differences are covered up culturally through the valorization of friendship.

42. Cavell, "Emerson's Constitutional Amending." Cavell writes, "From at least as early as 'Self-Reliance' Emerson identifies his writing, what I am calling his philosophical authorship, as the drafting of the nation's constitution; or I have come to say, as amending our constitution. When he says that, 'No law can be sacred to me but that of my nature,' he is saying no more than Kant had said—that, in a phrase from 'Fate,' 'We are law-givers,' namely to the world of conditions and of objects, and to ourselves in the world of the unconditioned and of freedom. But the next sentence of 'Self-Reliance' takes another step: 'Good and bad are but names readily transferable to that or this; the only right is what is after my constitution; the only wrong what is against it.' (The anticipation of Nietzsche's genealogy of morals is no accident.) Such a remark seems uniformly to be understood by Emerson's readers so that 'my constitution' refers to Emerson's personal, peculiar physiology and to be the expression of his incessant promotion of the individual over the social. Such an understanding refuses the complexity of the Emersonian theme instanced in his saying that we are now 'bugs, spawn,' which means simultaneously that we exist neither as individual human beings nor as human nations" (34).

43. This distinction is rendered in Nietzsche's aphorism concerning the origin of our concept of "knowledge" in *The Gay Science*, trans. Walter Kauffman (New York: Vintage Books, 1974), no. 355: "What do they want when they want 'knowledge'? Nothing more than this: Something strange is to be reduced to something *familiar*."

44. Cavell, "Emerson's Constitutional Amending," 36.

45. Emerson, "Self-Reliance," in *Essays and Lectures*, 259.

46. George Kateb sees Emerson's intervention into the debate concerning slavery as an exception to his philosophical stance concerning self-reliance, but I think

Cavell's understanding of this passage in "Self-Reliance" requires seeing Emerson as consistent in this case. Much hinges on how one assesses what Emerson means by the return of one's thoughts. See George Kateb, *Emerson and Self-Reliance* (Thousand Oaks: Sage Publications, 1995), 187. Referring to Emerson's support of the North in the Civil War, Kateb writes, "Emerson's moral commitments silence his existential passions." The use of the term *silence* as a technique of overriding, as a matter of suspending, is a concern shared by Cavell and Kateb. Moreover, both Cavell and Kateb do not see self-reliance as submission in the sense advanced by Christopher Newfield; see Newfield, *The Emerson Effect.*

47. Cavell, "Emerson's Constitutional Amending," 36.

48. Ibid., 37.

49. Ibid., 38.

50. It is worthy of note that this question of silence is important for Foucault for similar reasons. In "L'Ordre du discours" (translated as "The Discourse on Language"), his inaugural lecture at Collège de France, he asked, "What is so perilous, then, in the fact that people speak, and that their speech proliferates? Where is the danger in that?" See Michel Foucault, *The Archaeology of Knowledge and the Discourse on Language* (San Francisco: Harper & Row, 1972), 216.

51. Ludwig Wittgenstein, *Tractatus Logico-Philosophicus,* trans. D. F. Pears and B. F. McGuinness (Atlantic Highlands, NJ: Humanities Press, 1961), 74 (proposition 7).

52. Stanley Cavell, "Philosophy and the Arrogation of Voice," in *A Pitch of Philosophy: Autobiographical Exercises* (Cambridge: Harvard University Press, 1994), 16.

53. Cavell, "Emerson's Constitutional Amending," 39.

54. The question of silence in regard to Heidegger and the separation of philosophy and politics became the theme of discussion at a roundtable held at Amherst College in November 1995, to discuss a book on the relationship of Heidegger to Hannah Arendt in the wake of the publication of Elzbieta Ettinger's sensationalist study *Arendt /Heidegger* (New Haven: Yale University Press, 1995). The participants on the roundtable included Dana Villa, Bonnie Honig, and George Kateb. I am grateful to all of them for their thoughts on that occasion.

55. The will to self-justification doesn't simply haunt the bourgeois imagination on display in programs such as *Murder, She Wrote.* The most common way in which murders are solved in the United States (other than through straight confession) is through third parties who report the self-admission of the murderer. See Jack Katz, *The Seductions of Crime* (New York: Basic Books, 1989).

56. This point is made most directly and powerfully by Michel Foucault in *The History of Sexuality,* vol. 1: *The Will to Truth,* trans. Alan Sheridan (New York: Pantheon, 1979).

57. Jane Bennett, *Thoreau's Nature: Ethics, Politics, and the Wild* (Thousand Oaks: Sage Publications, 1994), 59.

58. For an analysis of this new fundamentalist impulse, see Connolly, *Ethos of Pluralization*, "Fundamentalism in America," 105–133. For an example of this fundamentalism at work, see "Symposium: The End of Democracy: The Judicial Usurpation of Politics," *First Things*, no. 67 (November 1996), with contributions by Robert H. Bork, Russell Hittinger, Hadley Arkes, Charles W. Colson, and Robert P. George, 18–42. This symposium has been widely commented on as a sign of a deep schism in the American Right. For a set of responses to this symposium, see *Theory and Event* 1, 2 (April 1997), at http://muse.jhu.edu/journals/tae.

59. This "secret" nihilism isn't really so secret. The idea that Leo Strauss and his followers are aristocratic Nietzscheans, publicly calling for civic virtue for the herd while preserving for themselves the privilege of dictating the conventions of morality from a stance beyond good and evil, has most directly been pointed out by Shadia Drury, *The Political Ideas of Leo Strauss* (New York: St. Martin's Press, 1990).

60. Henry David Thoreau, *Walden, or Life in the Woods and On the Duty of Civil Disobedience* (New York: New American Library, 1960), 163.

61. This passage paraphrases Emerson's assertion in "Experience": "I feel my heart beating with the love of the new beauty, I am ready to die out of nature and be born again into this new yet approachable America I have found in the West" (in *Essays and Lectures*, 485). I rely heavily on Cavell's gloss on that passage in his essay "Finding as Founding," in *"This New yet Unapproachable America,"* especially 115–118.

62. For one of the most important expressions of this sensibility, see Michael Sandel, *Democracy's Discontent: America in Search of a Public Philosophy* (Cambridge: Harvard University Press, 1996). Generally, Sandel suggests that at the heart of the formative project of democratic life is the need to cultivate a public morality that would enable people to be educated in the prerequisites for securing freedom. For Sandel, this project, which conjoins religion and morality in the service of democracy, is frustrated by the politics of the procedural republic, which brackets morality and religion too completely for them to be able to serve this tutelary function. Through his study, Sandel does not hesitate to identify the moral with the religious. But if Sandel notes there is a downside to the reliance on a republicanism blind to its own coercive force, as he does when he cites the work of Benjamin Rush during the American Enlightenment, for example (319–320), he seems less aware of how, for Rush and others like him, religion and reason together were to serve the interest of state power. Of course, this identification, while certainly worthy of contestation, is possibly less troubling than Sandel's identification of freedom with security, one traditionally made by anti-democratic forces under the guise of republicanism; see especially 317–328. For a critique of Sandel's evasion of this paradox, see William E. Connolly, "Democracy's Discontent," *Raritan* 16, 2 (Fall 1996), 140–149. For an earlier critique of the valences of Sandel's argument, see Dumm, *Michel Foucault*, 132–135. For a more detailed analysis of Benjamin Rush's moral politics, see

Thomas L. Dumm, *Democracy and Punishment: Disciplinary Origins of the United States* (Madison: University of Wisconsin Press, 1987), 89–96.

63. Friedrich Nietzsche, *Thus Spoke Zarathustra*, trans. R. J. Hollingdale (New York: Penguin, 1961), 42.

64. See Harold Bloom, *The American Religion: The Emergence of the Post-Christian Nation* (New York: Simon & Shuster, 1992). Bloom suggests, and I wouldn't disagree, that the American religion's foremost theologian is Emerson. Bloom also suggests that the American religion is post-Christian, most fully realized in a solitude that one has with a God who loves one. So Emerson as theologian of American religion may also be its foremost philosopher, as Cavell often seems to suggest. How one is to separate the two roles is yet another problem.

65. See *Time*, April 7, 1997, and *Newsweek*, April 7, 1997, for background information concerning the cults.

66. Stephanie Simon, Nick Anderson, and Tony Perry, "Thirty in Cult Left Recipes of Death: Believed Alien Ship Would Take Them to Heaven," *Los Angeles Times*, Friday, March 28, 1997, A1, A18.

67. Hannah Arendt, "The Conquest of Space and the Stature of Men," in *Between Past and Future* (New York: Penguin, 1977), 265–280. See George Kateb, "Hannah Arendt: Alienation and America," in Richard Poirier, ed., *Raritan Reading* (New Brunswick, NJ: Rutgers University Press, 1990), especially 198–201.

68. See Emerson, "Compensation," in *Essays and Lectures*, for a discussion of this sensibility. Also see Thomas L. Dumm, "Spare Parts," in Austin Sarat and Dana Villa, eds., *Liberal Modernism and Democratic Individuality: George Kateb and the Practices of Politics* (Princeton: Princeton University Press, 1996).

69. Charles Olson, *Call Me Ishmael* (New York: Reynal & Hitchcock, 1947), 14.

70. Ibid., 15.

71. This parenthetical speculation is designed only to acknowledge the work already done on this question by Olson and Cavell. Cavell's speculation on Lear's motives is to be found in his essay "The Avoidance of Love: A Reading of *King Lear*," in *Must We Mean What We Say?* (Cambridge: Cambridge University Press, 1976; originally published in New York: Scribner's, New York, 1969), 267–353.

72. Michael Rogin, *Subversive Genealogy: The Politics and Art of Herman Melville* (New York: Knopf, 1983).

73. Ibid., 109.

74. This reckoning of the respective weights of tragedy and comedy constantly shifts, not only in Melville's work but in Emerson's and Thoreau's as well. One need only re-read Emerson's "Experience" to note the movement from one to the other, or review the opening passages in Thoreau's *Cape Cod* to see the play of both melded into a sublime terror. So it may be that I am simply stupid to insist on an emphasis in Melville on the tragic, even in the confines of one novel, and will regret the claim

I make here. But I still make it, if only to note it for future thinking. A chapter other than this one would plumb the unfathomable connections between Ahab and King Lear, revisiting the ground that Charles Olson first opened in *Call Me Ishmael*, and encourage thinking about the argument concerning "openness" in *King Lear* noted by Stanley Cavell in his reading of the play. See Cavell, "Avoidance of Love."

75. Herman Melville, *Moby-Dick or the Whale*, Arion Press ed. of 1979 (reprint, Berkeley: University of California Press, 1983; originally published 1851), 77.

76. Ibid., 168.

77. On Emersonian hermaphrodism, see Kateb, *Emerson and Self-Reliance*, 121–128.

78. Rogin, *Subversive Genealogy*, 11.

79. Ibid., 142.

80. Ann Lauterbach, "The Night Sky, III," *American Poetry Review* 26 (March/April 1997), 23.

81. One might read Melville's critique of phrenology simply as a parody. One might also read Emerson's discussion of phrenology in "Experience" as parody as well, or at least as sarcasm. But the point for both is to criticize empiricism for its attempt to fix truth in determinate ways, especially through a static body.

82. Melville, *Moby-Dick*, 356.

83. Emerson, "Self-Reliance," 259.

84. Melville, *Moby-Dick*, 358.

85. Emerson, "American Scholar," 56.

86. Melville, *Moby-Dick*, 358.

87. Ibid., 360.

88. Gilles Deleuze and Félix Guattari, *A Thousand Plateaus: Capitalism and Schizophrenia*, vol. 2, trans. Brian Massumi (Minneapolis: University of Minnesota Press, 1987), 155.

89. Ibid., 243–245.

90. Ibid., 246.

91. Ibid., 247.

92. Melville, *Moby-Dick*, chap. 78, "Cistern and Buckets," immediately precedes the two chapters "The Prairie" and "The Nut."

93. Ibid., 168.

94. Lauterbach, "Night Sky, III," 25, citing Giorgio Agamben, *Stanzas: Words and Phantasm in Western Culture*, trans. Ronald L. Martinez (Minneapolis: University of Minnesota Press, 1993), 59.

NOTES TO CHAPTER 2

1. Stanley Cavell, "The Philosopher in American Life (Toward Thoreau and Emerson)," in *In Quest of the Ordinary: Lines of Skepticism and Romanticism* (Chicago: University of Chicago Press, 1988), 5. Cavell here summarizes (and, I

think, slightly transfigures) the argument concerning skepticism that he developed in his earlier work *The Claim of Reason: Wittgenstein, Skepticism, Morality, and Tragedy* (Oxford: Oxford University Press, 1979).

2. In describing how the shopkeeper who is given a slip of paper that says "five red apples" goes about his work of interpreting the meaning of those words, Wittgenstein says, "It is in this and similar ways that one operates with words" (*Philosophical Investigations*, trans. G.E.M. Anscombe, 3d ed. [New York: Macmillan, 1958], 3).

3. *Oxford English Dictionary*, s.v. "context."

4. The question of context is addressed by John Wikse in an early exploration of poststructuralism by an American political theorist; see his *About Possession: The Self as Private Property* (University Park: Penn State University Press, 1977), 49. Wikse notes that the distinction Michel Foucault draws between *connaissance* and *savoir* in *The Archaeology of Knowledge*, trans. A. M. Sheridan Smith (New York: Harper & Row, 1972), 15, points toward how one might develop a political epistemology sensitive to the notion of self-possession as a kind of technically *ecstatic, contextless* form of existence, a condition of being estranged from everything but one's self. For me, the play between context and contextlessness evokes a sense of being resigned that is deeply connected to the act of resignation.

5. Bob Woodward and Carl Bernstein, *The Final Days* (New York: Simon & Schuster, 1976), 451.

6. For details, see Seymour M. Hersh, *The Price of Power: Kissinger in the Nixon White House* (New York: Summit Books, 1983). Kissinger's failure to resign after threatening to do so, if the threat was made unconditionally, may be an example of what J. L. Austin has called an "unhappy" performative, not having the requisite intention. See J. L. Austin, *How to Do Things with Words*, ed. J. O. Urmson and Mirina Sbisà (Cambridge: Harvard University Press, 1962, reprint 1975), 39.

7. Bonnie Honig, "Declarations of Independence: Arendt and Derrida on the Problem of Founding a Republic," in Frederick Dolan and Thomas Dumm, eds., *Rhetorical Republic: Governing Representations in American Politics* (Amherst: University of Massachusetts Press, 1993), 201–225.

8. See *Oxford English Dictionary*, s.v. "resignation."

9. Jacques Derrida, "Declarations of Independence," trans. Tom Keenan and Tom Pepper, *New Political Science*, no. 15 (Summer 1986), 7–13. "In signing, the people say—and do what they say they do, but in differing or deferring themselves through [*différant par*] the intervention of their representatives whose representativity is fully legitimated only by the signature, thus after the fact or the coup [*après coup*]—henceforth, I have the right to sign, in truth I will already have had it since I was able to give it to myself" (10).

10. I take this argument to be consistent with that made by Stanley Cavell concerning the difference between the withdrawal from community and the withdrawal of consent. See Cavell, *Claim of Reason*, 24–25.

11. This idea parallels Cavell's claim concerning entering a political community; see ibid., 27.

12. This reference is designed as a gesture, barely scratching the surface of the complex analysis of specters that Derrida has undertaken. See Jacques Derrida, *Specters of Marx: The State of the Debt, the Work of Mourning, and the New International*, trans. Peggy Kamuf (New York: Routledge, 1994).

13. This seems to be the point of Jean Bethke Elshtain's reflection on Nixon at the time of his death; see her *Democracy on Trial* (New York: Basic Books, 1995), xvii. Elshtain confesses having been a "Nixon loather" and looks back abashed that she was able to hate so easily, writing, "I do not hate anymore. I have joined the ranks of the nervous." This latter-day conversion from hatred was made possible by members of Congress in the early 1970s who both investigated Nixon with the sense of carefulness the contract of government required and envisioned the trauma the contract's breaking would impose on the polity. Anticipating the trauma a broken promise will cause may signify a passage to a certain kind of maturity. Reflecting on one's bad behavior in a distant past is a different project, I think.

14. Woodward and Bernstein, *Final Days*, 455–456. This pattern of coming close to public breakdown and pulling back was noted prior to the Watergate scandal by Garry Wills, who pointed out that Nixon followed a similar script in the "Checkers speech" of 1952 and in his press conference after his defeat by Edmund Brown in the 1962 California gubernatorial election. See Garry Wills, *Nixon Agonistes: The Crisis of the Self-Made Man* (Boston: Houghton Mifflin, 1970).

15. William Shakespeare, *Titus Andronicus*, in *The Riverside Shakespeare* (Boston: Houghton Mifflin, 1974), 1025, 1.1.189–193; see also *Oxford English Dictionary*, s.v. "resign."

16. Shakespeare, *Titus Andronicus*, 1. 1.198–199.

17. William Shakespeare, *Richard III*, in *Riverside Shakespeare*, 738, 3.7.223–226.

18. The fungibility of the soul is associated with what might be called the migrations of sovereignty associated with the growth of modern power. On the subject of sovereignty, see Ernst Kantorowitz, *The King's Two Bodies: A Study in Medieval Political Theology* (Princeton: Princeton University Press, 1957); and Michel Foucault, *Discipline and Punish: The Birth of the Prison*, trans. Alan Sheridan (New York: Pantheon, 1977), especially part 1, "Torture." For an analysis of Foucault's work on these terms, see Thomas L. Dumm, *Michel Foucault and the Politics of Freedom* (Thousand Oaks: Sage Publications, 1996), 79–96.

19. For the most systematic investigation of the impact of money on politics over the course of the twentieth century, see Thomas Ferguson, *Golden Rule: The Investment Theory of Party Competition and the Logic of Money-Driven Political Systems* (Chicago: University of Chicago Press, 1995).

20. Alexis de Tocqueville, *Democracy in America*, trans. George Lawrence, ed. J.

P. Mayer (Garden City, NJ: Doubleday, 1969; from the 13th ed. of the original, 1850), 257–259.

21. For a fascinating reading of contemporary expressions of cynicism and stoicism in American culture, see William Chaloupka, "Praising Minnesota: The Coens' 'Fargo' and the Pressures of Stoic Community," *Theory and Event* 1, 2 (June 1997), at http://muse.jhu.edu/journals/theory_&_event/v001/1.2chaloupka.html.

22. See Ralph Waldo Emerson, *Essays and Lectures* (New York: Library of America, 1983), *Essays: First Series*, "Compensation": "The President has paid dearly for his White House. It has commonly cost him all his peace, and the best of his manly attributes. To preserve for such a short time so conspicuous an appearance before the world, he is content to eat dust before the real masters who stand erect behind the throne" (288).

23. This difficulty associated with being lost and found is marked by Stanley Cavell, in many of his meditations that connect themselves explicitly to Emerson's famous essay "Experience." Cavell also usefully thematizes the problem as philosophical and melodramatic in his thinking about Wittgenstein. See Stanley Cavell, *"This New yet Unapproachable America": Lectures after Emerson after Wittgenstein* (Albuquerque: Living Batch Press, 1989) 36–37. Ann Lauterbach has explored this theme poetically; see, most recently, her collection titled *On a Stair* (New York: Penguin, 1997). For an earlier approach to this question, see Dumm, *Michel Foucault*, chap. 2, "Freedom and Space." The idea that finding as founding presents America itself as a philosophical event is explored with great care by Simon Critchley in a meditation on Cavell; see *Very Little . . . Almost Nothing: Death, Philosophy, Literature* (New York: Routledge, 1997), especially 125–138.

24. I thank Bob Gooding-Williams for posing this question.

25. The phrase "unsigned resignation" was suggested to me by Lisa Disch.

26. Cavell, *Claim of Reason*, 27–28.

27. Ibid., 28.

28. Cavell suggests that *quiet desperation* is Thoreau's term for the everyday condition of living our skepticism, the tragedy of everyday life. See Cavell, *In Quest of the Ordinary*, 9.

29. Henry David Thoreau, *Walden, or Life in the Woods and On the Duty of Civil Disobedience* (New York: New American Library, 1960), 10; hereafter abbreviated *W*, when cited in the text.

30. Stanley Cavell, *The Senses of Walden*, rev. ed. (Chicago: University of Chicago Press, 1992), 61.

31. I borrow here from Cavell, *The Senses of Walden*, which is divided into three main chapters, "Words," "Sentences," and "Portions." The insight that *Walden* is importantly a book about language itself is a theme most thoroughly explored by Cavell.

32. In a discussion of Hegel's master and bondsman, Judith Butler, *The Psychic*

Life of Power: Theories in Subjection (Stanford: Stanford University Press, 1997) notes how the marking and remarking of the object, its signing and re-signing by bondsman and master—which culminates for Hegel in an achievement of self-recognition through the experience of absolute fear—is a scene of contestation. See especially 34–39. This moment might be considered an example of what Butler earlier notes is the form that power takes as a kind of *turning*. She writes, "The turn appears to function as a tropological inauguration of the subject, a founding moment whose ontological status remains permanently uncertain," 3–4. Resignation might be considered as another example of this turning.

33. Ibid., 4.

34. Ann Lauterbach, "The Night Sky, IV," *American Poetry Review* 26 (August 1997), 22.

35. Cavell, *"This New yet Approachable America,"* 36.

NOTES TO CHAPTER 3

1. These terms are familiar to most contemporary political theorists as belonging to John Rawls; see his *A Theory of Justice* (Cambridge: Harvard University Press, 1971). The idea of a scale of justice is implicit but strongly suggested in his discussion of two principles of justice (60–61). The critique that Rawls presents of his own theory of justice as "unrealistic" in the face of the fact of plurality is to be found in John Rawls, *Political Liberalism* (New York: Columbia University Press, 1993). To secure the concept of justice, Rawls suggests, it must be rooted in a political system of reasonable pluralism. The force of my argument here, while by no means addressing Rawls, is to suggest that one problem with reasonable pluralism is the way in which it seems to limit the range of what is to be considered reasonable. On the image of the scale of justice, see Dennis E. Curtis and Judith Resnik, "Images of Justice," *Yale Law Journal* 96, 8 (July 1987), 1727–1772. Curtis and Resnik focus primarily on the blindfold of justice, though they present a useful note (note 32, at 1741) on the history of the image of the scale.

2. One thinker to have trod this path, finding new passages that I have been happy to follow, and to whom this chapter is most directly addressed, is George Kateb.

3. See Jane Bennett, "Kafka's Genealogical Idealism," *Journal of Politics* 56, 3 (August 1994), 650–670.

4. Franz Kafka, "In the Penal Colony," from *The Penal Colony: Stories and Short Pieces*, trans. Willa Muir and Edwin Muir (New York: Schocken Books, 1961), 192.

5. Ibid., 223.

6. Ibid., 205.

7. Ibid.

8. Ibid., 209.

9. Ibid., 207.

10. Ibid., 198–199.

11. I think there is ample textual evidence to support a reading of "In the Penal Colony" as a feminist tale. For instance, the ladies' handkerchiefs can be interpreted to play a role as a form of cross-dressing and might even be understood as the officer's attempt to fashion breasts for himself. The officer early in the story "looked uncommonly limp, breathed with his mouth wide open and had tucked two ladies' handkerchiefs under the collar of his uniform" (Kafka, "In the Penal Colony," 192). Indeed, the major theme of this story is the breakdown of a *penal* colony.

But there is also reason to resist the psychoanalytical approach to understanding Kafka, as I discuss below.

12. Walter Benjamin, "Franz Kafka: On the Tenth Anniversary of His Death," in *Illuminations*, ed. Hannah Arendt, trans. Harry Zohn (New York: Schocken Books, 1969), 121.

13. Ibid., 131.

14. Benjamin, "Some Reflections on Kafka," in *Illuminations*, 143.

15. Though not, I think, consistent with the Sartrean idea of radical choice, even though the idea of nausea works so powerfully for Sartre as a metaphor, in ways that I think closely parallel this passage.

16. Ralph Waldo Emerson, "Compensation," in *Essays and Lectures* (New York: Library of America, 1983), 285.

17. Ibid., 286.

18. Ibid., 286.

19. Ibid., 287.

20. Ibid., 289–290.

21. Ibid., 290.

22. Ibid., 292.

23. Ibid.

24. Ibid., 299.

25. Ibid.

26. Ibid., 301.

27. Ibid., 301–302.

28. Ibid., 302.

29. See Emerson, "Spiritual Laws," in *Essays and Lectures*, 321. Emerson suggests that this essay is a continuation of "Compensation."

30. For a discussion of religiosity in Emerson that influences my imagination of Emerson without God, see George Kateb, *Emerson and Self-Reliance* (Thousand Oaks: Sage Publications, 1994), chap. 3, "The Question of Religiousness."

31. Ibid., 72.

32. See George Kateb, *The Inner Ocean: Individualism and Democratic Culture* (Ithaca: Cornell University Press, 1992).

33. Kafka, "In the Penal Colony," 224–225.

34. Ibid., 226.

35. Ibid.

36. Ibid., 226–227.

37. Giorgio Agamben, *The Coming Community*, trans. Michael Hardt (Minneapolis: University of Minnesota Press, 1993), 6–7. The artist whose work is being described is Robert Walser.

38. Ibid., 102.

39. Ibid., 103.

40. Ibid., 106.

41. Ibid., 85.

42. George Kateb, *Emerson and Self-Reliance* (Thousand Oaks: Sage Publications 1995), 195.

43. See *Monty Python and the Holy Grail*, directed by Terry Gilliam and Terry Jones, written by the Monty Python ensemble (Columbia Pictures, 1974; videotape, 1985).

44. Henry David Thoreau, *Walden, or Life in the Woods and On the Duty of Civil Disobedience* (New York: New American Library, 1960), 8. This reference to the ubiquity of shit is echoed in contemporary children's literature. See Taro Gomi, *Everybody Poops*, trans. Amanda Mayer Stinchecum (Brooklyn: Kane/Miller Book Publisher, 1993).

45. Thoreau, *Walden*, 59.

46. Ibid., 62.

47. Ibid., 64.

48. Thomas Bulfinch, *Mythology* (Toronto: Thomas Y. Crowell, 1970), 120.

49. Thoreau, *Walden*, 109.

50. Ibid., 108.

51. Ibid., 113.

NOTES TO CHAPTER 4

1. Stanley Cavell, "What Is the Emersonian Event? A Comment on Kateb's Emerson," *New Literary History* 25 (1994): 957.

2. This insight is developed in Michel Foucault's essay "Governmentality," in *The Foucault Effect: Studies in Governmentality*, ed. Graham Burchell, Colin Gordon, and Peter Miller (Chicago: University of Chicago Press, 1991), especially in his discussion of the influence of Machiavelli's *The Prince* on thinking about the art of governmentality. Foucault notes that authors influenced by Machiavelli's treatment place the prince in a position of external transcendence to the population and territory he is to control and yet also note the connections between the prince and others within the principality concerning the application of the art of government. "We have seen . . . that practices of government are, on the one hand, multifarious and concern many kinds of people: the head of a family, the superior of a convent, the teacher or tutor of a child or pupil; so that there are several forms of government

among which the prince's relation to his state is only one particular mode; while, on the other hand, all these other kinds of government are internal to the state or society. It is within the state that the father will rule the family, the superior the convent, etc. Thus we find at once a plurality of forms of government and their immanence to the state: the multiplicity and immanence of these activities distinguishes them from the transcendent singularity of Machiavelli's prince" (91).

3. Sir William Blackstone, *Commentaries*, 10th ed. (London, 1787), vol. 4, 162, as cited in Raymond B. Fosdick, *European Police Systems* (New York: Century Co., 1905), 3. It may be useful to note that this book on police was published in a series by the Bureau of Social Hygiene.

4. Theodore Lowi, *The End of Liberalism*, 2d ed. (New York: Norton, 1979), 273–274.

5. As I wrote the first draft of this essay in 1995, the most important indicator of police activity in its broadest sense, the population of those in prison, on probation, and on parole, had been released by the U.S. Department of Justice's Bureau of Justice Statistics. In 1994, the number of people in prison and jails was 1.5 million, a tripling of that population since 1980; another 3.5 million were on parole or probation. I wrote then that if current trends continued (and given the popularity of imprisonment as a political issue), by 1996 the population of those in the arms of the law would exceed the college student population of the United States (6 million), and in ten years the population of people in the arms of the law would exceed the current total population of New York City. The growth of prison populations is disproportionately distributed, with Southern states having the highest regional rate of imprisonment and two, Texas and Georgia, having the highest rates of annual increase, 28 percent and 20 percent respectively. Racial disparities are also intense. It is estimated by the National Center on Institutions and Alternatives that if current trends continue, an *absolute majority* of African American men between the ages of eighteen and forty will be in prisons or prison camps by the year 2010. See Fox Butterfield, "More in U.S. Are in Prisons, Report Says," *New York Times*, August 10, 1995, A14. An update on these figures for the most recent year available—1997, midyear—indicates that the growth continued through last year, with 1.7 million (1,725,842 men and women) in prison. Jails held about 558,000 adults, 322,700 of whom had not yet been convicted of a crime for which they were serving time. See "Nation's Prisons and Jails Hold More than 1.7 Million," press release of the U.S. Department of Justice's Bureau of Justice Statistics, January 18, 1998. The most recent update of probation and parole statistics indicates similar growth, to 3.9 million in 1996. See "Nation's Probation and Parole Population Reached Almost 3.9 Million Last Year," press release of the U.S Department of Justice's Bureau of Justice Statistics, August 14, 1997. Both of these reports are available at http:// www.ojp.usdoj.gov/bjs/. While rates of imprisonment themselves do not directly indicate a society that is more intensely policed, at a certain point, to paraphrase Hegel, quantity turns into quality. When I first began studying prisons in 1978,

335,000 people were in prisons and jails, a rate that most criminologists at the time considered to be high. Moreover, the idea that prisons are a substitute for, and are not themselves, mediating institutions is belied by the development of prison subcultures that are integrated into and give shape to the civic experiences of many citizens. For recent examples of how influential these subcultures are, see Nathan McCall, *Makes Me Wanna Holler: A Young Black Man in America* (New York: Random House, 1994); Sanyika Shakur [Monster Kody Scott], *Monster: The Autobiography of an L.A. Gang Member* (New York: Atlantic Monthly Press, 1993); and Luis J. Rodriguez, *Always Running: La Vida Loca, Gang Days in L.A.* (Willimatic, CT: Curbstone Press, 1993).

6. For the most thorough recent analysis of the restrictions in the national electoral system, see Thomas Ferguson, *The Golden Rule* (Chicago: University of Chicago Press, 1995).

7. See Benjamin Ginsberg, *The Captive Public: How Mass Opinion Promotes State Power* (New York: Basic Books, 1986).

8. This is, of course, a highly speculative guess. For a more informed presentation of this theme, see Claus Offe, *Disorganized Capitalism* (Cambridge: MIT Press, 1985). Some commentators from the Right have celebrated the now often noted growth of inequality of income in the United States. See, for example, David Frum, "Welcome, Nouveux Riches," *New York Times*, August 14, 1995, A15.

9. On the shift from individualized discipline to postdisciplinary strategies of social control, see Thomas L. Dumm, *united states* (Ithaca: Cornell University Press, 1994), chap. 4, "Rodney King, or the New Enclosures." These distinctions are rooted in the work done by Michel Foucault in *Discipline and Punish: The Birth of the Prison*, trans. Alan Sheridan (New York: Pantheon, 1977), and in *The History of Sexuality*, vol. 1, trans. Robert Hurley (New York: Pantheon, 1978). For an elaboration on these themes, see Thomas L. Dumm, *Michel Foucault and the Politics of Freedom* (Newbury Park: Sage Publications, 1996).

10. Sheldon Wolin, *The Presence of the Past* (Baltimore: Johns Hopkins University Press, 1989), chap. 10, "Democracy without the Citizen," 186–187.

11. Ibid., 187.

12. Ibid., 191.

13. Ibid.

14. For his discussion of this problem, see Wolin, "Fugitive Democracy," in Seyla Benhabib, ed., *Democracy and Difference: Contesting the Boundaries of the Political* (Princeton: Princeton University Press, 1996).

15. Theodore Lowi, *The End of the Republican Era* (Norman: University of Oklahoma Press, 1995).

16. Ibid., 216.

17. Ibid., 210–211. In the passage Lowi compares Allan Bloom to Robert Dahl, underlining the ironic dependence of moral absolutism on the toleration of liberals.

18. Ibid., 245–246. The question of how such articulations operate in the

American political system is the subject of a growing literature. For a sampling, see Frederick Dolan and Thomas Dumm, eds., *Rhetorical Republic: Governing Representations in American Politics* (Amherst: University of Massachusetts Press, 1993); Michael Rogin, *Ronald Reagan, the Movie and Other Episodes in American Political Demonology* (Berkeley: University of California Press, 1987); Anne Norton, *Republic of Signs* (Chicago: University of Chicago Press, 1993); Frederick Dolan, *Allegories of America: Narrative, Metaphysics, Politics* (Ithaca: Cornell University Press, 1994); and S. Paige Baty, *American Monroe: The Making of a Body Politic* (Berkeley: University of California Press, 1995).

19. The definitive study of such a moment in American history is Joseph Gusfield's book on the nineteenth-century temperance movement, *Symbolic Crusade: Status Politics and the American Temperance Movement* (Urbana: University of Illinois Press, 1963). A study of the contemporary demonization of drug culture that is similar in spirit but dramatically different methodologically is David Lenson, *On Drugs* (Minneapolis: University of Minnesota Press, 1995). I discuss Lenson's analysis below.

20. See Norbert Elias, *The History of Manners,* vol. 1 of *The Civilizing Process,* trans. Edmund Jephcott (New York: Pantheon Books, 1978), "On Blowing One's Nose," 152.

21. Norbert Elias, *Power and Civility,* vol. 2 of *The Civilizing Process,* trans. Edmund Jephcott (New York: Pantheon Books, 1982), 231.

22. Here we might note a parallel to a theme concerning normalizing processes developed by Foucault in *The History of Sexuality,* vol. 1, 139f., where he discusses the emergence of disciplines that individualize and also regulatory controls that direct a bio-politics of populations.

23. Elias, *Power and Civility,* 233.

24. Ibid., 333.

25. Iris Marion Young, *Justice and the Politics of Difference* (Princeton: Princeton University Press, 1990), 136.

26. Ibid., 137.

27. Ibid., 141. Also see Dumm, *united states,* 103.

28. Benjamin DeMott, "Seduced by Civility: Political Manners and the Crisis of Democratic Values," *The Nation* 263, 19 (December 9, 1996), 11–14.

29. Ibid., 13.

30. Ibid.

31. Jean Bethke Elshtain, *Democracy on Trial* (New York: Basic Books, 1995), 2.

32. Ibid., xii–xiii.

33. Ibid., 38.

34. I am thinking especially of William E. Connolly's *Identity\Difference: Democratic Negotiations of Political Paradox* (Ithaca: Cornell University Press, 1991). But there are differences between the two theorists. Connolly celebrates the cultivation and emergence of difference as a sign of pluralization and concerns himself with the

impulses that develop in the group in defense of themselves once they have *established* an identity. He notes the ubiquity and inevitability of the emergence of group identity and seeks a position from which he might engage in a critique that would not simply reinscribe the differences that separate groups. But he understands that this position cannot be one of a simple reconstitution of something called "the center."

35. Elshtain, *Democracy on Trial,* chap. 2 and 3.

36. Elshtain mentions religious fundamentalism once in *Democracy on Trial* (111–112), in the context of a discussion of Pope John Paul II's visit to Lithuania, but the mention is not germane to the discussion of that visit, which concerned itself with conflicts of national, not religious, identity.

37. See the symposium on "The End of Democracy? The Judicial Usurpation of Politics," *First Things* (November 1996), especially the contributions of Robert Bork and Hadley Arkes. Several members of the editorial board of *First Things* resigned in protest at the extremism of the symposium, including Gertrude Himmelfarb and Walter Berns.

38. C. Wright Mills, *The Power Elite* (New York: Oxford University Press, 1956). These days I am beginning to think that Mills was not only a better sociologist than Tocqueville but a better prophet as well, or that he at least is a better guide to understanding how intermediate institutions operate in a *mass* society than is Tocqueville.

39. For a more extended analysis of the homosocial dynamic of this identity group (one that blurs the distinction between public and private in a way Elshtain might condemn), see Dumm, *united states,* chap. 3, "George Bush, or Sex in the Superior Position."

40. This argument parallels that developed by Christopher Lasch in his final book, *The Revolt of the Elites and the Betrayal of Democracy* (New York: Norton, 1995), though Lasch doesn't analyze the elite as a group in political identity terms.

41. This is an old lesson in American political culture, going back at least as far as Mark Twain's analysis of the Gilded Age. It is thematized more forcefully by Thorstein Veblen, *The Theory of the Leisure Class* (New York: Viking, 1967; originally published, 1899). A fascinating recent study by Robert D. Putnam, with Robert Leonardi and Raffaella Y. Nanetti, *Making Democracy Work: Civic Traditions in Modern Italy* (Princeton: Princeton University Press, 1993), attempts to study comprehensively differences between northern and southern Italy precisely on the basis of deep-seated cultural and institutional differences dating to the late Middle Ages; see especially chap. 5, "Tracing the Roots of the Civic Community." Putnam and his associates focus on the civic republic and cite Machiavelli approvingly, that the barriers to a strong civic community are an absence of equality and the presence of corruption (132). One might note that there is little (no?) discussion of corruption of elites in most of the contemporary communitarian literature, and an extra-

ordinary amount of discussion of minorities and subalterns taking the quest for identity too far.

42. William Galston, *Liberal Purposes: Goods, Virtue, and Diversity in the Liberal State* (Cambridge: Cambridge University Press, 1991), 4.

43. See Alexis de Tocqueville, *Democracy in America*, trans. George Lawrence, ed. J. P. Mayer (Garden City, NY: Doubleday/Anchor Books, 1969), vol. 1, chap. 7, "The Omnipotence of the Majority in the United States," 257–259. There Tocqueville discusses the courtier spirit and notes how it adheres to American politicians: "Democratic republics put the spirit of a court within the reach of the multitude and let it penetrate through all classes at once. That is one of the main reproaches to be made against them" (258). "And I know of only one way of preventing men from degrading themselves, namely, not to give anybody the omnipotence which carries with it sovereign power to debase them" (259). I find in these sentences a telling description of the direction from which the greatest threat to contemporary democracy comes, which is not the threat of fragmentation that is identified with groups who, by challenging the majority, are lacking in such courtier spirit.

44. Tocqueville uses some of his strongest language to attack the courtier spirit in America among the politicians. "It is true," he writes, "that American courtiers never say 'Sire' or 'Your Majesty,' as if the difference really mattered; but they are constantly talking of their master's natural brilliance; they do not raise the question which of all the prince's virtues is most to be admired, for they assure him that he possesses all virtues, without having acquired them and, so to say, without desiring them; they do not give him their wives and daughters hoping he will raise them to the rank of his mistresses, but they do sacrifice their opinions to him and so prostitute themselves" (ibid., 258–259). I argue that the presence of the courtier spirit is especially strong these days among Republican politicians who seek support from the Christian Coalition. I think this is so because of the conjunction of electoral power with the specifically religious tenor of the coalition itself, which demands a submission to its core beliefs as a measure of loyalty to its political ends.

45. In this sense, one might argue that what we have witnessed through the past fifteen years has been the dramatic expansion of the realm of constitutive policy, as the realms of redistributive and regulatory policies have contracted. On these distinctions, see Lowi, *End of Liberalism*, 39; and the discussion of Lowi in Thomas L. Dumm, *Democracy and Punishment: Disciplinary Origins of the United States* (Madison: University of Wisconsin Press, 1987), 142–147. On the relationship of the Clinton administration's crime bill to communitarianism, see Sidney Blumenthal, "The Education of a President," *New Yorker*, January 24, 1994, especially 40–41.

46. For a discussion of the contemporary status of pluralism as a political ethos, see William E. Connolly, *The Ethos of Pluralization* (Minneapolis: University of Minnesota Press, 1995).

47. See Jerome Skolnick and David Bayley, *Community Policing: Issues and Practices around the World* (Washington, D.C.: National Institute of Justice, U.S. Department of Justice, 1988), 1–20.

48. Ibid., 82.

49. Ibid.

50. William Bennett, *The Devaluing of America* (New York: Simon & Schuster, 1992), 133, quoted in William E. Connolly, "Drugs, the Nation, and Free Lancing: Decoding the Moral Universe of William Bennett," *Theory and Event* 1, 1 (1997), 20, at http://muse.jhu/press/journals/theory_&_event/1.1.connolly.html.

51. Ibid., 21.

52. Skolnick and Bayley, *Community Policing*, 82–83.

53. Mark Harrison Moore, "Problem Solving and Community Policing," in *Modern Policing*, ed. Michael Tonry and Norval Morris; *Crime and Justice, A Review of Research*, vol. 15 (Chicago: University of Chicago Press, 1992), 152.

54. For an important perspective on this role of the welfare bureaucracy, see Barbara Cruikshank, "Welfare Queens" (paper presented for the panel "Liberalism and the Police," American Political Science Association, Annual Meeting, Chicago, Illinois, September 1995).

55. Michael Tonry, *Malign Neglect: Race, Crime and Punishment in America* (New York: Oxford University Press, 1995), 81–83.

56. Ibid., 111. Tonry's source is Alfred Blumstein, "Making Rationality Relevant: The American Society of Criminology 1992 Presidential Address," *Criminology* (January 1993), fig. 1.

57. Ibid., 110. Tonry here uses as his source the U.S. Department of Justice's Bureau of Justice Statistics, *Sourcebook of Criminal Justice Statistics* (Washington, D.C.: U.S. Department of Justice, 1991), tables 3.103, 3.104, 3.105. Whites use alcohol, marijuana, and cocaine at slightly higher rates than do blacks and Hispanics, and hallucinogens at a much higher rate. Blacks and Hispanics use heroin at a higher rate than whites.

58. Tonry, *Malign Neglect*, 104–107.

59. Ibid., 94.

60. Ibid., 97.

61. Lenson, *On Drugs*, 200.

62. Ibid., 23.

63. Connolly, "Drugs, the Nation, and Free Lancing," 40.

64. Michel Foucault, "Of Other Spaces," trans. Jay Misoweic, *diacritics* (Spring 1986), 27.

NOTES TO CHAPTER 5

1. For an important discussion of these issues at the close of the 1980s, see Diana Fuss, *Essentially Speaking: Feminism, Nature, and Difference* (New York:

Routledge, 1989), especially the discussion of Gayatri Chakravorty Spivak, "The Essentialism in Anti-Essentialism," 28–37. The primary essay by Spivak that Fuss explores is "Subaltern Studies: Deconstructing Historiography," in Gayatri Chakravorty Spivak, *In Other Worlds: Essays in Cultural Politics* (New York: Methuen, 1987). More recently, William Connolly, in both *Identity/Difference: Democratic Negotiations of Political Paradox* (Ithaca: Cornell University Press, 1991) and *The Ethos of Pluralization* (Minneapolis: University of Minnesota Press, 1995), has connected the question of identity to the politics of liberalism, especially American liberalism. Finally, Wendy Brown, *States of Injury: Power and Freedom in Late Modernity* (Princeton: Princeton University Press, 1995), focuses strongly on the connections between engenderment and *ressentiment* as they operate in reference to freedom and order in the late modern era. All these works provide implicit starting points for the reflections contained in this chapter. I also note that all these essays—including Spivak's, though she seems most tempted to the practice of strategic essentialism—are diagnostic in character and ambivalent and cautious in tone, a quality not shared by essentialists such as Bennett. See William Bennett, *The Devaluing of America: The Fight for Our Culture and Our Children* (New York: Simon & Schuster, 1992). For a discussion of Bennett in these terms, see William E. Connolly, "Drugs, the Nation and Free Lancing," *Theory and Event* 1, 1, January (1997) at http://muse.jhu.edu/journals/theory_&_event/1.1connolly.html.

2. This is an old question in modern political theory, dating at least to Thomas Hobbes and famously illustrated in the frontispiece to the first edition of *Leviathan*. See Thomas Hobbes, *Leviathan*, ed. C. B. MacPherson (New York: Penguin, 1968; originally published, 1651). It is the king's head depicted by Hobbes that Foucault suggested needed to be cut off; see Michel Foucault, "Two Lectures," in *Power/Knowledge: Essays, Interviews and Other Writings, 1972–1977*, ed. Colin Gordon (New York: Pantheon, 1980), 102. Wendy Brown usefully points out the difficulties Foucault had in escaping this hegemonic formulation; see *States of Injury*, 16–17. For a reflection on how this problem is articulated in reference to racialized bodies, see Lauren Berlant, "National Brands/National Body: *Imitation of Life*," in Bruce Robbins, ed., *The Phantom Public Sphere* (Minneapolis: University of Minnesota Press, 1993).

3. See Kaja Silverman, *Male Subjectivity at the Margins* (New York: Routledge, 1992). Silverman usefully deploys a Lacanian schema of "libidinal politics," relying on Jacques Lacan's elaboration of the ego (or the *moi*) and the idea of the fantasmic (from Jean Laplanche and Jean-Baptiste Pontalis), to elaborate an argument concerning the varying relationships between desire and identification in the establishment of male subjectivity. Silverman's project may be understood (in part) as an attempt to historicize the relationship of the phallus to the penis, to show how the dominant fiction of the Oedipus complex gives way to dissident organizations of male subjectivity as forces of historical trauma do their work, enabling a greater receptivity by males to feminine subjectivities; see, especially, 1–51. The fantasmic

may be understood as the imaginary site that operates to conceal the antagonisms of the social field. This realization is a primary point of entry for many of the analyses of popular culture found in the work of Slavoj Žižek; see, especially, *The Sublime Object of Ideology* (London: Verso, 1989). For an earlier attempt to describe the "center" in reference to American political culture, see Thomas L. Dumm, *united states* (Ithaca: Cornell University Press, 1994), chap. 3, "George Bush, or Sex in the Superior Position."

4. This is another way (admittedly awkward) of reasserting what has been put forward with greater clarity by Connolly in *Ethos of Pluralization*, especially chap. 6, "Tocqueville, Religiosity, and Pluralization."

5. See, for instance, Michael Kimmel, *Manhood in America* (New York: Free Press, 1996); Christopher Newfield, *The Emerson Effect: Individualism and Submission in America* (Chicago: University of Chicago Press, 1996); Calvin Thomas, *Male Matters* (Urbana: University of Illinois Press, 1996); and Kim Townsend, *Manhood at Harvard* (Boston: Norton, 1996). These titles hardly exhaust the list of recent works one might cite but are important for their varying attempts to outline manhood in reference to distinctively American ideological formations. Sometimes this effort fails. The difficulty with Kimmel's study in particular is that it primarily updates general cultural histories, merely highlighting the role of men *qua* men in the making of it. This exercise is similar to a *Saturday Night Live* skit many years ago, in which Dan Ackroyd parodied hagiographic public television shows that celebrate the accomplishments of various marginalized groups by having a show celebrating the accomplishments of . . . men.

6. Henry Clay, cited in Kimmel, *Manhood in America*, 26.

7. Ibid., 50–59.

8. David Reisman, *The Lonely Crowd* (New Haven: Yale University Press, 1953), chap. 1. Reisman's study is a template for Kimmel's, and to a certain extent Newfield's, in that what he describes as a characterological shift, from tradition-directed to inner-directed to other-directed persons, establishes a series of historical correspondences: feudal, market, and corporate work organization; subsistence, productive, and consumptive modes of economic life; and agricultural, industrial, and postindustrial modes of production. Of course, this familiar division predates Reisman, but his book is an important predecessor to these studies in the sense that he argues concerning a distinctively American mode of character. Moreover, he exhibits the familiar collapsing of a history of culture into a history of men: "This is a book about social character and about the differences in social character between *men* of different regions, eras and groups" (1; my emphasis). For other studies that take the gendered character of the emergence of corporate culture as their direct object, see Ann Douglas, *The Feminization of American Culture* (New York: Knopf, 1977); and Cathy Ferguson, *The Feminist Case against Bureaucracy* (Philadelphia: Temple University Press, 1984).

9. Fox Butterfield, *All God's Children: The Bosket Family and the American Tradition of Violence* (New York: Knopf, 1995).

10. Here I am following Žižek's explication of what he terms "the ideological *sinthome*"; see his *Looking Awry: An Introduction to Jacques Lacan through Popular Culture* (Cambridge: MIT Press, 1991), especially 140, where he discusses the pathetic expression of identification with those who suffer an unbearable experience: "We are all that!" (Some examples: We are all Jews! We are all boat people! We are all going to die someday!) See also Žižek, *Sublime Object of Ideology*, "From Symptom to *Sinthome*."

11. Žižek, *Sublime Object of Ideology*, 75

12. Ibid.

13. This priority does not mean that the self is not a social self. *How* the self is social, and how the relation of the self to other is constituted, is Emerson's text.

14. George Kateb, *Emerson and Self-Reliance* (Newbury Park: Sage Publications, 1995), 197.

15. Ralph Waldo Emerson, *Essays and Lectures* (New York: Library of America, 1983), "Compensation," 287.

16. Emerson, "Swedenborg; or the Mystic," in *Representative Men*, in *Essays and Lectures*, 680; quoted in Kateb, *Emerson and Self-Reliance*, 124.

17. Kateb, 17–18.

18. Ibid., 124.

19. Kateb fully acknowledges this limit, noting that the only time Emerson wrote of homosexual love was in an essay he composed at the age of seventeen. He also notes that it remains for Whitman to link mental hermaphrodism and active bisexuality (ibid., 128). We may also note that in the famous first meeting between Emerson and Whitman (a day they spent together), while strolling on the Boston Common, Emerson urged Whitman to tone down some of the explicit references to sex in the "Children of Adam" section of *Leaves of Grass*. See Robert Richardson, Jr., *Emerson: The Mind on Fire* (Berkeley: University of California Press, 1995), 528–529.

20. Emerson, "Experience," in *Essays, Second Series*, in *Essays and Lectures*, 473.

21. Ibid., 485.

22. Ibid., 492.

23. Newfield, *The Emerson Effect*, 65.

24. Ibid., 32–33.

25. This is where Newfield and Kateb are probably most at odds. Kateb would point readers toward "Compensation" as a doctrine of pluralization that is remarkable for the difficulty of its demands on those who would act on it, even as Emerson urges them. Newfield would minimize or overlook this essay's point and note the larger work of reassurance accomplished in such essays as "Nature" and "Self-Reliance." For an extended analysis of the force of reassurance, see William Corlett,

Community without Unity: A Politics of Derridian Extravagance (Durham: Duke University Press, 1989), part 2.

26. While the phrase "inner ocean" comes from the title of George Kateb's *The Inner Ocean: Individualism and Democratic Culture* (Ithaca: Cornell University Press, 1992), the structural limits of liberal solidarity are enunciated more explicitly by Richard Rorty in *Contingency, Irony, and Solidarity* (Cambridge: Cambridge University Press, 1989).

27. For a discussion of the problem of determining the embedded character of alternatives to dominant orders, see Connolly's discussion of Thoreau in "Tocqueville, Religiosity, and Pluralization," in *Ethos of Pluralization*, 173–178.

28. The desire for completion is, in Lacan's understanding, always retrospective. See his discussion of the "mirror stage" and "the body in pieces" in Jacques Lacan, *Ecrits: A Selection*, trans. Alan Sheridan (New York: Norton, 1977), 1–7. For a discussion of Lacan's essay in the context of fascism, see Susan Buck-Morss, "Aesthetics and Anaesthetics: Walter Benjamin's Artwork Essay Reconsidered," *October* 62 (Fall 1992), 3–41.

29. See Wilson Carey McWilliams, *The Idea of Fraternity in America* (Berkeley: University of California Press, 1973).

30. On the end of disciplinary society, see Dumm, *united states*, especially chap. 4, "Rodney King, or the New Enclosures"; and Thomas L. Dumm, *Michel Foucault and the Politics of Freedom* (Newbury Park: Sage Publications, 1996), especially chap. 4, "Freedom and Seduction." For an argument that is quite similar in focus, see Michael Hardt, "The Withering of Civil Society," *Social Text* (December 1995), 27–44.

31. See William Chaloupka, "Right-Wing Militancy, Legitimacy, and the Politics of Resentment" (unpublished manuscript, Department of Environmental Studies, University of Montana).

32. Jan Swafford, *Charles Ives: A Life with Music* (New York: Norton, 1996), 202–205. In these passages, the key work by Ives that Swafford is discussing is titled *The Amount to Carry—Measuring the Prospect* (New York: Ives & Myrick, 1920).

33. Ibid., 211.

34. Ibid., 210.

35. Ibid., 211, citing Charles Ives, *Essays before a Sonata and Other Writings*, ed. Howard Boatwright (New York: Norton, 1972), 8. The *Essays before a Sonata* were written to accompany the publication of Ives's Piano Sonata no. 2, *Concord, Mass., 1840–60*, better known as the *Concord* Sonata, the four movements of which were named after Emerson, Hawthorne, the Alcotts, and Thoreau.

36. Swafford, *Charles Ives*, 388.

37. Ibid., 405.

38. Ibid., 416–417.

39. Townsend, *Manhood at Harvard*, 102. Townsend here is characterizing the views of Dudley Sargent, who was a professor of physical education. Sargent advo-

cated gymnastics but opposed football and intercollegiate sports generally as being corruptive. For this view, he was dismissed from his professorship by the Harvard Board of Trustees (101).

40. Ibid., 147–148.

41. John Wikse, *About Possession: The Self as Private Property* (University Park: Penn State University Press, 1977), 10–11.

42. Townsend, *Manhood at Harvard,* 149.

43. Ibid., 9.

44. Swafford, his biographer, doesn't suggest this at all (though I think he lays good ground for asking the question). One might wonder what Ives would have been like had he not suffered the psychic disabilities and limits brought on by his homophobia. Of course, these comments are highly speculative—I can barely hum a tune.

45. The phrase "how to raise your kids gay," is taken from an essay of that title by Eve Sedgwick in *Tendencies* (Durham: Duke University Press, 1993).

46. The narrative line of *Toy Story* is framed by two incidents concerning Mr. Potato Head's anxieties, which together seem to quote, in parody, David Lynch's *Blue Velvet.* The first incident has to do with Mr. Potato Head's dismemberment by Andy's toddler little sister. His ear is the subject of a brief visual close up after he is hurled to the floor (covered in baby slobber). The toys come to life immediately after this visual joke. At the end of the movie, Mr. Potato Head's wish for a Mrs. Potato Head is fulfilled, a gesture that evokes the saccharine conclusion to *Blue Velvet* when the young couple comes together, and normalcy is restored.

47. Randy Newman enjoys a distinguished position in the history of American popular music, as a writer of songs that rely on ragtime motifs. His most critically celebrated song cycle was the 1974 album *Good Old Boys* (Warner Brothers), which attempted to limn the collective mind of Southern disenfranchised white men. Newman's satirical songs have not become less sharp in focus in recent years, but they seem to be less recognized as satire. For an early critical analysis of Newman's work, see Greil Marcus, *Mystery Train: Images of America in Rock 'n' Roll* (New York: Dutton, 1975).

48. Toni Morrison, *Playing in the Dark: Whiteness and the Literary Imagination* (Cambridge: Harvard University Press, 1992), chap. 3.

49. For an example of this psychology at work in the white collar world, see Rick Bragg, "Big Holes Where Dignity Used to Be," *New York Times,* March 5, 1996, A1. This article tells the story of James Sharlow, a plant manager for Kodak, laid off at age forty-nine from a $130,000 job. Like many other laid-off executives, to sustain his sense of purpose and worth, he dresses for work every day even though he no longer has a job to go to. Instead, he attends motivational meetings with other laid-off executives. In March 1996 he had not worked for close to two years and had applied for over three thousand jobs in his field.

50. This quote is not transcribed from notes from the movie but taken from

Disney's Toy Story, adapted by Betty Birney (New York: Golden Books, 1995). I use this occasion to thank two important informants with regard to the film, Irene Bright-Dumm and James Bright-Dumm. Without their persistence, I probably would not have seen the film in the first place. I also relied on their expertise while reconstructing the plot of the film, since they screened it more often, and more attentively, than I did.

51. Silverman, in *Male Subjectivities at the Margins*, provides an analysis of male terror of castration in *The Best Years of Our Lives* that is relevant to this recuperative moment as well; see 67–90. For a take on dismemberment that resolves the crisis of identity in a more insidious manner, see Ronald Reagan in *King's Row*. Michael Rogin's analysis of Reagan in that role can be found in his *Ronald Reagan, the Movie and Other Episodes in American Political Demonology* (Berkeley: University of California Press, 1987).

The war trauma being negotiated in *The Best Years of Our Lives* has its parallel in the panic of those faced with potentially diminished lives because of the structural unemployment created of the end of the industrial era. The uncertain ability to negotiate an identity in an era of truncated economic opportunities shakes up loose assumptions about the value of who one is. The question is: Is the shift in the form of civilization as epoch-changing as that which occurred during and after World War II?

52. This is an allegorical example of a commonplace in American movies, especially if one considers the mutant toys as stand-ins for blacks. The role of blacks as mediators for whites is a common one in American cinema. For analyses of the film relationship of blacks and other ethnic groups, see Michael Rogin, *Black Face, White Noise* (Berkeley: University of California Press, 1996); and Robert Gooding-Williams, "Black Cupids, White Desires: Reading the Representation of Racial Difference in *Casablanca* and *Ghost*," in Cynthia Freeland and Thomas Wartenberg, eds., *Philosophy and Film* (New York: Routledge, 1995).

53. A key moment is when Buzz notes the imprint inside his sleeve that indicates he was, in fact, made in Taiwan. This moment is foreshadowed when Buzz is first introduced to the toys of Andy's room, and the toy pig, by way of introduction, asks him where he's from, then adds, "I'm from Mattel. Well, not actually Mattel, but a smaller company purchased by Mattel in a leveraged buy-out."

54. Interestingly, in this regard it departs from the recent tendency in Disney children's films to thematize explicitly issues of race and gender difference, as in *Beauty and the Beast, The Lion King*, and, most controversially, *Pocahontas*.

55. Hobbes, *Leviathan*, book 1, chap. 13, suggests that one enters into society to avoid death and get the things necessary for commodious living (188).

56. Dumm, *united states*, chap. 4, "Rodney King, or the New Enclosures"; and Hardt, "The Withering of Civil Society."

57. Thanks to Paul Gilroy for pointing this out to me.

58. For a sustained study of the history of monstrosity in the West, see Marie Helene Huet, *Monstrous Imagination* (Cambridge: Harvard University Press, 1993).

59. Patricia Williams, "Pre–Old Law, Post–New Man and the Adventures of Everywoman" (unpublished essay, based on a lecture presented at Amherst College in 1991). Parts of this essay were subsequently published as "Law and Everyday Life," in Austin Sarat and Thomas Kearns, eds., *Law in Everyday Life* (Ann Arbor: University of Michigan Press, 1993).

60. Donna J. Haraway, *Simians, Cyborgs, and Women: The Reinvention of Nature* (New York: Routledge, 1991), "A Manifesto for Cyborgs."

61. "Toy Story," *Business Week*, October 30, 1995, 46.

62. The post–World War II cultural description of the devolution of masculinity probably begins with Arthur Miller's *The Death of Salesman* and works its way through to David Mamet's *Glengarry, Glen Ross*. An alternative tradition has its moments as well, from Ragni and Rado's *Hair* to Tony Kushner's *Angels in America*.

NOTES TO CHAPTER 6

1. Edmund Plowden, *Commentaries or Reports* (London, 1816), cited in Ernst Kantorowitz, *The King's Two Bodies: A Study in Mediaeval Political Theology* (Princeton: Princeton University Press, 1957).

2. On the genealogy of this knowledge, see Thomas Tierney, "The Birth of Anatomy," *Theory and Event* 2, 1 (1997), at http://muse.jhu.edu/journals/theory_&_event?toc.

3. Michel Foucault, *Discipline and Punish: The Birth of the Prison*, trans. Alan Sheridan (New York: Pantheon, 1977), 29.

4. For an elaboration of this interpretation of *Discipline and Punish*, see Thomas L. Dumm, *Michel Foucault and the Politics of Freedom* (Thousand Oaks: Sage Publications, 1996).

5. Michel Foucault sustains this critique most thoroughly in "Two Lectures," in *Power/Knowledge*, ed. Colin Gordon (New York: Pantheon, 1980).

6. Foucault, "Truth and Power," in *Power/Knowledge*, 121.

7. In response, Foucault calls for the creation of a new right, one that would be located at the level of the specific and local resistances of subjects in opposition to the forces of normalization; see "Two Lectures," 108.

8. For the argument concerning the emergence of postdisciplinary society in the United States, see Thomas L. Dumm, "The New Enclosures," in Robert Gooding-Williams, ed., *Reading Rodney King, Reading Urban Uprising* (New York: Routledge, 1993). An expanded version of this essay appears as "Rodney King, or the New Enclosures," in Thomas L. Dumm, *united states* (Ithaca: Cornell University Press, 1994). On the emergence of postdisciplinary society, also see Michael Hardt, "The End of Civil Society," *Social Text* (September 1995). Also see the round-

table "Immigrant Acts: Rethinking American Studies in the Transnational Era," at the 1996 American Studies Association, Annual Meeting, Kansas City, Missouri.

9. Michael Paul Rogin, *Ronald Reagan, the Movie and Other Episodes in American Political Demonology* (Berkeley: University of California Press, 1987), chap. 3, "The King's Two Bodies: Lincoln, Wilson, Nixon, and Presidential Self-Sacrifice," 82.

10. Ibid., quoting Nixon's interview with David Frost, *New York Times*, May 20, 1977, 16.

11. Ibid., 84.

12. See Stephen Skowronek, *The Politics Presidents Make: Leadership from John Adams to George Bush* (Cambridge: Belknap Press of Harvard University Press, 1993), 407ff.

13. On Skowronek's characterization of the varieties of presidential politics in political time, see ibid., chap. 3. For his distinction between political and secular time, see ibid., chap. 2, "Power and Authority," especially 30.

14. Ibid., 43.

15. Ibid., 446. As I prepare the final draft of this chapter, President Clinton has admitted an inappropriate relationship with Monica Lewinsky. The fate of his presidency (almost astonishingly) seems to be in some doubt.

16. Ibid., 444–445. Skowronek is unclear about the path to disgrace. In Nixon's case, the primary offense of office he committed in was in the name of an exercise of his power. In Clinton's case, the primary offense is marginal to that exercise. This may, however, be a difference that does not matter.

17. Hal Foster, "Death in America," *October* 75 (Winter 1996), 50. Foster here is summarizing the arguments of Claud LeFort and Jürgen Habermas on the crisis of political representation that attends mass democracy in the wake of the democratic decapitation of the king. LeFort refers to it as a "disincorporation" of the body politic. As Foster notes, this subject is also treated by Michael Warner in "The Mass Public and the Mass Subject," in Bruce Robbins, ed., *The Phantom Public Sphere* (Minneapolis: University of Minnesota Press, 1993).

18. Lauren Berlant, *The Queen of America Goes to Washington City: Essays on Sex and Citizenship* (Durham: Duke University Press, 1997), 12.

19. Anne Norton, *Republic of Signs* (Chicago: University of Chicago Press, 1993).

20. Jodi Dean, "The Truth Is out There: Aliens and the Fugitivity of Postmodern Truth," *Camera Obscura* (Fall 1996), 1. Also see Jodi Dean, *Aliens in America* (Ithaca: Cornell University Press, 1998).

21. Ibid., 21–22.

22. William Corlett, *Community without Unity: A Politics of Derridian Extravagance* (Durham: Duke University Press, 1989).

23. For a discussion of "minority readings" in this context, see chap. 5, "Toy Stories."

24. The Wally Benham Society is the oldest of RV societies that meet annually at different spots throughout the country for weeklong jamborees. Wally Benham invented the Jetstream trailer. There are now multiple such societies, composed primarily of retirees who sometimes sell their wheelless homes to go permanently on the road.

25. The contemporary use of TV stars can most convincingly be traced, I think, to Robert Zemeckis's use of Michael J. Fox in *Back to the Future* (1985). Zemeckis has gone on to make *Forrest Gump* (1994), which is perhaps the most thoroughgoing celebration of the "ordinary," in opposition to the "eventful," that has ever been made. More generally, one might note that what was once an opposition between TV and film has collapsed over the past fifteen years, as television values have thoroughly infiltrated popular film. Penny Marshall (Laverne of *Laverne and Shirley*), Rob Reiner (Meatball of *All in the Family*), and, perhaps most important of all, Ron Howard (Opie of *The Andy Griffith Show* and Richie Cunningham of *Happy Days*) are among the most respected and powerful directors in commercial film at this time.

26. Rogin, "The King's Two Bodies."

27. The discussion of Clinton as the last president of the Republican era is suggested by Theodore J. Lowi's analysis of the Clinton presidency in the paperback edition of *The End of the Republican Era* (Norman: University of Oklahoma Press, 1995; reprint, 1996).

NOTES TO CHAPTER 7

1. That conference, "Modern Communication and the Disappearance of Art and Politics," resulted in an edited volume that contains Jean Baudrillard's "Transpolitics, Transsexuality, Transaesthetics," as well as a useful response by Ron Silliman, "What Do Cyborgs Want? (Paris, Suburb of the Twentieth Century)," which together provoked the event I describe below. See William Stearn and William Chaloupka, eds., *Jean Baudrillard: The Disappearance of Art and Politics* (New York: St. Martin's, 1992), 9–26, 27–37.

2. Ibid., 26.

3. On the writing and early recording history of "Wild Thing," see Chip Taylor, "Rough Mix: How I Wrote 'Wild Thing,'" *Musician* 16 (March 1996).

4. For a sustained analysis of the relationship of beer to the bloodiness of fascism, see Klaus Theweleit, *Male Fantasies*, vol. 1: *Women, Floods, Bodies, History*, trans. Stephen Conway, in collaboration with Erica Carter and Chris Turner (Minneapolis: University of Minnesota Press), 1987.

5. On Thoreau and resignation, see chap. 2.

6. Jane Bennett, *Thoreau's Nature: Ethics, Politics, and the Wild* (Thousand Oaks: Sage Publications, 1994), 3.

7. Nicholson utters these lines in the 1995 melodrama film directed by Rob Reiner, also starring Demi Moore and Tom Cruise, *A Few Good Men*. The question of being able to handle the truth is deeply evocative of a passage of analysis in Stanley Cavell's essay on the relationship of Emerson's thought to Nietzsche and Heidegger, "Aversive Thinking," where *hand*someness, clutching, and grasping are all brought into play in relationship to thinking about the humanity of truth. See Stanley Cavell, *Conditions Handsome and Unhandsome: The Constitution of Emersonian Perfectionism* (Chicago: University of Chicago Press, 1990), 38.

8. For a report, see David S. Bennahum, "Just Gaming: Three Days in the Desert with Jean Baudrillard, DJ Spooky, and the Chance Band," *Lingua Franca* (February 1997), 59–63.

9. One important example of what I am calling mediated uncanniness is Marjorie Garber's tour de force "Jell-O," in Marjorie Garber and Rebecca Walkowitz, eds., *Secret Agents: The Rosenberg Case, McCarthyism and Fifties America* (New York: Routledge, 1995). In that essay, Garber connects the phrase Harry Gold is reported to have said when he handed over a ripped Jell-O box as his sign—"Benny sent me"—to the prosaic but eerie fact that Jell-O was the sponsor of the *Jack Benny Show* on the radio at that time. This is eerie in the sense that the guilt of Julius Rosenberg hinged on the fact that Gold came from Julius, not from Benny, and the reconstruction of the phrase became a matter of contestation throughout the spy trial. Such a mediated uncanniness in this case might serve as an exemplary proof, though whether it would be sustained in a court of law is another question.

10. Stanley Cavell, *In Quest of the Ordinary: Lines of Skepticism and Romanticism* (Chicago: University of Chicago Press, 1988), especially, "Emerson, Coleridge, Kant"; and Cavell, *Conditions Handsome and Unhandsome*, especially "Aversive Thinking."

11. Elinor Ostrom, "A Behavioral Approach to the Rational Choice Theory of Collective Action: Presidential Address, American Political Science Association, 1997," *American Political Science Review* 92, 1 (March 1998), 18.

12. Jean Baudrillard, *Simulations*, trans. Paul Foss, Paul Patton, and Philip Beitchman (New York: Semiotext(e), 1983), 13.

13. Ralph Waldo Emerson, "The American Scholar," in *Essays and Lectures*, ed. Joel Porte (New York: Library of America, 1983), 58.

14. Michel Foucault, "The Masked Philosopher," in *The Essential Works of Michel Foucault*, Vol. 1, *Ethics, Subjectivity, and Truth*, ed. Paul Rabinow (New York: New Press, 1997), 323; Jacques Derrida, *Specters of Marx: The State of the Debt, the Work of Mourning, and the New International*, trans. Peggy Kamuf (New York: Routledge, 1994); Stanley Cavell, *Contesting Tears: The Hollywood Melodrama of the Unknown Woman* (Chicago: University of Chicago Press, 1996); Judith Butler, *Gender Trouble: Feminism and the Subversion of Identity* (New York: Routledge, 1990);

Gilles Deleuze and Félix Guattari, *Kafka: Toward a Minor Literature*, trans. Dana Polan (Minneapolis: University of Minnesota Press, 1986); and William E. Connolly, *The Ethos of Pluralization* (Minneapolis: University of Minnesota Press, 1986; for example. As many know, these are only samples culled from large and distinctive bodies of work. But a gesture is a gesture.

Index

About the Author

Thomas L. Dumm teaches politics at Amherst College. He is founder and co-editor of the online journal *Theory and Event* and the author of several previous books, including *Democracy and Punishment, united states,* and *Michel Foucault and the Politics of Freedom.*